# EXPERIMENTAL DESIGN

Dedicated to our teacher, colleague and friend Helmut Lortz [1920-2007].

# EXPERIMENTAL DESIGN

## VISUAL METHODS AND SYSTEMATIC PLAY

ARMIN LINDAUER   BETINA MÜLLER

**PLEASE TURN THE PAGE.** "Though this be madness, yet there is method in it."[1]
The 'madness' of passionately collecting certain items over the years is a widespread
phenomenon amongst designers. Graphic designers collect prizes, artists collect
vanguards, art historians collect footnotes. Scientists, especially professors,
collect 'experimental methods'. Armin Lindauer and Betina Müller, close acquaintances
since their student days at the Berlin University of the Arts, have in the meantime
dedicated themselves to research and teaching. Armin, at Mannheim University of Applied
Sciences and Betina, at Potsdam University of Applied Sciences. Both of them have
now compiled an exemplary collection of 'visual creativity' with a great deal
of patience and verve, daring the gap, in order to represent and compare experimental
design in arts, design and science. As graphic designers committed to arts rather than
science, they have succeeded in properly conveying structural design processes
and even in defining chaos as a consequence of order.

**If you do not bother with** the explanations and digressions and just focus on the
illustrations of series and sequences, you will miss the actual question and preventive
challenge of their bold ideas. Above all, the notorious page flipper will miss
the phenomenon of self-similarity as well the nasty surprise that not everything that
is infinitely varied is an experimental concept. Students will appreciate this book,
in particular those who see it as more than just a source of inspiration.
For ultimately, arts and science are about using innovation to overcome conventional
classification systems and perhaps even reinvent them.


Uwe Loesch

**PROLOGUE**   This book shows how and where experimental methods are used to support decisions relating to design and art, which connections exist between creativity and method and the role of intuition. It explains that design and art do not only come into being by intuition, but that, similar to science, they employ methodical procedures that lead to approaches and solutions, and that also in design, experiments can be carried out in the sense of a test setup or a test arrangement. Such a test setup consists first of indicating analogies and affinities between artistic and scientific methods and then of introducing methods developed by individual artists for their own special needs, which can be recognised as a unique canon. Although processes designed by artists can only be transposed to deviating applications to a lesser extent, they can nevertheless serve as a template, model or sample by adapting them to meet specific requirements.

**Two aspects of methodical procedures** make a particular contribution to clarifying questions of design. One leads to concretisation of form, colour, composition, expression and other elementary design parameters and the other leads to findings and ideas and thus to creativity in the broadest sense of the word. In this context, the self-invented test setup plays an important role. The individual arrangement of the experiment is a partial result. The risk that this could lead to a limitation of creativity can be counteracted by flexibly manipulating the test setup.

The chapter BASIS already shows that simple and systematic exercises can yield creativity and surprising results. The chapter INTERPRETATION then leads to the topic of techniques of representation, also referred to as media. The chapter VARIATION searches for a creative link, which is enhanced by adding a number of other signs in the chapter RELATION. Finally, the chapter SEQUENCE achieves the greatest degree of freedom, containing only a few definable constants.

**A seeming contradiction** exists between postulated methods and anticipated results. Although methodical processes are underpinned with much exemplary work, you should not come to the automatic conclusion that they necessarily lead to relevant results. Instead, the focus lies on presenting different systematic approaches and methods. Of course they do not exist for their own sake, because ultimately, it is the constant interaction between systematic variation and intuitive selection that delivers results. Moreover, the book shows **not only final works and small cabinet pieces**, but also the creative process and the visual design methods behind them. In doing so, it intends to not only present single results, but a whole host of variations and alternatives. Deviations and results that seem at first sight to be absurd are also shown, because they are a significant aspect of the creative process. Mostly, however, only a fraction of the countless possibilities are presented here, despite it being our declared goal to articulate as many principles as possible. Instead of merely focussing on results, the approach here is an open-ended process. Also, not everything that presents itself as a series can be described as 'experimental', which would require clearly defined frame conditions and constant and variable parameters. As a whole, this chapter shows that there are more similarities and connections between scientific and artistic work than generally supposed, and that both use specific methods to gain knowledge and foster the creative process. In that sense we can also say that there is method in design.

For over two decades, Betina Müller and I have searched, collected and compiled works dealing with experimental design using methodical design methods as we understand it. We collected a part of **the materials** in the archives of the Berlin University of the Arts, which keeps almost five hundred semester protocols, i.e. students' papers from Lortz's class with whom we also once studied. Prof. Helmut Lortz taught for twenty-nine years as head of the class for Experimental Graphics at the former Hochschule der Künste Berlin, today known as the Berlin University of the Arts. At the end of each semester, every student was required to submit a 'picture protocol' in the form of a bound book. Our task was to analyse and assess this comprehensive collection of ideas, proposals, systematics and methods from three decades. Today, we are teachers ourselves; I work at Mannheim University of Applied Sciences and Betina at Potsdam University of Applied Sciences. What we experienced as students has found its way into our research and teaching, developing further over two generations of teaching designers and many generations of students. In that way, many new works using these methods have emerged. When conducting our picture research, we also discovered various excellent works by other authors that have completed, supported and broadened the subject. We discovered works in completely different areas such as advertising, product design, poster design and in free art, at the same time finding lots of similarities in science. Ultimately, a visual and methodical approach independent of the target and discipline was our guiding principle. All works prove that the application of methods in design, such as the systematic variation of a figure or a theme, is not an isolated procedure from a specific discipline. As a matter of fact, practical examples show that not only free-floating creativity is produced, but that methods lead to concrete applications and results.

It will only be possible to touch on many topics in the following, in
DRAFTING A SYSTEM OF VISUAL METHODS, and few will be discussed appropriately
or even adequately. It is thus expressly noted that the purpose of the text
is primarily an accompanying and supplementary one. Its intention is to create
an associative space which places the illustration in a more comprehensive
context with the aim of leading to people's own explorations and research. In
addition, I realised during the writing process that some of my considerations
were part of a greater context and had already been dealt with much more
comprehensively in other disciplines. Where I deemed it to be necessary,
I indicated that. The concept of 'series', which appears now and then in the
text, is mostly understood in the sense of a loose sequence of ideas about
a limited theme. Normally, it deals with variations displaying different
characteristics. Since this concept is used in a general, unspecific way,
I took advantage of this openness in our application, without striving for an
exact definition.

We had great fun collecting, selecting and compiling an immense amount of
different works. Many pictorial works require onlookers that are willing to
accept different systems as well as their upheaval, and moreover let themselves
be seduced by randomness. This book delivers neither complete concepts nor
recipes, but rather offers a diversity of experiments that should inspire
people to conduct their own experiments and investigations. It is **an invitation**
to experience the potential and limits of visual and creative methods, to
engage with the methodical and thus pay the necessary attention to one's
intuition.

Armin Lindauer, January 2015

"Imagination is the most scientific of our faculties,

because it alone is capable of understanding the universal analogy."[1]

his stays in Étretat on the French northern coast, Gustave Courbet[1819–1877]

**DRAFTING A SYSTEM OF VISUAL METHODS** The concepts "experimental art" and
many versions of the picture LA VAGUE. The Städel Museum Frankfurt
"experimental graphics" are used for artistic and applied works. The title
possesses one of these paintings, knows of "about sixty tableaus
EXPERIMENTAL DESIGN was chosen for this book because it is more general
of which, high tide and breakers which Courbet painted between 1865 and 1869
and therefore more comprehensive. What does "experimental" mean in connection with
coast of Normandy and completed in his studio. They express man's
design? THE BROCKHAUS encyclopedia delivers the following definitions of
for life and are a symbol of political hope for renewal and experience of
experiment", which may be allocated to the following four concepts: 1. general,
"[29]. The motif mostly only shows sky and sea, sometimes with a piece of beach
2. natural sciences, 3. psychology and 4. social sciences; the concepts experimental

An experiment is generally a methodical investigation based on
a test setup designed on invention of a scientist. Empirical information or data are
collected by means of systematic processes. Furthermore, scientific approaches include

research a phenomenon, the theme is methodically analysed using a test setup,

"Imagination is the most scientific of our faculties,
because it alone is capable of understanding the universal analogy."[1]


**DRAFTING A SYSTEM OF VISUAL METHODS**   The concepts 'experimental art' and
'experimental graphics' are used for artistic and applied works. The title
EXPERIMENTAL DESIGN was chosen for this book because it is more general and
therefore more comprehensive. What does 'experimental' mean in connection with design?
The BROCKHAUS encyclopedia delivers the following definitions of 'experiment',
which may be allocated to the following four concepts: 1. general, 2. natural sciences,
3. psychology and 4. social sciences; the concepts experimental art-house film,
experimental philosophy, experimental archaeology, experimental poetry, experimental
music, experimental economics and experimental psychology are additionally mentioned.
Experimental art and experimental design are not included.

**An experiment** in the scientific sense means a methodical investigation based on
a test setup designed or invented by a scientist. Empirical information or data are
collected by means of systematic processes. Further scientific approaches include
observation of nature or thought experiments. The former is mainly done in
natural sciences such as physics, biology and astronomy, the latter in humanities
such as philosophy, theology and mathematics. The scientific experiment uses
experimental design with the aim of researching a special area, a subarea or a
specific aspect. It is characterised by a test setup, a documentation and assessable
results and should be repeatable and quantifiable. However, the quality of the
results is completely open; they can be either valuable or totally worthless.

Constant frame conditions have to be created for a scientific experiment in order
to yield reproducible results. This is why only one single parameter or
influencing factor, a **'ceteris paribus'** (Lat. for "all other things being equal
or held constant"), is investigated: "a formulation used in connection with
experiments [...] which means: 'under the presumption that all except the (afore)
mentioned frame conditions (premises) remain equal'."[2] Therefore, in order
to draw conclusions and achieve verifiability, the observed or measured change needs
to be traced back to the variable. Hence, scientific experiments are generally
simplified models of reality in which individual parameters are investigated.
Usually, experiments are carried out using methods, which are described as targeted,
science-based, proven technology, i.e. as instructions for implementing a concept.
It is "a well-planned (methodical) process with a subject and target — a skilled
technique for solving practical and theoretical tasks"[3]; accordingly, methodology
means "science in general, i.e. the procedure of a science"[4].

1 Charles Baudelaire (1821–1867), THE BIRTH OF IMPRESSIONISM:
EDOUARD MANET, PIERRE-AUGUSTE RENOIR, CLAUDE MONET, film by Alain Jaubert, Paris 2000.
2 www.en.wikipedia.org/wiki/ceteris_paribus (retrieved 3/6/2014).
3 Bibliographisches Institut (ed.), BROCKHAUS ENZYKLOPÄDIE, Mannheim, Vienna, Zurich 1982, Vol.18, p.348.*
4 Ibid., p.349.*

The basic structure of a normal working procedure is outlined as follows:
In order to deal with a task or research a phenomenon, the theme is methodically analysed using a test setup, thus creating a broad range of variations. Selection follows variation. Again, this selection is further explored by varying partial and sub-aspects taking place during a continual change of **variation and selection**, which may, in the best case, lead to relevant results. During this process, methods are continually adapted according to the progress of work and to current knowledge. With the number of variations per step, the probability of achieving better results increases, whilst the 'right' selection determines quality. Since every variation directly generates countless possibilities, many of which are not useful, a selection must be made immediately. Those with potential have to be found and subsequently followed up. It should be noted that this is particularly the case with "mechanisms postulated by evolutionary biology — variation and selection"[5]. Here, diversity is created by a spontaneous variation of genes, and selection takes place according to the most suitable adaptation. This natural process, which can be described as biological creativity, follows a similar pattern to human creativity,[6] evolution historian Thomas Junker believes, further stating that "human imagination activity [...] is similar to genetic diversity created by mutation and recombination, which is a prerequisite for the evolution of organisms"[7]. However, "in contrast to human inventions, creative improvements in evolution [...] are not caused by targeted change, but by random variations, which subsequently prove to be more or less advantageous"[8]. The essential difference between them is therefore that the controlled process requires less time than the random one — "Cultural evolution [...] runs at a speed that is a thousand times higher than biological evolution"[9].

Scientific processes should be logical, rational and objective, but it is still impossible to determine all **facts and figures.** They are always incomplete, probably systematically erroneous and often superimposed by randomness; in mathematical statistics, this phenomenon is known as 'stochastic failure'. However, in order to be able to draw conclusions and evaluate, the process of collecting has to be terminated sooner or later. Finally, the collected material is assessed and extrapolations are made. At this stage even science needs to make use of intuition, which — alongside the hard facts of experiments and data collection — plays an important role in scientific work as well.

This leads to a further common trait of artistic and scientific work: Both of them not only draw from intuition, but also from **visual ideas** that precede the actual creative process. In art and in design, we would expect to encounter these ideas, but we are surprised how often they are described in science. In his book THE ACT OF CREATION, Arthur Koestler states a number of famous examples, amongst others Max Planck: "Max Planck, the father of quantum theory, wrote in

5 Thomas Junker, DIE 101 WICHTIGSTEN FRAGEN: EVOLUTION (THE 101 MOST IMPORTANT QUESTIONS: EVOLUTION), Munich 2011, p.11.*
6 Thomas Junker, DIE EVOLUTION DER PHANTASIE. WIE DER MENSCH ZUM KÜNSTLER WURDE (EVOLUTION OF IMAGINATION. HOW MAN BECAME AN ARTIST), Stuttgart 2013, p.92.
7 Ibid.*  8 Ibid., p.48.*  9 Ibid., p.124.*

his autobiography that the pioneer scientist must have 'a vivid intuitive imagination, for new ideas are not generated by deduction, but by artistically creative imagination'".[10] Then he goes on to Michael Faraday, "who also [was] a 'visionary' not only in the metaphorical but in the literal sense. He saw the stresses surrounding magnets and electric currents as curves in space, for which he coined the name 'lines of forces' and which, in his imagination, were as real as if they consisted of solid matter. He visualized the universe patterned by lines of force — like the familiar diagram of iron filings around a magnet"[11]. Further descriptions can be found in Jürgen Neffe's Einstein biography. "As a pupil, Einstein [...] maintained that he had already conducted a gedankenexperiment"[12] asking himself: "What would it be like to follow a ray of light? What would it be like to ride on it?"[13] Mathematician Benoît Mandelbrot, famous for his discovery of fractal geometry, also referred to his visual imagination capacity: "My whole life long I've dealt not with formulae but with pictures. [...] During an algebra course, I suddenly saw geometrical images that corresponded to algebraic equations in my mind, and with these pictures in my mind, the solutions became evident. In that way I discovered an ability that I didn't know I possessed until then, namely that I could immediately convert equations into pictures in my mind."[14] This frequently observed phenomenon probably led to a statistical survey that Koestler mentioned: "Hadamard's inquiry among leading mathematicians in America revealed that practically all of them avoided not only the use of mental words but also the mental use of algebraic or any other signs. On the testimony of those original thinkers who have taken the trouble to record their methods of work, not only verbal thinking, but conscious thinking in general plays only a subordinate part in the brief, decisive phase of the creative act itself."[15] — "In fact, the majority of mathematicians and physicists turned out to be 'visionaries' in the literal sense-that is visual, not verbal thinkers."[16] These observations are of significance insofar as they show that 'visual ideas' that are usually attributed to art, are also found surprisingly often in natural sciences, and indeed that scientists rely on them in order to achieve knowledge and formulate theories.

Another similarity is that **aesthetic experiences** are not only made in art but also in science. Formulae, physical laws, chemical compounds, molecules, reaction chains: all of these can be perceived as being as beautiful as an image. In mathematics, we know that there is 'beauty in an equation' or 'elegance in a proof'. Scientific journalist Gábor Paál writes about the relationship between science and art, that both process knowledge and that every cognitive process has a basic aesthetical dimension. "On an abstract level, even criteria resemble one another: Simplicity, elegance, harmony, symmetry, inner consistence, originality and a certain amount of complexity"[17] In WAS IST SCHÖN? (WHAT IS BEAUTIFUL?), he deals with the subject in more depth: "Just like art, science is inconceivable without a feeling for aesthetics."[18] "Aesthetical

10 Arthur Koestler, THE ACT OF CREATION, London 1964, p.147.
11 Ibid., p.474.*
12 Jürgen Neffe, EINSTEIN, EINE BIOGRAFIE (EINSTEIN, A BIOGRAPHY), Reinbek bei Hamburg 2005, p.145.*
13 Ibid., p.81.*
14 Interview in: FRACTALS — HUNTING THE HIDDEN DIMENSION, produced and directed by: Michael Schwarz, Bill Jersey, 2008.*
15 Koestler 1964, p.208.
16 Ibid., p.322.
17 Gábor Paál, "Wahre Schönheit — Schöne Wahrheit?"* (True Beauty — Beautiful Truth?), in: ATTEMPTO, June 2013, p.2.*
18 Gábor Paál, WAS IST SCHÖN? ÄSTHETIK UND ERKENNTNIS (WHAT IS BEAUTIFUL? AESTHETICS AND COGNITION), Würzburg 2003, p.161.*

15 DRAFTING A SYSTEM OF VISUAL METHODS

19 Ibid., p.168.* 20 "Stimmen aus der Wissenschaft: Wie wichtig ist Schönheit für ihre Forschung?" ("Voices from the world of science: How important is beauty for your research?"), in: ATTEMPTO, June 2013, p.6.*
21 James D. Watson, DIE DOPPELHELIX (THE DOUBLE HELIX), Reinbek bei Hamburg 1989, p.164.*
22 Quoted in: Ricarda Stiller, Universitätsmuseum: "Warum Schönheit die Wissenschaft antreibt" ("Why Beauty Drives Science"), in: STUTTGARTER ZEITUNG, 21/5/2013.*
23 Quoted from: not specified, "Der Forschung Kern", in: FTE INFO, MAGAZIN FÜR EUROPÄISCHE FORSCHUNG, special edition Kunst und Wissenschaft, March 2004, p.19.*

values, however, not only influence the power, but also the kind of scientific principles. They also have an influence on the kind of subjects that science deals with", he says, stating further "that aesthetic subjects have a decisive effect on the implicit self-conception of many sciences"[19]. Johannes Kabatek, Professor for Romance Linguistics, also sees aesthetic motives in his subject area: "Just as with all sciences, the beauty of linguistics lies in the aesthetics of the successful explanation. A linguistic line of argument, terminology, or a semantic or syntactic analysis is only beautiful if it is clear and if complex things are represented in such a way that we can recognise a certain order, system or structure in the ocean of complexity."[20] Biochemist and co-discoverer of the DNA (deoxyribonucleic acid) James Watson reports the following about a critical colleague who saw the model of a double helix for the first time: "Just like most people she realised how attractive these complementary base pairs were and accepted the fact that the structure was too beautiful to be wrong".[21] Many scientists therefore think that the beauty of a model, a hypothesis or explanation has a value of its own. The physicist and Nobel Prize holder Werner Heisenberg is said to have formulated this in the following ironic manner: "A theory needs not be true, but beautiful."[22] Thus aesthetical experiences are also sought after and had in sciences, and beauty happens — supposedly — only in a different environment, in a different context. The French poet Saint-John Perse was convinced of the similarity of experiences made by researchers and artists, as the "questions are always the same and they are posed on the same precipice, and only the investigation methods are different."[23] It is easy to believe that art is primarily guided by aesthetics, but that this is also often the case in the sciences, is surprising.

In creative professions, it is not common to proceed with the help of a test setup or an experimental investigation. Mostly, the incalculable brilliant idea is considered as far too important. The concept of the '**experimental**' is increasingly used in design, especially by students who understand it as 'trying out'. These experiments are easily associated with being random or aimless. In free arts, however, 'experimental' is often used in the sense of works which cannot be easily assessed or measured. Here, one gets involved with radical subjectivity that seeks to withdraw from any assessment. In contrast to this, experimental design as we understand it uses a test setup similar to a scientific experiment, and a test series as an instrument and method. Claudia Giannetti quotes Peter Weibel on this subject, who thought that "science may stand out on grounds of its methodological character, whereas art [...] is not generally considered as a method. [...] Art and science can only be compared seriously, if we accept that both are methods. That does not mean that we declare that both possess the same methods. We only want to say that both have a methodological approach, even if their methods are different or may differ"[24].

In the following, we will show that numerous methodical processes are also used in design and that despite the prevailing difference to science, they still deliver convincing and coherent results. Today, individual scientific disciplines are highly specialised and each subject area has its own **repertoire of methods.** Their origin lies in the observation of nature and the collection of facts and figures. But which methods, comparable with those in science, can be used in future when dealing with questions of design? Are there similarities or will visual design have to develop new independent forms? Can, for example, well-known procedures of science also be used here for finding solutions? One model, for example, the morphological matrix[216], is used in various different disciplines. Findings about a new subject are made by combining two parameters. Changing these parameters enables targeted control over the direction of the investigation. Examples of design work based on this tool are shown on pages[278/373]. Also the morphological box, a matrix extended spatially by Swiss astrophysicist Fritz Zwicky, is very helpful when it comes to design. In that context, a problem is divided into three dimensions and then investigated. These first examples already illustrate that it is definitely possible and meaningful to use methodical procedures to clarify design-related problems.

A further significant aspect of experiments — be they artistic or scientific — is **the safeguarding of results.** Alternative scenarios can be played out during the investigation of partial aspects or variants. What is part of common practice in science, is also practiced by many designers. Uwe Loesch once remarked on this subject during an interview at a symposium "Even if I find the solution at first sight, I still try out lots of other alternatives just to find out if it was really the best one."

Sometimes, a systematic approach helps to overcome **functional fixedness,** as psychologists call it. Since we tend to solve problems in ways we are already familiar with, we are prevented from finding other possibly better solutions, i.e. from being creative. But how can we leave the beaten track, if pure reflection fails? In such cases, test setups and systematics are excellent auxiliary means. They run according to principles and fixed programmes, generating variants that would not be selected intuitively. Well-known approaches are inevitably abandoned, and what at first sight seems to be a restraint to creativity, turns out to be an extension thereof, delivering potentially surprising results.

Hence, just like the scientific experiment, the design experiment should also be based on constant conditions and only investigate one variable, if possible, in order to achieve traceable and assessable results. The 'correct' reduction of complexity generates insight. One decisive advantage is direct comparability:

24 Quoted in: Claudia Giannetti, "Kunst, Wissenschaft und Technik" ("Art, Science and Technology"), in: MEDIEN KUNST NETZ, www.medienkunstnetz.de/themen/aesthetik_des_digitalen/kunst_wissenschaft_technik (retrieved 3/6/2014).*

25 Cf. www.en.wikipedia.org/wiki/Isle_of_the_Dead_(painting) (retrieved 22/1/2015).
26 Rolf Lauter, "Schreiender Papst" ("Screaming Pope"), www.rolf-lauter.com/index.php?option=com_content&view=article&id=24&Itemid=33&kunstler=Bacon
(no longer retrievable, last retrieved 15/8/2014).
27 Ibid.  28 Ibid.

**Difference** makes everything visible and thus assessable. The better form, the more appropriate technology and the more intelligent content is found more quickly and easily.

Now, how can the **experiments** as described above be employed in art and design? When and where are methodical processes introduced to art and design work? Which historical and modern examples can be considered here? How and where have visual artists, or more generally, designers, dealt with systematic research of visual phenomena? First of all, we are fascinated by the endurance and devotion with which some artists always pursue the same theme or motif — sometimes a whole life long. The objects of their obsession can vary greatly. Swiss Arnold Böcklin[1827–1901] painted five versions of TOTENINSEL (ISLE OF THE DEAD) between 1880 and 1886. The subject of death had an extraordinary effect on his life and work and, as a consequence, he even painted his initials on one of the island's burial chambers from the 3rd version onwards.[25] It has been documented that the repetition was due to demand and in one case even to a lack of money rather than to artistic requirements, which is why this aspect has not been considered more closely here. "Between 1949 and the early Sixties" the Irish painter Francis Bacon[1909–1992] "painted more than 40 versions"[26] of THE SCREAMING POPE after a reproduction of Diego Velázquez's painting INNOCENT X.[1650]. He never saw the original painting. His compositions are based on two other motifs: The first is "a still photograph from Sergei Eisenstein's BATTLESHIP POTEMKIN showing a screaming nanny with broken glasses"[27], the other is a photo of "Pope Pius XII on his throne"[28]. THE SCREAMING POPE can be interpreted as a metaphor of despair expressing the pain over the absence of redemption in this world. These clearly differentiated compositions, formats and colouring, however, are individual solutions that are difficult to compare. That is why this series of paintings is not appropriate for our considerations. The Japanese artist Katsushika Hokusai[1760–1849] created a hundred drawings and prints of Mount Fuji, including the well-known series of coloured woodcuts THIRTY-SIX VIEWS OF MOUNT FUJI. Ultimately, however, this series does not show the desired consistency; that is why we selected the following works with regard to their special relevance for an experimental approach, considering the accessible and available pictorial material for a closer look: LA VAGUE by Gustave Courbet[>28–29]; LA CATHÉDRALE DE ROUEN by Claude Monet[>30–31]; SAVIOUR'S FACE and ABSTRACT HEAD by Alexej von Jawlensky[>32–33]; THE PAINTER by Pablo Picasso[>34–35]; HOMAGE TO THE SQUARE by Josef Albers[>36–37] and WASSERTÜRME (WATER TOWERS) by Bernd and Hilla Becher[>36–37].

**Gustave Courbet**[1819-1877] painted many versions of the picture LA VAGUE[>28-29] during
his stays in Étretat on the French Atlantic coast. The Städel Museum Frankfurt,
which possesses one of these paintings, knows of "about sixty tableaus
of water whirls, high tide and breakers which Courbet painted between 1865 and 1869
on the coast of Normandy and completed in his studio. They express man's
struggle for life and are a symbol of political hope for renewal and experience of
nature"[29]. The images mostly only show sky and sea, sometimes with a piece of beach
on the lower edge or a boat that appears in different places. Those versions
showing only the sky and the sea seem to be more convincing and modern, from today's
point of view. In its transcendent meaning, the motif stands for the eternally
recurrent, for birth and death. Moreover, it has been given a political dimension
insofar that it has been interpreted as a symbol of emerging democracy of the
Third French Republic of 1871. We will never know whether these many versions have
more to do with commercial success or if they were the result of the painter's
drive to better comprehend the motif. It is evident, however, that he attained both
better form and stronger expression after repeating the motif so often.
Courbet most probably wanted to heighten form and expression and to draw a more
striking quality from the motif. Although some of the variations already
display far-reaching similarities, they still do not have the conceptual and formal
clarity of Monet's 'Series' created some twenty years later.

**Claude Monet**[1840-1926] started painting in an impressionist manner at the end of
the 1860s. His picture titled IMPRESSION[1872] that gave this trend its name, is a
view of Le Havre harbour. It was only almost twenty years later that Monet
painted his first pictures en serie: he began to paint multiple versions of the
same motifs — first of all from different perspectives and compositions.
In 1890/1891, after these early approaches, he began to consequently pursue and
repeat a certain motif for the first time in MEULES (HAY STACKS). However, the
pictures still differ distinctly. "Only from 1890 on did Monet use the word 'serie'
and exhibited the greatest part of his works under this title."[30]
Almost at the same time, in 1881, he painted twenty-three tableaus named PEUPLIERS
(POPLARS) that show unmistakably similar, often nearly identical compositions,
so that his intention, to represent light at different times of the day and seasons,
strikes us. One year later, between 1892 and 1894, he created thirty-eight tableaus
showing LA CATHÉDRALE DE ROUEN[>30-31]. This is the most consequent of Monet's
initial series. All of the pictures show the Cathedral's façade, almost from the
front, although they have little differences in frame and perspective.
The portal is in the middle of the picture, and the towers are at the sides.
Monet used this strict, formal, and therefore highly modern structure,
to investigate light. Due to the high level of abstraction, almost identical

29 Description of the collection, www.staedelmuseum.de/sm/index.php?StoryID=1047&ObjectID=184 (retrieved 4/6/2014).
30 Edition Montparnasse (ed.), THE BIRTH OF IMPRESSIONISM, documentary by Alain Jaubert, 1988.

31 Volker Rattemeyer, Renate Petzinger (eds.), JAWLENSKY. MEINE LIEBE GALKA!, exhibition catalogue of the Museum Wiesbaden, Wiesbaden 2004, pp. 63.*

composition and the repetition, the actual motif is objectivised and pushed into the background, whilst the beholder's attention is focussed on the differences in light and colour shades, which become the true object of investigation.

**Alexej von Jawlensky** [1864–1941] moved from St Petersburg to Munich in 1896 and came into contact with Modernism and especially with German Expressionism. His early oeuvre is attributed to this period and art critics regarded it as more valuable than his later works. Volker Rattemeyer found that "a re-evaluation of the oeuvre from the end of the 1960s"[31] had taken place, which is especially true for the series from 1914 onwards. At the outbreak of World War I, Jawlenski went into exile in Switzerland and at fifty years of age, he began the picture series VARIATIONEN ÜBER EIN LANDSCHAFTLICHES THEMA. He made little additions to the title of the series VARIATION, such as "Mountain and Lake", "Bright Morning", "Tragic", "Tenderness", and many others — his catalogue of works lists 284 paintings. His method of repeating the same motif in the same style emerged from this initial series, sparking and acting as a transition to the HEADS he painted in the following two decades. He developed his repertoire from his Expressionist portraits which he stylised and simplified. From 1917 to 1937, he painted four comprehensive series he called MYSTICAL HEAD, SAVIOUR'S FACES, ABSTRACT HEAD and MEDITATION. He gave additional names to these titles, just as he had done with his landscape variations. From 1917 onwards, he painted 115 versions of MYSTICAL HEAD which appear less serial in a formal sense. Some of these heads are frontal, some are semi-profiles, some have a neck and others do not. In 1917, he also began his SAVIOUR'S FACES series[32–33], which is attributed to Constructivism and consisted of 87 pictures upon completion. This series is already distinctly more consequent, but still shows a significant break. Some heads have open eyes, some of them closed, as if he was not able to decide between the introverted and extraverted gaze. The heads of the two subsequent series always have closed eyes. In 1918, Jawlensky began his third ABSTRACT HEAD series[32–33], which is characterised by an even greater reduction and geometrisation. Instead of the painter's gesture, the pictures show clear surfaces, vivid colours and a balanced brightness. In 1921, he returned to Germany from exile and settled down in Wiesbaden. It was there that, in 1934, he painted most of his 274 ABSTRACT HEAD versions and between 1934 and 1937, nearly all 580 versions of MEDITATION. Between the series, we can observe transitions, overlaps and developments that sometimes reflect a process and sometimes are spontaneous. Despite his consequent serial mode of working, the series are never closed or consistent, because the individual works often differ distinctly in their format and colouring. Moreover, the beginning and end of the series are not really distinguishable as there is a continuous change and processual development with varying setbacks and progress. Thus, every picture has remained unique despite its serial character, something that is also expressed in the additional subtitles. Jawlensky's principally empirical approach is faced with an astonishing formal consequence. From what we know today, it is hard to say if and to what extent he was aware of the modernity of his approach, because we have no evidence or remarks of his own about his art. Volker Rattemeyer writes "that Jawlensky [...] considered all theoretical explanations of his own work as a speculation"[32]. The fact that these series are probably not completely consequent and less clear, does not detract from their unique quality. They rather reveal an early conception of modern artistic methodology. Rattemeyer thinks that "Jawlensky was searching for [...] a Utopian form, subject to the paradox that serial work would continually revive this search without moving towards a climax, that this unique picture would therefore never come into being, but that it would be the ultimate sum of the serial total"[33]. Accordingly, Jawlensky's picture series challenged the individual single picture as a unique work of art, as is the case with other series, too.

**Pablo Picasso**[1881-1973] and his ground-breaking works are well-known. From the mid-20th century onwards, the public and critics seemed rather helpless in the face of his late oeuvre. Between the end of World War II and the late 1960s, abstraction dominated the international art establishment. Picasso himself commented on his late oeuvre, which was a blend of Cubism, Expressionism and child-like exposé — hardly classifiable by the art establishment — as follows: "I was able to draw when I was young just like Raphael, but it took me my whole life to learn to draw again just like a child." And he commented on abstraction: "There is no such thing as abstract art. One always has to begin with something. And then one can remove all traces of what is real."[34] The series THE PAINTER presented here [34-35] was created between 10th and 24th October, 1964, i.e. within two weeks, and consists of 29 pictures. They are paint-overs of the reproduction of his oil canvas using gouache and Indian ink. They show the painter's head, his hand, his drawing tools and an easel with part of the canvas. Why did Picasso, who was said to have great graphical mastery, paint 29 variations of the same motif that he had already painted before? What drove him to engage anew with this subject? Format, motif, composition and colour palette have all remained more or less the same. The subject of his investigation is ultimately the changing of expression through the varying of his exposé. In that context it is astonishing that his self-imposed limitation to paint over his own picture with a similar motif, by no means seems to weaken his creativity and his desire for the object; on the contrary, it is stimulated. Throughout his whole life, Picasso repeatedly dealt with the same themes and motifs in extensive series, but he was rarely as formally consequent with any of his work as with this series.

32 Ibid., p.58.*
33 Ibid., p.73.*
34 Dietmar Elger, ABSTRAKTE KUNST (ABSTRACT ART), Cologne 2008, p.26.*

Josef Albers [1888-1976] began to study in 1920 and from 1925 onwards he taught at the Bauhaus, until he emigrated to the U.S. in 1933. It was there that he first taught at different universities before he came to Yale University in 1950. In the same year he began his picture series HOMAGE TO THE SQUARE [>36-37], which he worked on for twenty-five years. He created over a thousand works on this subject: Paintings, drawings, prints and murals. His pictures always consist of three or four differently coloured squares that are nested within one another, closer to the lower edge of the painting than to the upper edge, i.e. mostly in a 1:3 ratio. This arrangement already creates a spatial effect. Albers exclusively used industrial colours, in order to achieve comparability amongst different colour combinations. With the help of this simple geometric figure, Albers explored the subjectivity of our colour perception. He wanted to investigate the interaction of surfaces, which seemed sometimes brighter and sometimes darker, appearing sometimes in the background and sometimes in the foreground, sometimes standing high and sometimes low, and sometimes both at the same time, creating a floating impression. He called these changing appearances objectively existing facts, "factual facts" on the one hand, and subjectively sensual visual experiences, "actual facts", on the other. Albers thought that only appearances were not deceiving. In 1963 he published his findings in a trendsetting treatise, INTERACTION OF COLOR, a study on the theory of colour. In his treatise, Josef Albers did not investigate the square, but the colour and the title HOMAGE TO THE SQUARE he chose, does not really represent the subject. We can suppose that he chose the square because of its neutrality and lack of direction, i.e. as a figure that suppresses emotional aspects to a minimum. He himself said: "Colour is the core of my language. It is self-sufficient. I do not worship the square. The square is only a tray upon which I spread out my ecstasy using colour"[35], and "When I paint, I see and think primarily in — colour. Mostly colour in movement. Not as following form. [...] But as colour in constant inner movement."[36] These extensive series explore the phenomenon and physiology of our colour perception.

At first, Bernd [1931-2007] and Hilla Becher [born in 1934] merely aimed to document industrial buildings in their photographs. In that sense, their photographs are intentionally objective and neutral, and their stylistic devices are the central perspective, freedom from distortion, overcast daylight and mostly a slightly elevated position. They usually feature industrial architecture such as water and shaft towers, gasometers, blast furnaces and factory buildings. By arranging similar objects in tableaus, they created typologically organised series, so-called 'typologies'. Thus presented, their comparative arrangements lead to knowledge about architecture, especially industrial architecture and the history of industry. From their numerous series, we have chosen WASSERTÜRME (WATER TOWERS) [>36-37],

35 Quoted in: GOTTHARD GRAUBNER. GESPRÄCH MIT JOSEF ALBERS (INTERVIEW WITH JOSEF ALBERS), exhibition catalogue, Museum Quadrat Bottrop, Düsseldorf 2011, p. 95.*
36 Ibid., p. 117.*

because they are fundamental and archetypical examples of the work of the two artists. Despite the documentary objectivity and clarity of their photographs, their series emanate great visual strength, formulating a unique artistic position. This was soon noticed in the art world and the pieces were subsequently regarded as conceptual art, which led to an even greater perception and acknowledgement of their works far beyond photography. It goes without saying that not all design experiments lead to such convincing results. Nevertheless, despite the primacy of intuition in art, it seems that some artists have developed and implemented methods that bear similarity to scientific ones. They designed test arrangements, carried out test series and invented processes tailored to their individual requirements. It is evident that they use methods that have proved successful in the field of art and which have usually helped to develop works with an unmistakable personal character.

Eadweard Muybridge[1830-1904] is considered to be a **borderliner** between science and art. By means of a photographic series, he systematically investigated human and animal movement sequences[38], which he photographed from 1872 to 1885, using cameras placed in a row. His photographs represent anatomical, kinetic and physiological studies on the one hand and a high aesthetic quality on the other. Is this extraordinary and striking combination of science and art a coincidence or do other examples also exist?

In his book WISSENSCHAFT ALS KUNST, Paul Feyerabend writes about the relation-ship between science and art: **"In the beginning, all objects were 'arts'** (Greek: technai), that means, they were only distinguished by their results (the art of navigation was different from the art of healing, and this again differed from the art of rhetoric), but not by their methods. They gathered experiences and classified them as well as possible [...] they also included the correct recognition of symptoms (of the weather or a disease), which means that you could not separate them from the process of learning and practice [...] and 'objectivise' them".[37] A few pages further on, he says: "From Antiquity to the Renaissance, painting, sculpture and architecture were mere handicrafts. [...] Medieval universities then took up music and poetry in the liberal arts, but painting remained amongst the guilds."[38] The 12th-century drawing HORTUS DELICIARUM by Abbess Herrad von Landsberg illustrates this principle: "Philosophy stands as a symbol in the middle of the septem artes liberales. From it stems the tripartite stream of Grammar, Rhetoric and Logic and the quadripartite one of Music, Arithmetic, Geometry and Astronomy."[39] Up to Renaissance, artists were craftsmen. A change was triggered by exceptional artists such as Leonardo da Vinci, who advanced into areas that had, until then, been occupied by other arts.

37 Paul Feyerabend, WISSENSCHAFT ALS KUNST (SCIENCE AS ART), Frankfurt/Main 1984, p.8.*
38 Ibid., p.22.*
39 Kunstgewerbemuseum Zürich (ed.), ORNAMENT? OHNE ORNAMENT, 5 Volumes, Vol.2: Roland Gross, SYMMETRIE, exhibition catalogue, Zurich 1965, p.5.*
40 Cf. Leonardo da Vinci, THE NOTEBOOKS OF LEONARDO DA VINCI, J.P.Richter (ed.), New York 1970 [London 1883], Vol.3, Chapter 39, see also www.en.wikiquote.org/wiki/Leonardo_da_Vinci (retrieved 22/1/2015).*

41 Ursula Brandstätter, GRUNDFRAGEN DER ÄSTHETIK (FUNDAMENTAL QUESTIONS OF AESTHETICS), Cologne, Weimar, Vienna 2008, pp. 40.*
42 Feyerabend 1984, p. 78.*

Leonardo worked as an engineer, anatomist, architect, cartographer, town-planner and botanist. He worked on anatomic studies, invented catapults, rockets, printing presses, robots, windmills, tanks, irrigation systems, flying machines, etc. In his records, he wrote the amazing sentence: "If you are not a mathematician, do not read me, because principally, that is what I am."[40] Whether this really corresponds to his self-conception or whether it was his intention to upgrade his own work, we do not know. Trained sculptor Michelangelo also worked interdisciplinarily as a painter, architect and engineer; and Albrecht Dürer's UNDERWEYSUNG DER MESSUNG, MIT DEM ZIRCKEL UND RICHTSCHEYT (INSTRUCTIONS IN MEASUREMENT WITH COMPASS AND RULER) has more to do with geometry and mathematics than with art. The central perspective was discovered by Renaissance artists and is used today in almost all disciplines to represent their ideas and models — from architecture to artificial film worlds, from medicine to biology and from astronomy to nuclear physics. Their discoveries and inventions led to a scientification of arts and ultimately, to their enhancement. However, in the age of Enlightenment, science and art were split apart. A type of science developed that wanted to be objective and neutral, and a type of art developed that turned to the subjective, the sensual and the emotional. Ursula Brandstätter explains this in more detail: "A major break in the relation-ship between science and art happened in the 18th century, the age of enlightenment, in which reason began to dominate all other human abilities. At the same time analogous thinking and metaphorical recognition were pushed into the background — i.e. out of the scientific realm and into the special realm of art — scientific and artistic methods, tasks and functions began to drift apart. [...] While sciences were increasingly geared towards the ideal of objectivity and the intersubjective generalizability of its findings, art gained a special role as refuge for subjectivity, individuality and originality that had been ousted from the realm of science."[41] This separation was maintained up until the 20th century, with each scientific discipline developing its own highly specialised methodology. From the 1980s onwards, there has been an increasing discussion about the new rapprochement between science and art. Proof of this is a whole host of essays, writings, exhibitions and symposiums, in which the objectivity and neutrality of sciences are challenged and the development of the arts is discussed, turning again to scientific methodology. This development peaked in Paul Feyerabend's provocative and much discussed hypothesis: "[Th]e analogous situation in the sciences can be best described [in its relationship to the arts, author's note] and the many overlaps between the two [...] as follows, namely that sciences are arts in the sense of this progressive understanding of art. [...] If we lived in a time in which man had a naive faith in the healing power and 'objectivity' of arts [...], then it would be opportune to point out that arts are sciences."[42] One well-known example in physics clarifies impressively the relativity of scientifically gained knowledge. Today, the phenomenon of light is chiefly explained using two completely different models: Depending on which phenomenon is observed, it is either described as an electromagnetic wave or as a light quantum, or photon. There is an interaction between the test setup and the object to be identified, which forces the light to behave as a wave in one case, and as a particle in the other. Both models are correct and incompatible. This one example stands for many others and shows that the way in which something is observed has a decisive influence on our perception and cognition. Furthermore, the example reveals that the insights into reality that science is able to yield are only valid in certain contexts.

In the following, we would like to introduce further design methods and examples from different disciplines such as advertising, posterdesign, art history, documentation and representation techniques such as photography, painting and object art, using **exemplary selected recent works**. We have selected design processes that, despite their different concepts and implementation, employ methods that show how broad the range of possibilities is. We would like to describe these methods as 'experimental design'. The first example is Absolut Vodka's international advertising campaign[>pp.254]. It is probably one of the most famous series worldwide involving one single product based on one single principle: the variation of its packaging, the bottle. A second set of examples is Günther Kieser's famous Jazzposters[>pp.150], which he designed over many decades with much enthusiasm and overflowing imagination. He repeatedly changed music instruments into fantastically impossible objects. This series does not boast formal completeness, but instead adopts the technique of treating similar motifs in a similar manner. DAS GROSSE SCHWEINEBUCH OR: DAS SCHWEIN IN DER BILDENDEN KUNST DES ABEND-LANDES (PIGART)[>pp.116] by Michael Ryba shows pictures, sculptures, objects and artifacts of art history, whose main characters are lovingly replaced by pigs. The serial character emerges through the pig's recurrent appearance as a motif and by referring to well-known art historical standards. In spite of this inevitably extensive stylistic shift, a clearly definable content-based fabric is woven. TAG UM TAG GUTER TAG (DAY BY DAY, GOOD DAY)[>112-113] is a series of five thousand paintings by the artist Peter Dreher, showing one and the same glass. At first sight, these pictures look like a repetition of the same picture, but on closer inspection it is clear that they all differ in terms of shade and reflection. Half of the pictures were painted by day and the other half by night. "In 1972, a first single picture of a glass was created. Since 1974, at least 50 pictures have emerged every year, showing an empty water glass upon a white table surface against a white background. The glass resembles a real glass in size. The outer conditions such as lighting, distances and picture format remain unchanged."[43] It is the minimal differences between the pictures that make the work special and turn the series into a collection of subjective snap-shots. Over a period of more than four decades, this conceptual serial painting developed into the artist's oeuvre. PARLAMENTE HOUSES OF PARLIAMENT)>pp.222 is a photographic work by Jörg Hempel showing deserted plenary halls in different countries. Central perspective, homogeneous lighting and similar shooting positions establish comparability, thus emphasising differences and even enabling or provoking interpretation and appraisal. These inner spaces narrate the culture and history of the respective country by means of their architecture, furnishings and decoration and we are inclined to interpret the images as revealing country-specific traits or even the presence of certain regimes.

The above-described examples show that **methods** are also implemented successfully in design and that it can also be useful to design individual processes to meet one's own needs. And still there are no valid methodologies available, i.e. no repertoire of standardised methods such as are used in science. But even if there were, they would probably only yield the expected, as once something is invented, its repetition is no longer a creative act. Artistic methods therefore cannot be re-used to create creativity. Strictly speaking, the creative act in science is therefore not scientific, because it is unique. Only subsequent experimental evidence that must be reproducible fulfils scientific criteria. In an exaggerated sense, we can say that science as we understand it today only confirms hypotheses and theories, whereas establishing them is an artistic act in itself or, as Friedrich Kittler remarks: "Science creates knowledge by means of art."

Design research therefore has to invent, try out and discard its own variety of methods. We need a pluralism of methods, a concept which has been borrowed from Karl Popper's epistemological work THE LOGIC OF SCIENTIFIC DISCOVERY[44]. If methodology in design means a **variable system** that allows for systematics and their modification, a system that is controllable and influenceable and individually adaptable, this tool can develop remarkable potential. If the methods are understood and used as such, they can become part of the creative process that will further new knowledge and help to reduce the process of trial and error by means of targeted and methodical experiments. Only if we can achieve the selected targets more efficiently by means of designed or invented methods, can they be appraised as useful and valuable.

In the following, we would like to emphasise further relationships between scientific and artistic **creativity** and for that reason, the concept needs to be briefly outlined. If the expression 'vertical and horizontal thinking', which can be found in many publications, is strongly abbreviated, it can be described as follows: 'Vertical thinking' means logical thinking — to draw conclusions that are assessed as being right or wrong, useful or useless. It is especially used in logic, philosophy and mathematics; Edward De Bono also calls it "selective thinking"[45],

44 Herbert Keuth (ed.), KARL POPPER. LOGIK DER FORSCHUNG (THE LOGIC OF SCIENTIFIC DISCOVERY), Berlin 2004.*
45 Edward de Bono, NEW THINK. THE USE OF LATERAL THINKING IN THE GENERATION OF IDEAS, New York 1968.*
46 Ibid., p.10 (German edition 1989).*

because it distinguishes between right and wrong. In contrast, "horizontal thinking" means creative thinking. It is described as thinking in alternatives and makes comparisons, establishes analogies, figures out possibilities, searches for other ways, works with parallels, associations and diversity and in that way, leads to a wide range of results. It thus creates possibilities and because of that, it is also called "generative thinking" or, as De Bono put it: "lateral thinking". He equates it with creative thinking, making the following remark: "Lateral thinking is closely related to intuition, creativity and humour. All four processes have the same basis."[46] Both 'modes of thinking' are reflected in the categorisation of creativity techniques. Here, too, we chiefly distinguish between two groups: The 'intuitive' method works on a similar basis to horizontal thinking, using chains of association, analogies and alienation, aimed at helping to overcome rigid approaches and establish new connections. Here, almost a dozen main methods and countless variants are commonly used — including well-known ones such as brainstorming or mind mapping, and less well-known ones such as semantic intuition or analogy. 'Discursive' methods work in a manner similar to vertical thinking — i.e. they are logically conclusive. Here, fewer methods are generally used, perhaps only half a dozen, such as the morphological matrix, the relevance tree analysis or functional analysis. Creativity techniques (heuristics) are processes which focus on problems that cannot be resolved by means of logic or because of a lack of data or proven knowledge. "Such techniques include suppositions, analogies, hypotheses, models and thought experiments, amongst others."[47] Methods are also employed that can be used to find solutions in open situations, which are today known as creativity techniques. Many of the works presented are based upon or drawn from them. Visual creativity should also be stimulated using various methods, in order to achieve targeted results more quickly. However, that does not mean that a method immediately transforms into creativity; it is rather used as a means and tool.

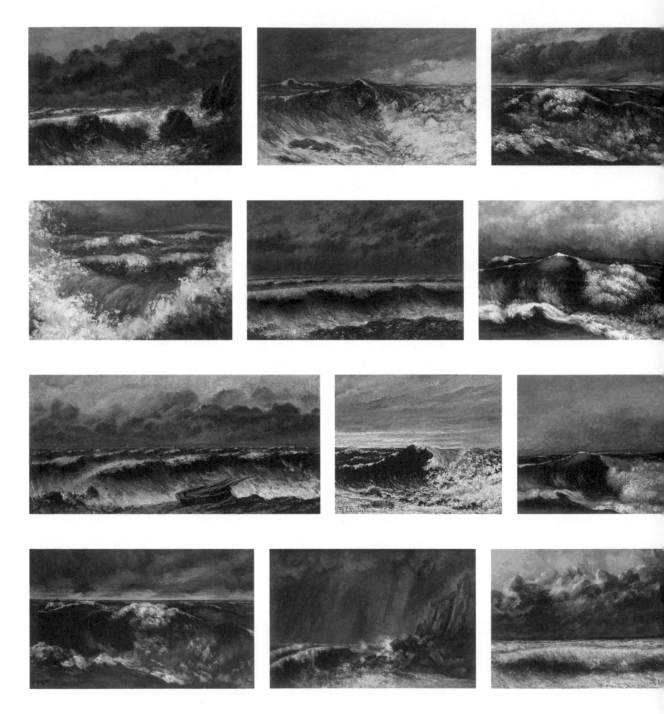

LA VAGUE (THE WAVE), 1865–1869, Gustave Courbet.

103×73 cm    100×65 cm    100×65 cm    100×65 cm    100×65 cm

100×73 cm    106×73 cm    110×73 cm    106×74 cm    106×73 cm

91×63 cm    100×65 cm    100×65 cm    106×73 cm    92×65 cm

ROUEN CATHEDRAL, 1892–1894, Claude Monet.

×65 cm     100×65 cm     100×65 cm     100×65 cm     100×65 cm

×65 cm     100×65 cm     100×65 cm     100×65 cm     100×65 cm

×73 cm     106×73 cm

Daniel Wildenstein (ed.), MONET ODER DER TRIUMPH DES IMPRESSIONISMUS, catalogue raisoné, Cologne 1996.

**31 DRAFTING A SYSTEM OF VISUAL METHODS**

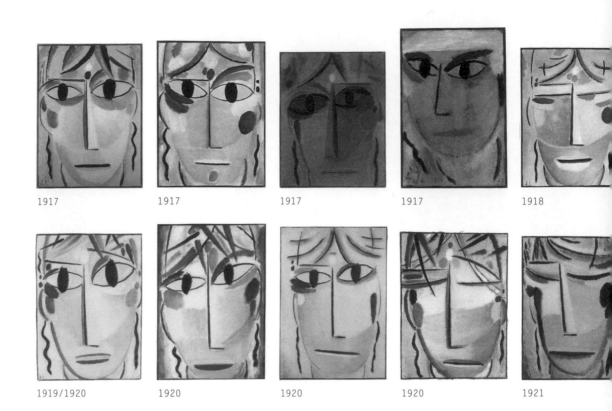

1917    1917    1917    1917    1918

1919/1920    1920    1920    1920    1921

SAVIOR'S FACES, 1917–1937, Alexej von Jawlensky (18 of 87 paintings according to catalogue raisoné).

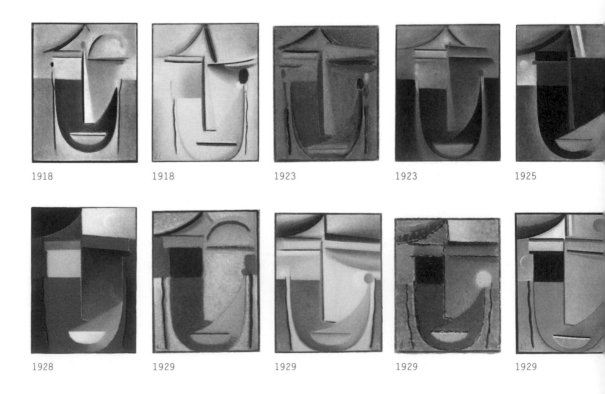

1918    1918    1923    1923    1925

1928    1929    1929    1929    1929

ABSTRACT HEADS, 1918–1937, Alexej von Jawlensky (20 of 274 paintings according to catalogue raisoné).

1919    1919    1919

1921    1922    1931

1926    1926    1927    1928

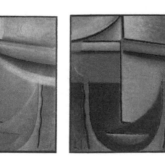  

1931    1931    1933    1935

Volker Rattemeyer, Renate Petziger (eds.), JAWLENSKY. MEINE LIEBE GALKA!, Wiesbaden 2004.

33 DRAFTING A SYSTEM OF VISUAL METHODS

The prints are based on
the oil painting
in the format 92×73 cm.
The prints are reproductions
painted over with gouache
and china ink each 98×75 cm.

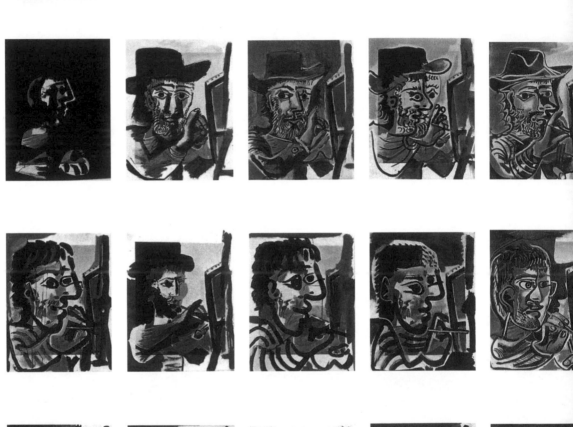

THE PAINTER, 10th to 24th October 1964, Pablo Picasso.

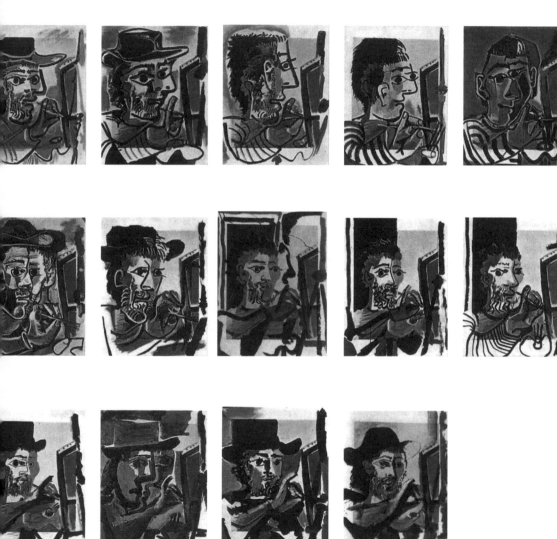

Ingo F. Walther (ed.), PABLO PICASSO, Cologne 2002.

35 DRAFTING A SYSTEM OF VISUAL METHODS

HOMAGE TO THE SQUARE, 1950–1976, Josef Albers.

WT 7, 1967–1982
9 black-and-white
photographs all
from Germany,
40×30 cm.

WT 12, 1972–1987
9 black-and-white
photographs;
7 from France,
1 from Italy,
1 from Germany,
40×30 cm.

WATERTOWERS, Bernd and Hilla Becher.

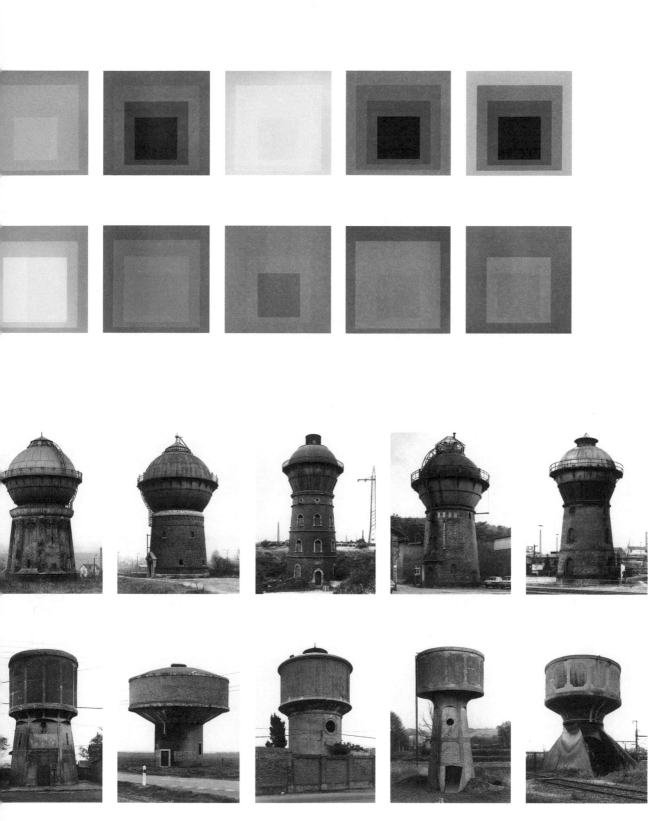

Bottom: BERND & HILLA BECHER – TYPOLOGIEN INDUSTRIELLER BAUTEN, Düsseldorf 2003.  Top: Josef Albers, FORMULATION : ARTICULATION, London 2006.

37 DRAFTING A SYSTEM OF VISUAL METHODS

**38 DRAFTING A SYSTEM OF VISUAL METHODS**

Eadweard Muybridge, THE MALE AND THE FEMALE FIGURE IN MOTION, 60 CLASSIC PHOTOGRAPHIC SEQUENCES, Dover Publications, New York 1984.

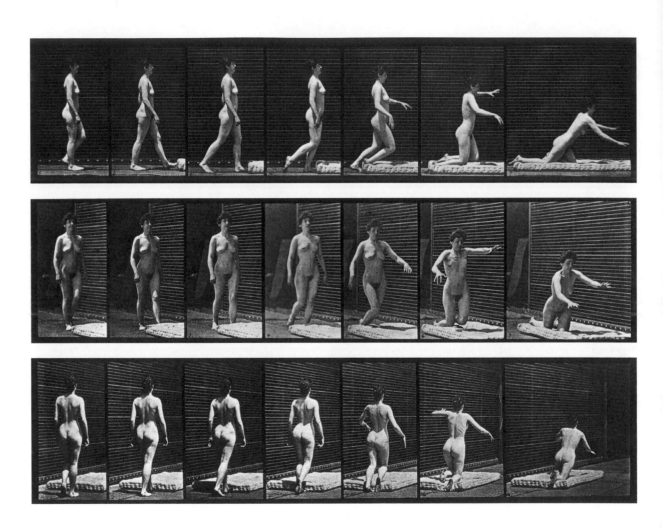

STUMBLING AND FALLING ON THE GROUND, 1884/1885 (3 of 6 sequences of a tableau), Eadweard Muybridge.

SNOW CRYSTALS, 1931 (12 of more than 5000 photographs), Wilson A. Bentley.

Wilson A. Bentley, William J. Humphreys, SNOW CRYSTALS, Dover Publications, New York 1962.

**39 DRAFTING A SYSTEM OF VISUAL METHODS**

This fractal was generated with the Ultra Fractal 3 programme. The pictures showing the section of the next picture were edited by the authors.

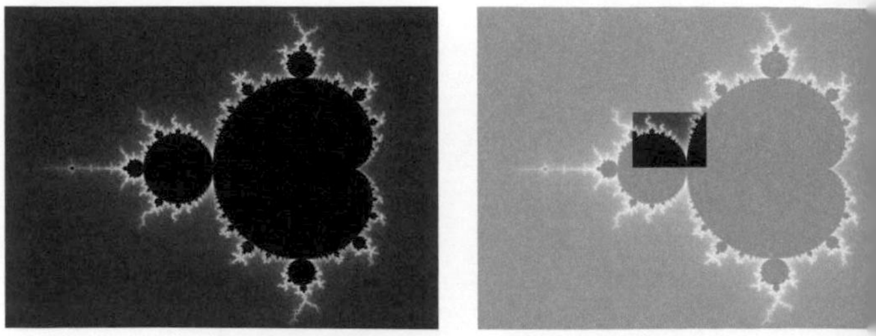

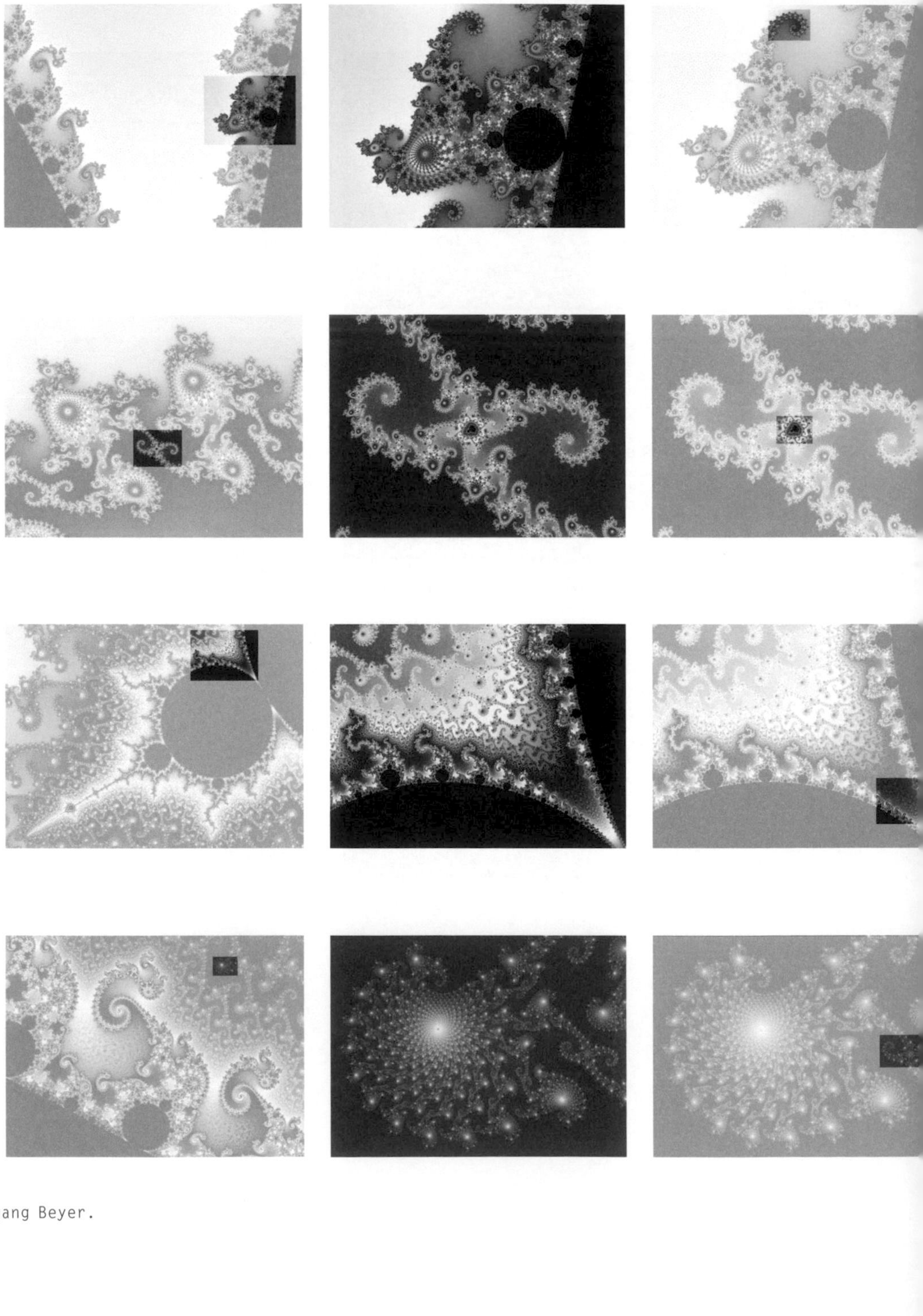

FRACTAL, 2006, Wolfgang Beyer.

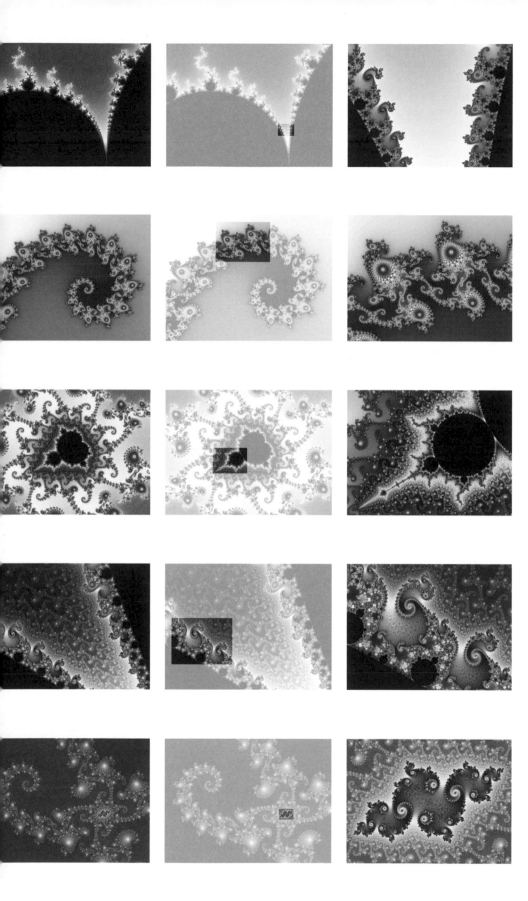

41 DRAFTING A SYSTEM OF VISUAL METHODS

Closely related to creativity is **intuition** – defined as inspiration, intuitive or anticipatory understanding or immediate insight into connections without rational or deliberate derivation. To act intuitively can also mean leaving a well-known, well-trodden path of solution and following one's flash of intuition. The physicist and Nobel Prize winner Gerd Binnig writes about how intuition is dealt with: "In science, intuitive thoughts are deemed unacceptable. [...] However, the rejection of intuitive thoughts seems exaggerated. All important scientific works are actually based on intuition. But, it seems we should not admit that."[48] Why, then, despite methodology and systematics and the collection of data and information, does intuition play such an important role in art, just as it does in science? The reason is, as already mentioned, that facts are never complete, often erroneous and what's more, subject to varied interpretations. If ultimately, data collection has to be terminated and permanently incomplete information evaluated – be it because of a lack of time or too great a complexity – then intuition comes into play. The subconscious is, it is speculated, in a better position to consider and evaluate a large amount of information. Goethe's well-known quotation, "Unless you feel, naught will you ever gain"[49], probably describes this context best. The ability to deal intuitively with matters stems from many years of dealing with a subject, from countless repetitions and therefore, from great experience. The one leads to the other: experience and findings that are gained by means of different methods foster intuition. In his short contribution on YouTube, psychologist and management consultant Peter Kurse says the following: "If you act intuitively, you should be able to look back on a long history of learning to the point of exhaustion."[50] Moreover, he says that there is only a chance of making the right decision intuitively, if the experiences on which it is based are still valid. In THE ACT OF CREATION, Arthur Koestler deals with intuition, writing: "The creative act is not an act of creation in the sense of the Old Testament. It does not create something out of nothing; it uncovers, selects, re-shuffles, combines, synthesizes already existing facts, ideas, faculties, skills."[51] Koestler describes the creative act in a brilliantly extensive line of argument that is warmly recommended to anyone who wants to learn more about this subject. We would like to present a very brief description of one aspect of his thoughts relating to the similarity in the process of both making jokes and discoveries in science and art: "The logical structure of the creative process is the same in all three cases: it consists of the discovery of hidden similarities",[52] connecting hitherto "mutually incompatible frames of reference"[53]. Koestler calls this process "bisociation" in order to express the fact that at least two different frames of association are involved. He explains bisociation with reference to Gutenberg, Kepler and Darwin. In Gutenberg's days, books had already been printed with woodblocks for almost one hundred years. Whole pages were

**42 DRAFTING A SYSTEM OF VISUAL METHODS**

**48** Gerd Binnig, AUS DEM NICHTS. ÜBER DIE KREATIVITÄT VON NATUR UND MENSCH (EX NIHILO. ON CREATIVITY OF NATURE AND MAN), Munich, Zurich 1989, p.219.*
**49** Johann Wolfgang von Goethe, FAUST. EINE TRAGÖDIE (A TRAGEDY), www.en.wikiquote.org/wiki/Goethe%27s_Faust (retrieved 22/1/2015).
**50** Peter Kurse, Short presentation "Wie reagieren Menschen auf wachsende Komplexität?" ("How do People React to Growing Complexity?"), Video online at: www.youtube.com/watch?v=m3qqDOeSahU (retrieved 4/6/2014).*
**51** Koestler 1964, p.120.* **52** Ibid., p.17.* **53** Ibid.,* p.25.*

cut into the wood, coated with paint, covered with paper and then transferred
by means of a frictional tool. Seals and coins had long been cast, preferably using
an alloy of lead — and there were coin mints made of steel with which coins were
minted by means of a hard blow. There were also screw presses, which were used
in various different areas such as in paper and wine production, coinage, or even as
instruments of torture. Gutenberg's achievement consisted of connecting these
isolated systems to form a new unit. He divided the printing plate into single,
reusable characters totalling 290 letters and ligatures, casted them from lead and
printed them using a screw press.[54] Koestler describes Darwin's achievement
as follows: "Charles Darwin is perhaps the most outstanding illustration of the
thesis that 'creative originality' does not mean creating or originating a system
of ideas out of nothing but rather out of the combination of well-established
patterns of thought — by a process of cross-fertilization, as it were."[55]
"Towards the end of the 18th Century, so much proof [...] had been gathered that
evolution theories emerged simultaneously in several European countries [...] —
i.e. fifteen years before Darwin's birth."[56] Accordingly, Darwin reassembled facts
that scientists of his time had already known, using them to develop his
revolutionary theory of evolution. Koestler further writes about creativity when
working with data evaluation, stating: "Scientists [...] consider themselves
as rag and bone men rummaging in the garbage bin of 'empirical data' without having
a clear idea that the art of collecting rags is also subject to intuition."[57]

Both Gutenberg and Darwin had the creative power to recognise commonly known
connections and structures and to assemble them in such a way that new knowledge
emerged and new conclusions could be drawn. By **selecting the right combination,**
they succeeded in creating an innovative technology and in discovering
a revolutionary model of nature. This power is the expression of creative
intelligence that is able to recognise relevant patterns within seemingly chaotic
structures of the available material. In this context, the ability to be
familiar with as many reference systems as possible and to shift between them
without limitation, plays a decisive role. Whether knowledge is gained by
collection, observation or an experiment — it is ultimately these special abilities
that decide upon success or failure.

Two further aspects that often accompany discoveries, are briefly outlined
in the following. The first states that the actual discovery nearly always follows
**countless failures:** "People who try to be creative will naturally make a lot
of mistakes. There is so much scrap."[58] The creative scientist thus needs a high
degree of stability — psychologists call it frustration tolerance —, in order
to be able to bear these failures. We know from many biographies that artists, too,

54 Cf. ibid., pp.122–125.*
55 Ibid., p.131.*
56 Ibid., p.134.*
57 Ibid., pp.137.*
58 Binnig 1989, p.62.*

possess this special quality, particularly with regard to their activities. Their findings also require countless exercises and endless studies, intensively working on a subject or with a medium for years or even decades.

The second aspect is that **scientific discoveries are often made more than once**: "In 1922, Ogburn and Thomas attracted general attention with their publication of approximately 150 inventions and discoveries that had been already independently made by different people. Only a few years before, Merton had come to the paradox conclusion that 'the phenomenon of the multiple independent scientific discovery was more the rule than the exception'."[59] Thus, discoveries are not unique isolated events, but are rather embedded in a temporal and social context, which is crucial for their success, but not for their creative performance.

In order to release creativity and intuition, a number of other frame conditions are required, revolving around concepts such as **freedom, play, pleasure, interest, leisure and chaos**. Although none of these concepts can be fully represented here, I have noted some fleeting personal thoughts and associations in the section that follows. I gladly leave the definition, discourse and discussion to experts from the area of psychology, sociology and philosophy.

**Freedom** neither has a psychological or sociological meaning here, it is neither positive nor negative freedom, it is neither personal, sovereign nor civil; I simply wish to make some remarks on 'inner freedom': It describes the state in which abilities and talents can be used without constraints and fears such as conventions, morals, role patterns, drives, etc. It refers to freedom in the sense of absence of the fear of failing or not meeting requirements. Since search and trial are always prone to failure, it is of utmost importance to let mistakes happen and accept the mishap. It is precisely the unsuccessful experiment that has the potential to bring forth valuable results. It is only possible to recognise this fact, even to provoke errors, control them or to deliberately take advantage of them — as in the work of Fons Hickmann[>138] —, if one has inner freedom. The common notion "one learns from one's mistakes" is not really appreciated in the workplace, but it is especially true for the creative design process. In DAS GLEICHE NOCHMAL ANDERS, Samuel Beckett writes ironically, that "being an artist means to fail as no other would dare to fail, because failure is the artist's world"[60]. The foreword says that "'failure' is the essence of making art, it is the reason for and motor of today's artwork, i.e. it is not a negation, but an optimal condition."[61]

We are allowed to make mistakes when we **play**, because playing is not a 'serious' thing, and that is its decisive advantage. Playing means trying out, attempting, exploring and repeating actions until they succeed. Mostly, parts of a larger whole

**59** Koestler 1964, p.109.*
**60** Samuel Beckett, DAS GLEICHE NOCHMAL ANDERS. TEXTE ZUR BILDENDEN KUNST, Frankfurt/Main 2000, p.59.*
**61** Ibid., p.15.*

are practiced in this way. It seems to happen playfully, without any great effort, or we do not notice the effort, and success comes automatically, as a side-effect. This apparent lightness and aimlessness, however, is learning in reality, i.e. "learning for life" and is thus survival training in the best sense of the word. Observations from the animal world prove this hypothesis to be true. We develop many of our mental and physical abilities by playing, something which is easy to see when you watch children playing. The emphasis on the pleasure of playing, the continuous shift between tension and relaxation reduces the aspect of strain. That is the main reason why playing is important, especially for creative work. This is proven by the biographies of eminent scientists and artists, who have maintained this playful element as an adult. Sigmund Freud described Leonardo da Vinci as follows: "Throughout his whole life, the great Leonardo remained childlike in some aspects. People say that all great men have to maintain a childish element. Even as an adult, he continued to play."[62]. When playing, one tends to forget oneself — even though one is wide awake and fully conscious at the same time. In Anglo-American countries, this state is known as 'flow' and the German Jewish teacher Kurt Hahn called it "creative passion" at the beginning of the 20th century. Schiller's well-known statement is still valid today: "Man only plays when, in the full meaning of the word, he is a man, and he is only completely a man when he plays."[63] In his book HOMO LUDENS, the Dutch historian Johan Huizinga investigated the meaning of play for many cultural areas. He describes it as the origin of all great cultures: "In the following, I would like to show that culture emerges from playing, and that culture is initially enacted. [...] In these plays, the community expresses the meaning of life and the world. However, this should not be understood in the sense that enactment changes into culture, but rather that culture, in its original phases, has something playful about it, and that it is even enacted in the forms and atmosphere of a play."[64]

One essential driving force of playing is **pleasure,** which is often a mere functional pleasure. Psychologists describe the desire to do something for its own sake, for the sake of mere pleasure, as 'intrinsic motivation'. You could also call it joy or sheer pleasure in doing something. It means pleasure instead of burden, pleasure and enjoyment in fulfilling a task in the sense of feeling self-awareness and knowledge of the world, and sometimes it just helps to satisfy one's curiosity. In art, pleasure is not only crucial for the creative act, but has always been present as a theme in works of painting, sculpture and handicrafts. It is not only the creation and representation of beauty and perfection that are able to arouse pleasure, but also the observation and knowledge of it. As Auguste Renoir put it: "I love pictures that arouse in me the desire to walk around in them, if they are landscapes or, if they are women, then to caress them."[65]

62 Quoted in: Frank Zöllner, LEONARDO DA VINCI. COMPLETE PAINTINGS AND DRAWINGS, Cologne 2003, p. 6.*
63 Friedrich Schiller, "III. Über die ästhetische Erziehung des Menschen. Fortsetzung", in: DIE HOREN, 2nd Volume, 1795.
64 Johan Huizinga, HOMO LUDENS. A STUDY OF THE PLAY-ELEMENT IN CULTURE, Boston 1971 (German edition 2006, p. 57).*
65 www.gutezitate.com/zitat/277551 (retrieved 22/1/2015).*

Should there be a profound **interest** and desire to explore new things, that is, curiosity in the best sense of the word, then there is a need to experience the world by exploring it, to fathom out things and test various different considerations, thus bringing forth the necessary patience, passion and devotion for a scientific or artistic profession. "Interest" stems from Latin and consists of the parts "inter" meaning 'between, amidst', and "esse", meaning 'to be'. How passionate and enduring one's 'being', or ultimately one's 'remaining' is, depends on one's emotional connection. And still: "It is not the love of doing something that is crucial, but the distance."[66]

**Leisure,** here, means creative leisure as a precondition for culture, art and creativity, corresponding to the Latin word 'otium', meaning leisure, peace, study and learning, but also hesitation and slowness. In this context, stopping and lingering are essential for perceiving, receiving and feeling. This temporal infinity is an important prerequisite for acquiring knowledge and becoming aware of connections in order to find solutions. It is much easier for this to take place in a state of leisure. Cicero once uttered the well-known words "otium cum dignitate"[67], meaning "leisure with dignity", referring to the state in which men spent their time doing scientific and philosophical work. We gladly adopt this meaning to describe creative design work.

In his MINIMA MORALIA, Theodor W. Adorno writes that "the purpose of today's art is to bring order into chaos"[68]. A very interesting thought, indeed. But what if one notices that **chaos** is already there? One day I noticed that my working methods had become somewhat chaotic, although I tried to work systematically. But the results do not reveal the chaos that had preceded them — on the contrary, they appear quite orderly. Somehow, then, the work has its order. This probably happens by way of constant and permanent repetition, editing and rearranging it, i.e. it happens by itself, as it were, which is a really wonderful process that one should let happen. It would, however, be nice if one could better understand how it worked — because one could then retrieve it more easily, whenever necessary. Our mind is probably a structured and pattern-forming system in its own right that classifies the world, putting it in order, so to speak. It is an order that is created in us and through us to make the world more comprehensible in its infinite complexity and enable us to deal with it more easily. It is assumed that we are very creative in installing an order into a world that appears to be chaotic, and that we strive for logic and intuition when doing so. Hence, the orders we find, and frequently also invent, are patterns formed from chaos. We would like to point out that this is a basic idea of radical constructivism to which Paul Watzlawick has made major contributions. He has accordingly maintained "that we do not just encounter the world, but that we invent our own world"[69]. Recent brain research

**46 DRAFTING A SYSTEM OF VISUAL METHODS**

**66** Armin Lindauer, HELMUT LORTZ. DENKZETTEL, Mainz 2003, p.122.*
**67** Cicero, DE ORATORE, www.en.wikipedia.org/wiki/Otium (retrieved 22/1/2015).
**68** Theodor W. Adorno, MINIMA MORALIA. REFLECTIONS FROM A DAMAGED LIFE, Berlin, Frankfurt/Main 1969, p.298. (German edition).*
**69** Cf. Paul Watzlawick, HOW REAL IS REAL?, New York 1976. Audio lecture broadcasted by Deutschlandradio (retrievable at YouTube). at the beginning of the 90s, speaker's introduction.

results prove that we believe that we map the world, but in truth, we construct it.[70] Whether and to what extent these invented patterns are relevant or whether they are often simply incorrect, is another significant aspect that is often the subject of experimental psychology research; however, we would like to refer to the literature on that subject.

A popular direction of applied design, the graphic design of the 1990s, appears to embody the complete opposite of the methodical approach. Remember the atomisation of 'Bauhaus / Swiss / Ulm Design' by David Carson by means of **deconstructing** font, type area and picture. A new tool made this possible: the Apple Macintosh. What is interesting about it is that the Apple computer's design was the complete opposite of the graphic design that it generated. Whereas the former was completely sober and clear, without any ornaments, entirely according to Bauhaus tradition, the latter tries to generate a free-riding, seemingly random design that is characterised by fragmented, broken forms. Such 'deconstructive' trends are also found in philosophy, especially in Jacques Derrida's works of the second half of the 20th century — and directly connected to Derrida — in architecture since the 1980s. At the beginning of the 20th Century, cubists had already dissected and reassembled their pictorial motifs. A closer look at their works, however, reveals that their dissection of form immediately led to new structures and patterns. This is also the case with recent deconstructions. In his essay ENTROPY AND ART, Rudolf Arnheim reveals a similar contradiction: "Simple forms are [...] the tangible result of physical forces, whose balance is achieved through the best possible arrangement. This is true both for organic and inorganic systems and creates symmetry in crystals, flowers, animal bodies, etc."[71]

We can tell from nature that not only the right angle or the grid — synonyms of Modernism — ensure structural **order**. Nature is full of countless complex order systems and there are no signs of arbitrariness, let alone randomness. By contrast, Arnheim refers to the second law of thermodynamics, writing: "that the world of matter is moving away from states of order towards a growing disorder and that the final state of the universe will be a maximum of disorder."[72] We have to take into consideration that this disorder signifies the entropic chaos of physics, meaning a "degradation of the degree of order, where forms, functional connections and local affiliations are destroyed"[73]. Arnheim compares this initially irresolvable contradiction with two eruptive currents of modern art that either have "a tendency to extreme simplicity" — exemplarily referring to Minimal Art, or "by contrast [...]" attempt to "randomly or deliberately create disorder" — referring here to Jackson Pollock's action painting.[74] Yet, upon closer inspection you can see that his own pictures certainly consist of regular structures and that they show virtually ideal repetitions. In the opposite sense, then, it is not easy to

70 Cf. Wolf Singer, ICONIC TURN (FELIX BURDA MEMORIAL LECTURES) — VOM BILD ZUR WAHRNEHMUNG, www.youtube.com/watch?v=5YMOoTXtYFM (retrieved 5/6/2014).*
71 Rudolf Arnheim, ENTROPIE UND KUNST: EIN VERSUCH ÜBER UNORDNUNG UND ORDNUNG, Köln 1979, pp.14–15.*
72 Ibid., pp.20.*  73 Ibid., p.22.*  74 Ibid., p.20.*

work chaotically, in an environment that is without structure or order, or
as Einstein once put it: "Every order is the first step on the road to a new chaos."
But the reverse could also be true: "Every chaos is the first step on the road
to a new order."

We can see an interesting connection between creative and **chaotic systems** —
they are described as chaotic only when the laws that affect them are known,
but their results are not precisely foreseeable. One well-known example of this
phenomenon is the weather — we know its system, yet our ability to forecast
the weather is evidently very limited. This is revealed in Snowflakes[>39]
which always form hexagons, but none are identical. A third well-known example
is dust formation, whose sudden appearance is still not exactly predictable.
Despite their random behaviour, these phenomena all have characteristic patterns
and are thus known as 'complex dynamic systems'. One special variation of these is
seen in fractals[>40-41]. This word was coined by Benoît Mandelbrot who explains
it in great detail in his book THE FRACTAL GEOMETRY OF NATURE from 1977.
"Although we strictly define the concept 'fractal quantity', 'natural fractal'
or just 'fractal' is often only used to describe a natural pattern in everyday
language."[75] Fractals are mathematical quantities that are able to calculate
and represent natural patterns and living systems. You can find them everywhere —
in crystals, plants and living organisms; in mountains, woods and clouds;
in the ramification systems of ferns, rivers, trees, cauliflower, blood vessels and
lungs. Since they exist in so many different systems and can only be distinguished
by the variation of their ramifications, they are of far-reaching significance.
One main characteristic of the pictorial representation of fractals is that large
and small segments possess similarities, i.e. a segment of a figure might
resemble the original figure, but will never be identical to it. Accordingly,
they develop repetitive, or mathematically speaking, periodical structures that
are more or less predictable, but not in detail. Mandelbrot writes thus:
"They possess the same degree of irregularity and/or fragmentation in all size
ranges."[76] By means of fractals, i.e. special mathematical algorithms, it will be
possible to artificially reproduce complex natural processes and phenomena.
Although these prototypes are determined by a pictorial idea, e.g. by 'clouds' or
'mountains', they remain unpredictable and incalculable in their exact development.
Fractal geometry has enabled us, for the first time, to mathematically
reproduce processes and images from nature, such as are required for films and
animations, revolutionising production. Having quickly recognised this enormous
potential, scientists, film artists and designers have been generating artificial
worlds for some decades that are impossible to distinguish from real ones.
Art and mathematics, pictures and algorithms all come together at this point and
achieve a closeness that one would not have deemed possible before.

75 Benoît B. Mandelbrot, DIE FRAKTALE GEOMETRIE DER NATUR (THE FRACTAL GEOMETRY OF NATURE), Basel, Boston 1987, p. 16.*
76 Ibid., p. 13.*

Gerd Binnig also refers to a remarkable series of processes that in his opinion are fractal processes. He names evolution, coincidence, mutation, reproduction and the primordial soup.[77] This is interesting because it reveals an enlightening connection between mathematics and the creative process. In mathematics, the repeated use of the same function and calculation method is known as **iteration**. And the calculation of the fractals described above is also iterative. It is worth noting that creativity is also described as an iterative process. Robert Dilts, author, trainer and representative of neurolinguistic programming, prefers to speak of it as "reiterative" — "permanent repetition" — and writes of it "that according to the law of required variability, the process of creativity requires permanent actualisation, extension and revision of its own creative strategies [...]"[78]. "If you try something out and it does not work out, then you return to the starting point and try something else. Instead of giving up [...] you change it a bit and try it again. You constantly make slight alterations, and then, all of a sudden, it seems as if you had made a quantum jump",[79] He continues: "The paradox of creativity is that in truth, the main part of it is a highly reiterative (repeating itself) and permanently progressive process that is based on feedback."[80]

Other striking **analogies** can be found between experimental design and fractal geometry. Both of them are active within known reference systems and are therefore calculable to a certain extent and both have an unpredictable part, despite known frame conditions. It is possible to steer the fractal geometry system by changing algorithms that we previously referred to as ramification laws, and to control design experiments through variation of visual signs. Order and creative disorder, system and chaos are closely interwoven. According to Mandelbrot, it is the element of randomness, of the unpredictable, which is inherent in both chaotic systems and experiments, that has the creative potential to generate new solutions. "These useful fractals contain randomness both in their regularities and irregularities."[81] Perhaps that is why we tend to speak of 'creative chaos'.

There is, however, a decisive difference between **pure coincidence** and chaotic systems, namely its supposed incalculability. And yet, coincidence also possesses creative moments, for, as we all know, randomly found forms and figures often have surprisingly great powers of persuasion. Many artists make use of this principle of randomness and adopt techniques that are implicitly random. That was the guiding principle of Dadaism. However, it is a real challenge to deliberately produce a credible coincidence. As opposed to the truly coincidental, the intentional is mostly more conspicuous. True coincidence expresses itself in its greater relevance, at least in the best of cases, and that is why artists often search for the border between control and coincidence. As Gabriel García Marquez said: "If, however, one should choose the realm of arbitrariness and imagination,

77 Cf. Binnig 1989, pp. 152–160.*
78 Robert B. Dilts, KNOW-HOW FÜR TRÄUMER, STRATEGIEN DER KREATIVITÄT (TOOLS FOR DREAMERS), Paderborn 1994, p. 89.*
79 Ibid., p. 376.* 80 Ibid.* 81 Mandelbrot 1987, p. 13.*

**49 DRAFTING A SYSTEM OF VISUAL METHODS**

82 Quoted in: Gottlieb Guntern (ed.), IRRITATION UND KREATIVITÄT, Zurich 1993, pp. 214. 83 Adorno 1969, p. 298. 84 Binnig 1989, p. 172.*
85 Gottfried Boehm, "Die Wiederkehr der Bilder", in: iedem (ed.), WAS IST EIN BILD?, Munich 1995, pp. 11–38, here p. 13.
86 Willibald Sauerländer, "Iconic turn? Eine Bitte um Ikonoklasmus", in: Hubert Burda, Christa Maar (eds.),
ICONIC TURN. DIE NEUE MACHT DER BILDER, Cologne 2004, pp. 408.*
87 Statista – The Statistic Portal: www.de.statista.com/statistik/daten/studie/207321/umfrage/upload-von-videomaterial-bei-youtube-pro-minute-zeitreihe/
(retrieved 5/6/2014).*
88 Cf. Benjamin Schischka, "Zuckerberg. Facebook-User laden täglich 350 Millionen neue Fotos hoch", in: PC WELT, 31/1/2013.*

then there is a logic to it that should be respected in the same way. Arbitrariness, too, has its own laws, and if one indulges in arbitrariness, then one should know its laws in order to be able to keep them. [...] Hemingway's advice has taught me that you can always invent anything you want, as long as you are able to do it credibly."[82] According to this, then, a new logic emerges with its own laws. It is probably a supposed arbitrariness that holds creative potential, or as Adorno put it in his MINIMA MORALIA, aphoristic as he was: "Artistic productivity is the power of the arbitrary in the involuntary."[83] However, it could be that there is no such thing as mere coincidence, but that we are just not able to recognise, understand or produce the rules governing it, because our abilities are far too limited to grasp its infinite complexity. Gerd Binnig comments on this phenomenon as follows: "What is apparent chaos? It is a chaos that we do not understand, in which we fail to see any order. In this respect, every kind of research is chaos research. All behaviour seems chaotic until we recognise the order in it."[84]

One particular phenomenon that exists in both science and art is known in visual culture as **iconic turn**.[85] Gottfried Boehm coined the concept in 1994 in the essay "Die Wiederkehr der Bilder". In his text he states that "there is a shift from the linguistic to the visual information level, from the word to the picture, and, even scarier, from the argument to the video"[86]. It is easy to establish that there are clear signs of an enormously increasing proliferation of images in our mind. All new media are, above all, dominated by pictures, not texts. Operating of computers, smartphones and other terminals using icons is only one of many examples. Further examples are the myriads of photos and films permanently taken using various different devices, the increasing number of available broadcasting stations, professional journals and special magazines, countless online images and films, offers from search machines and websites and interactive applications of computer games and simulations, etc. New operating and control elements that appear as 'shapes' are another sign of the increasing dominance of images. We prefer an image to the briefest of texts, because it is much quicker to identify a shape or figure than a text. In the following, two statistical values emphasise the significance of the increasing proliferation of images: In 2013, an average of 72 hours of video material were uploaded on YouTube per minute, which corresponds to around a hundred thousand hours per day,[87] while a quarter of a million images per minute, thus 350 million images per day were uploaded on Facebook.[88] As expected, these numbers have been surpassed by far in the meantime. It is not only the dominance of images in general that is increasing, but also images from specialised disciplines that seek to represent and disseminate their concerns and theories in this way. In medicine, for example, computer tomography is investigating every inch of the human body by means of increasingly complex and detailed imaging techniques; empirical data, statistics and complicated information are today transformed into images in almost all areas. History, architecture, accidents and catastrophes are re-enacted by means of 3D animation. The fantastic images of the Hubble telescope are assembled from thousands of individual shots by experts in the field of imaging and visualisation technology and artificially coloured.[89] The HUBBLE EXTREME DEEP FIELD image published in 2012, for example, is composed of 2000 single exposures that were created within a 10-year period using a shutter speed of two million seconds. Photos of the smallest imaginable images from electron microscopes are black and white, because the represented resolution of a surface is smaller than the wavelength of visible light. Whenever they are in colour, they have always been coloured by hand previously. These new scientific images are artificial sophisticated models, aesthetic visual worlds that reach far beyond any objective description, thus creating new realities in their own right. The emergence and possibilities of the computer as an imaging and image-manipulating medium play a highly important role here. Its generative power combined with new imaging technology brings forth new images of the world, new 'world images' as it were. Evidently, the enormous proliferation of technical and digital images is not only prevalent in design and art, but also in the sciences. In doing so, these sciences are showing us 'artificial images' of a non-existent reality, and in their footage, the media are showing us artificially generated reproductions of a supposed reality. Thus we are increasingly fed with fiction. This quality has always been attributed to art, especially since its split with the sciences. Today, however, scientific images are turning into artificial models of the world that are as fictional as their artistic counterparts. Ursula Brandstätter believes: "The sciences and arts are united in their fictional approach to reality."[90]

The essence of new media probably becomes most tangible within the flood of information, of unclassified knowledge and a **wild growth of images**. But wild growth always implies devaluation, and the yearning for images and information swells to an ear-deafening noise. Significance and value can only be gained through selection, structuring and classification. Ultimately, the individual ability to recognise patterns in the chaotic mass of images and information will determine the quality of selection. The programming language Processing[>134/345], for example, is able to create countless variants in a very short time. The results, however, always depend on the clarity of the input, on the installation of the test setup, i.e. the more precise a way in which the tools are used — in this case, formulae and algorithms — the more calculable, exact and better the results will be. This powerful tool splendidly supports experimental processes, however the appraisal and interpretation of results still remains in the user's hand. Evgenij Feinberg describes the situation as follows: "After all, [...] computer science has led to the fact that an enormous amount of computing work and other logical

89 BEHIND THE PICTURES, www.hubblesite.org/gallery/behind_the_pictures (retrieved 5/6/2014); "Hubble images are made, not born. Images must be woven together from the incoming data from the cameras, cleaned up and given colors that bring out features that eyes would otherwise miss."
90 Brandstätter 2008, p.55.*

formalisable intellectual work, which has always hidden the intuitive elements
in scientific and technical activities, could be delegated to the machine,
thus relieving the brain. Thus, more and more features are dominating the structure
of the scientific working process, bringing it closer to the process of creative
work and scientific work in the humanities."[91]

Regardless of this, we would like to type the following on the touchscreen of the
prophets of computer salvation: There is (still) no such thing as **critical reason**
in the algorithms of design and information machines, but there is also no critical
reason in the test setups of science either, nor in the design methods presented
here, whether they may be called grid, matrix, chain of associations, analogy
or metamorphosis. Today, evaluation, assessment and conclusion still depend on man.
Only if computers learn to reproduce creative processes, producing and, above all,
assessing the random and the chaotic, will they be able to deliver creative results.

And yet **systematics, methods and experiments** can be useful and valuable in design
too. They can contribute to resolving visual problems and phenomena and provide
excellent support in searching for and finding ideas. Systematic approaches,
generating many different variations, developing one's own professional or personal
repertoire of methods can help to make targeted and relevant decisions or findings
quicker and more easily. They cannot replace the creative idea and intuition.
Today, we only evaluate phenomena as valuable, new and surprising if they have been
acknowledged and selected as such by man. Human creativity remains on top in
areas where grids, methods, design programmes, computers and the internet are not
able to be creative and cannot establish new connections between different
reference systems by themselves.

Armin Lindauer

"Man can draw a completely illogical conclusion from logical developments
that will still be correct."[92]

**91** Evgenij L.Feinberg, ZWEI KULTUREN. INTUITION UND LOGIK IN KUNST UND WISSENSCHAFT
(TWO CULTURES. THE CREATIVE ACT IN ART AND SCIENCE), Berlin, Heidelberg 1998, p.273.*
**92** Interview with Frank Schirrmacher, in: FORUM – DAS MLP-MAGAZIN, March 2010.*

**1. BASIS**   This chapter investigates the potential and visual quality of basic
design elements such as dots, lines, area, space, form, rhythm, contrast
and composition. The square serves as a design surface because of its neutrality
and lack of direction. As a defined place, the dot is a mobile compositional element
with which possible positions are systematically played out within
a predefined area[>76-77] on different grids. The method of using a grid helps to find
positions that were selected neither by intuition, nor for aesthetical reasons.

Simple principles of order such as sequencing, agglomeration, grouping, sprawl,
symmetry, asymmetry, structure, grid, focus, contrast, dynamics and statics
can thus be tried out. This method is also suitable for more complex applications
such as composition, symmetry, perspective, proportion and golden ratio,
as its potential is twofold. It not only provides basic design experience, but
allows for formal experiments that lead to results, which — perhaps somewhat
surprisingly — already generate content-related meanings[>60-61]. Slight alterations
mostly suffice to perceive an abstract figure in terms of its content.
It becomes clear that certain constellations are swiftly interpreted and that
an immediate shift occurs between the abstract and concrete view.

In the next step, this strictly systematic approach is abandoned in order to play
with the given elements. The working surface is also incorporated into the
design as an independent element[>59/62]. It now becomes evident that despite quite
limited preconditions, an astonishing amount of possibilities emerge that
have much more potential than the mere shifting of points on a grid would suggest.

These relatively simple exercises often help to build up basic experience and
acquire a design repertoire at the same time. They do not have to yield any valid
visual results at first, but rather aim to experience and investigate visual
phenomena. At this stage however, they already need to be observed closely;
they sensitise and help to resolve compositional problems and formulate initial
content-related messages. In that way, they gradually lead to complex tasks
which can later be used to communicate the same message. Getting to know
and understanding structural systems and their purpose, and finally, finding out
how to transfer them freely, is the object of these investigations.

## dots of various sizes

presentations of a grey gradients in black-and-white with points
of different sizes and varying grid widths

dot sizes

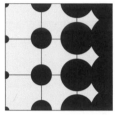 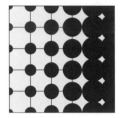 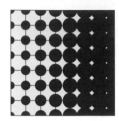

## dots of identical size

presentations of a grey gradients with dots of identical size

dot sizes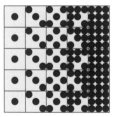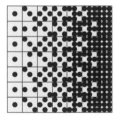

different distances between dots of identical size

## position

neutral

lying

floating

falling

coming

going

drowning

fleeing

## size

small

medium

format filling

format busting

## order

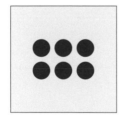

structured

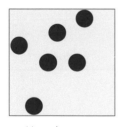

scattered

lined-up

clustered

## proportion

earth and moon

moon and earth

earth and jupiter

earth and sun

**57 BASIS** Depending on their position and size, the dots are given attributes. Armin Lindauer

rhythm

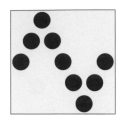 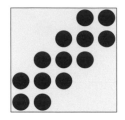 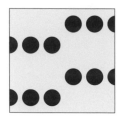 

brightness

  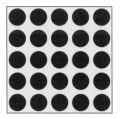 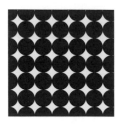

form 1

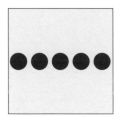 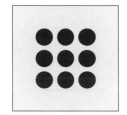 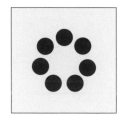 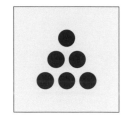

form 2

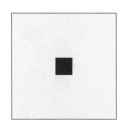   

motion

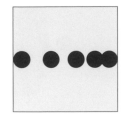 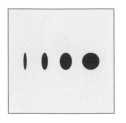  

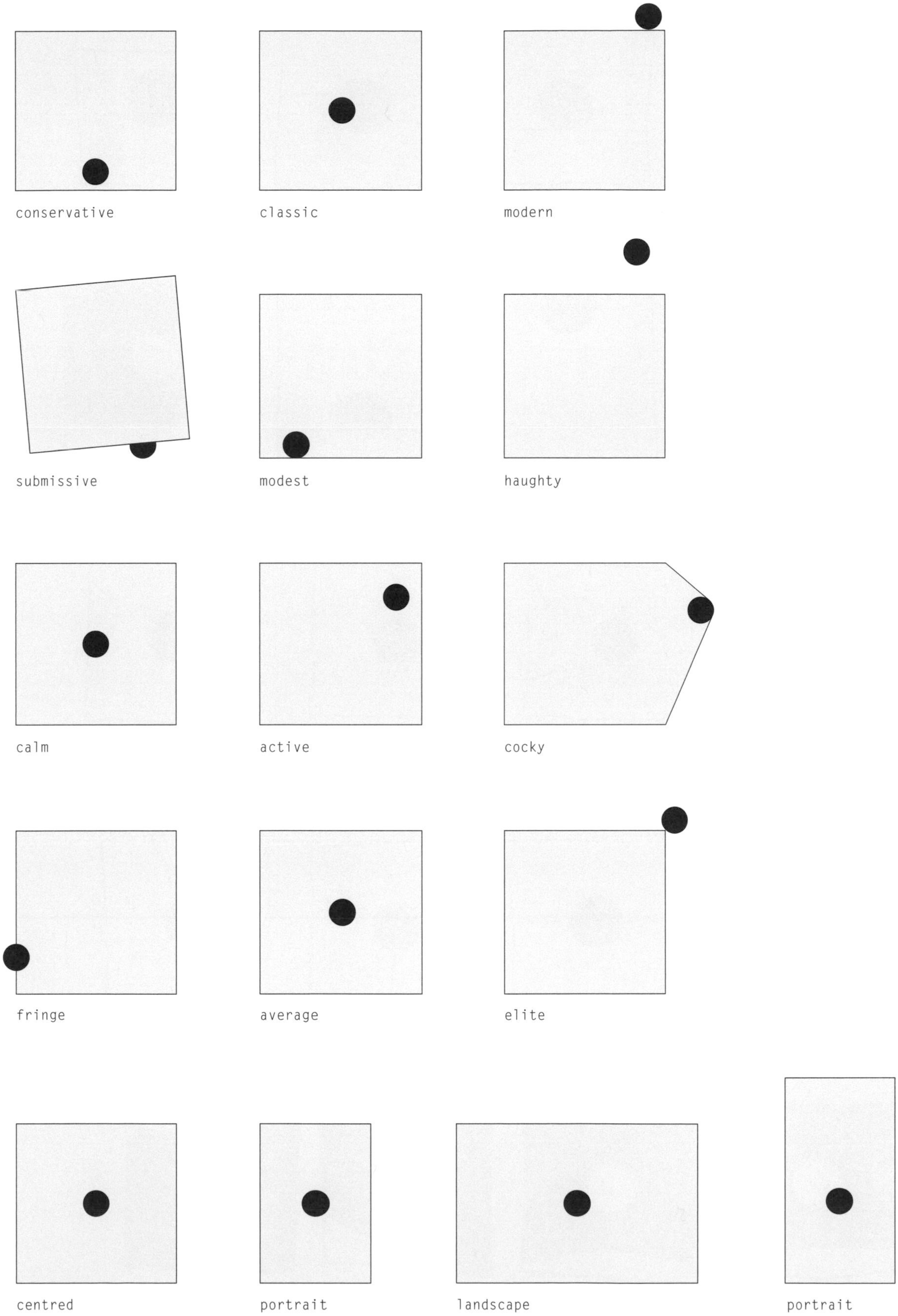

conservative

classic

modern

submissive

modest

haughty

calm

active

cocky

fringe

average

elite

centred

portrait

landscape

portrait

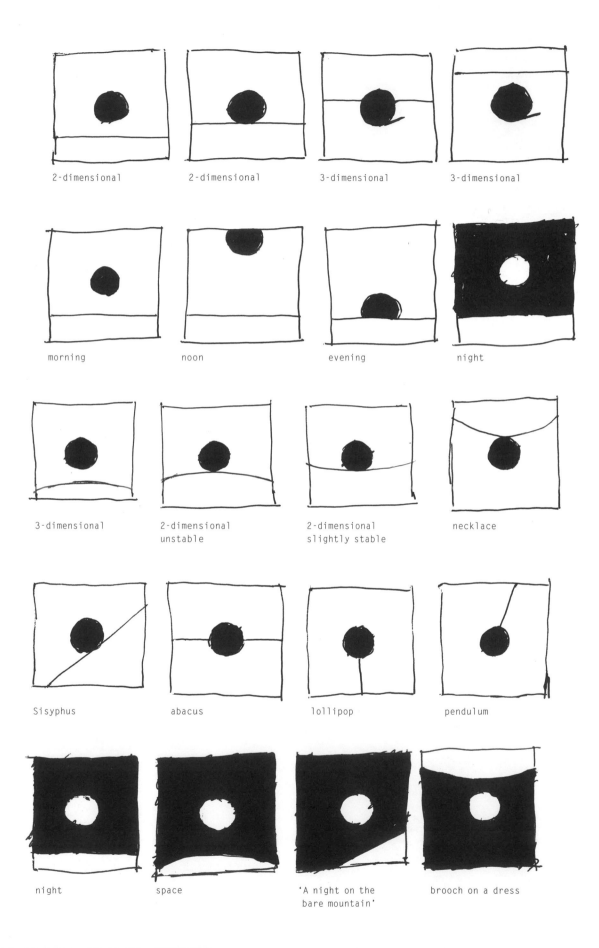

2-dimensional  2-dimensional  3-dimensional  3-dimensional

morning  noon  evening  night

3-dimensional  2-dimensional unstable  2-dimensional slightly stable  necklace

Sisyphus  abacus  lollipop  pendulum

night  space  'A night on the bare mountain'  brooch on a dress

1 dot and 1 line

belly button  billiards  pendulum  note

2 dots and 2 lines

neutral  astonished  angry  very angry

neutral  not friendly  irritated  oohhhhh

dot and figure

human  soldier  man  woman

square head  egg head  alien  in love

**61 BASIS** Simple elements become interpretable figures through the way they are arranged.

not-yet square

doing-it square

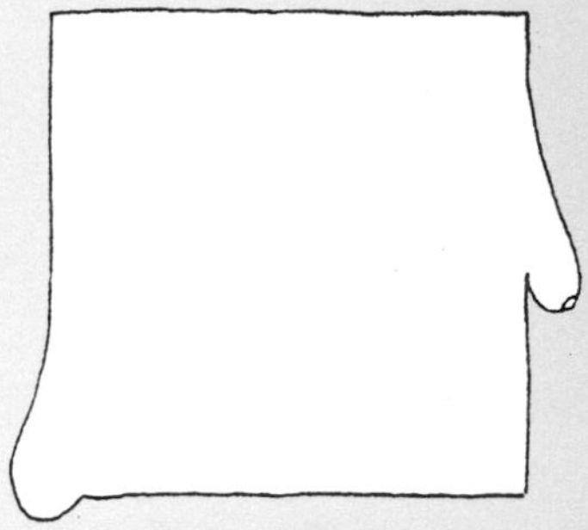

not-anymore square

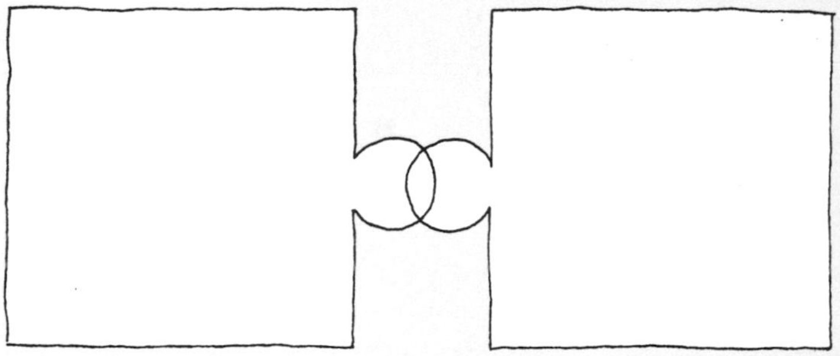

married squares

divorced square

aroused square

ready square

limp square

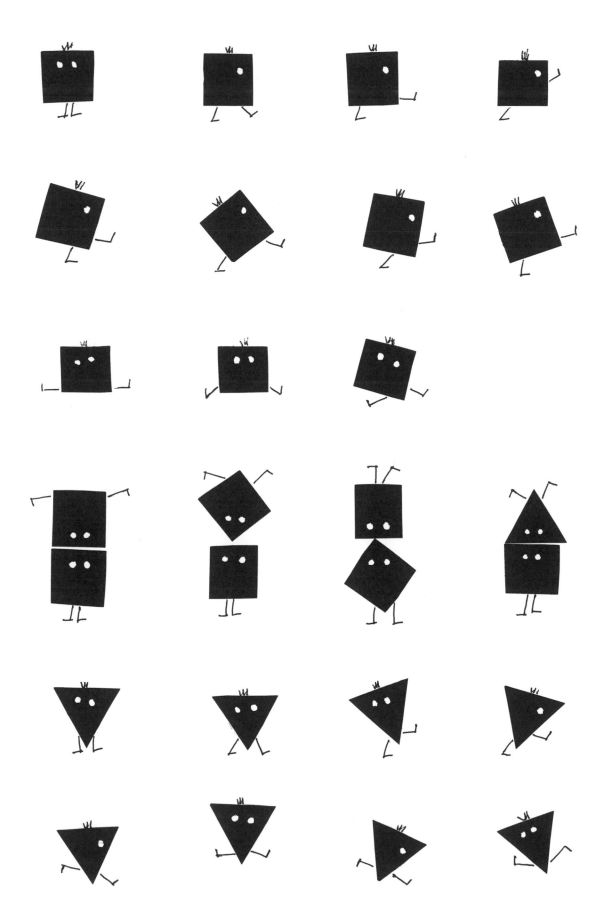

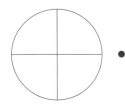

The basic elements
are quadrants and dots.

 www.vimeo.com/19559401

66 **BASIS** "Understanding Data – Eine gestalterische Exploration zur grafischen Dateirepräsentation" ("Understanding Data – a creative exploration to a graphical representation of files"), visualisation of file sizes in an exhibition. Dorothée Stietz

Visualisation of file sizes by means of a square (2-dimensional) and cube (3-dimensional). Dorothée Stietz

1 KB

1 MB

1 GB corresponds to a square with
an edge length of approx. 54.5 cm.

1 KB = 1000 bytes
1 MB = 1000 KB
1 GB = 1000 MB

Industry calculates units
of measure with 1000 units.
IT calculates units of measure with
1024 units.

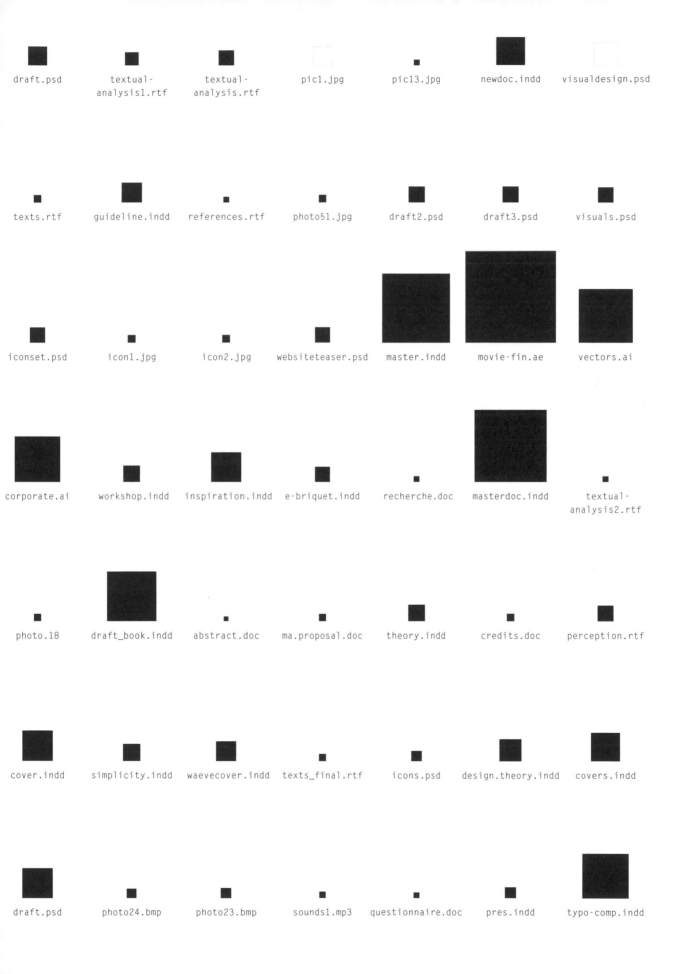

draft.psd · textual-analysis1.rtf · textual-analysis.rtf · pic1.jpg · pic13.jpg · newdoc.indd · visualdesign.psd · texts.rtf · guideline.indd · references.rtf · photo51.jpg · draft2.psd · draft3.psd · visuals.psd · iconset.psd · icon1.jpg · icon2.jpg · websiteteaser.psd · master.indd · movie-fin.ae · vectors.ai · corporate.ai · workshop.indd · inspiration.indd · e-briquet.indd · recherche.doc · masterdoc.indd · textual-analysis2.rtf · photo.18 · draft_book.indd · abstract.doc · ma.proposal.doc · theory.indd · credits.doc · perception.rtf · cover.indd · simplicity.indd · waevecover.indd · texts_final.rtf · icons.psd · design.theory.indd · covers.indd · draft.psd · photo24.bmp · photo23.bmp · sounds1.mp3 · questionnaire.doc · pres.indd · typo-comp.indd

69 BASIS File size is represented by the size of the square.

## linear basic form

diagonal line

radial lines

vertical lines

crossed lines

line jumble

lined surface

## circular basic form

circular area

amorphous area

ring

centred rings

agglomeration
of rings

drawn-out ring

## angular basic form

square

grey square

cuboid

triangle

trapezoid

pentagon

The density of the lines
shows how long a file
has been edited.

short editing time                              long editing time

The longer the file
is edited the longer
the shape becomes.

short editing time                              long editing time

The share of black
in the circle segment
indicates the up-to-
dateness of the file.

hardly current                                  current

The age of the file
is indicated by
the annual rings.

young (1 year)                          old (10 years)

Each time the file
is saved another line
is added.

hardly any saving activity              a lot of saving activity

Each time the file
is saved another ring
is added.

hardly any saving activity              a lot of saving activity

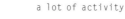

The inclination
of the line illustrates
the file activity.

hardly any activity                     a lot of activity

The higher, more pointed
and upward inclined (towards
the right) the triangle,
the more file activity.

hardly any activity                     a lot of activity

The area is deformed to
demonstrate file activity:
The more the file is
edited the more irregular
the surface becomes.

hardly any activity                     a lot of activity

The cursor movement
is shown by the density
and number of paths.

little cursor activity                  a lot of cursor activity

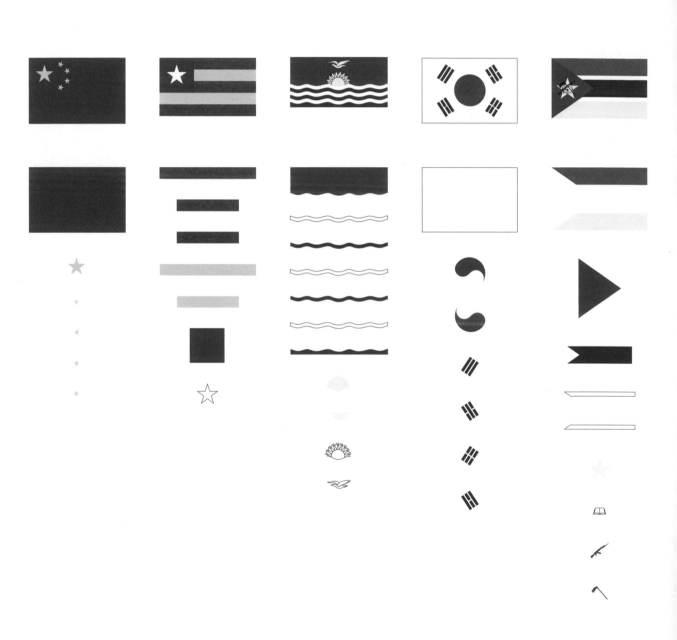

**72 BASIS** Graphical analysis of country flags by separating and listing the visual elements. In reading direction: China, Togo, Kiribati, South Korea, Mozambique, U.S.A., Brazil, Great Britain, Germany (official flag of the federal authorities), Jamaica. Anja Gollor

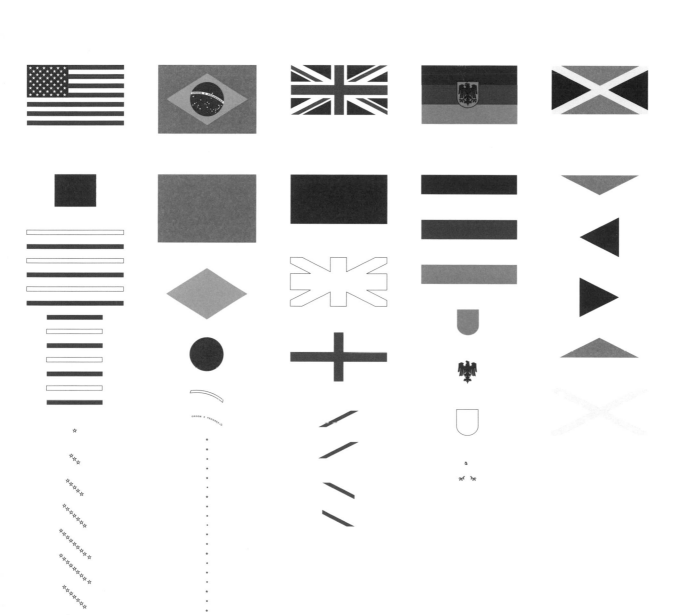

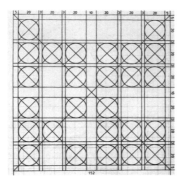

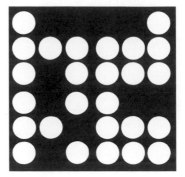

hdkb

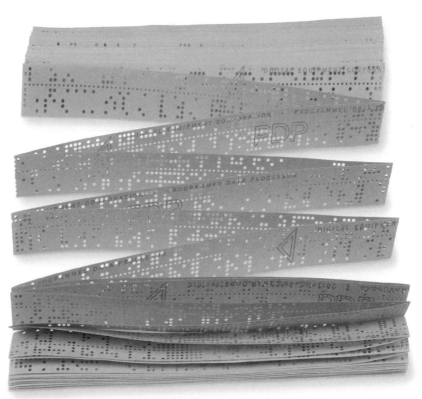

Inspiration drawn from the storage
media of the punched tape.

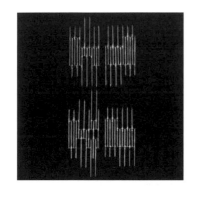

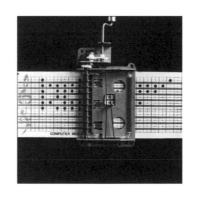

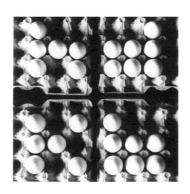

**75 BASIS** Free interpretation of the logo of the Berlin University of the Arts. Students of Lortz' class

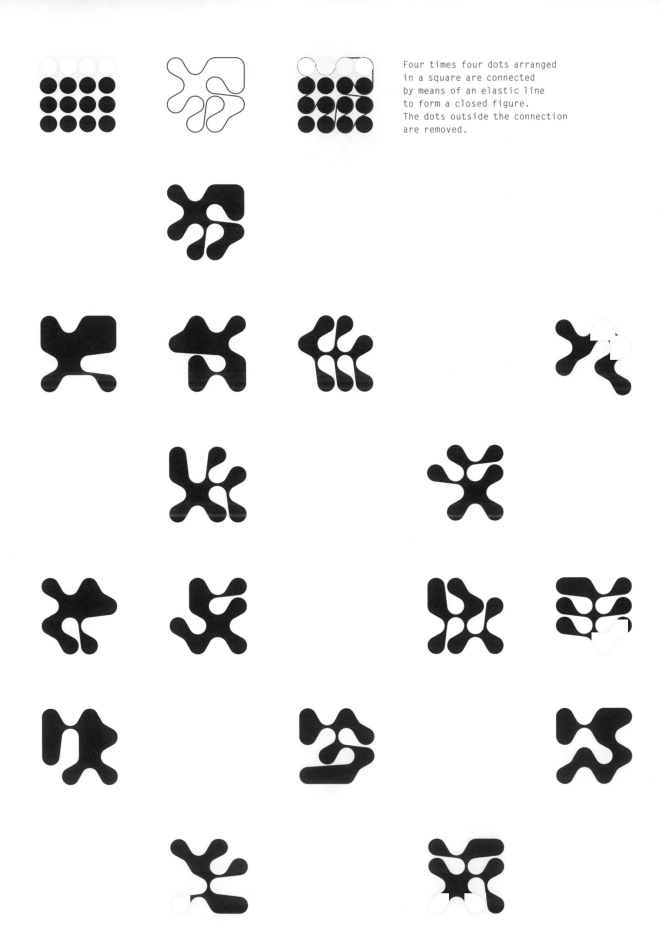

Four times four dots arranged
in a square are connected
by means of an elastic line
to form a closed figure.
The dots outside the connection
are removed.

Four dots in the same position
are combined using different numbers of lines
of varying length and direction.
The square and the dots remain constant.
The connecting lines are varied,
either systematically or intuitively.

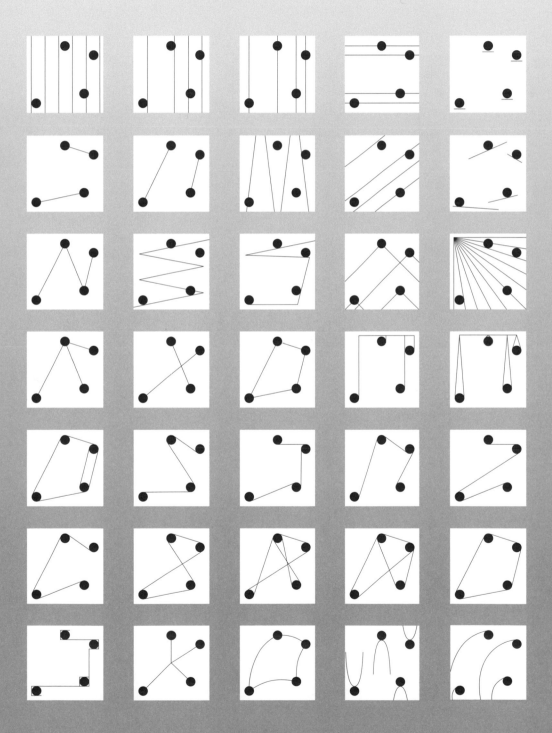

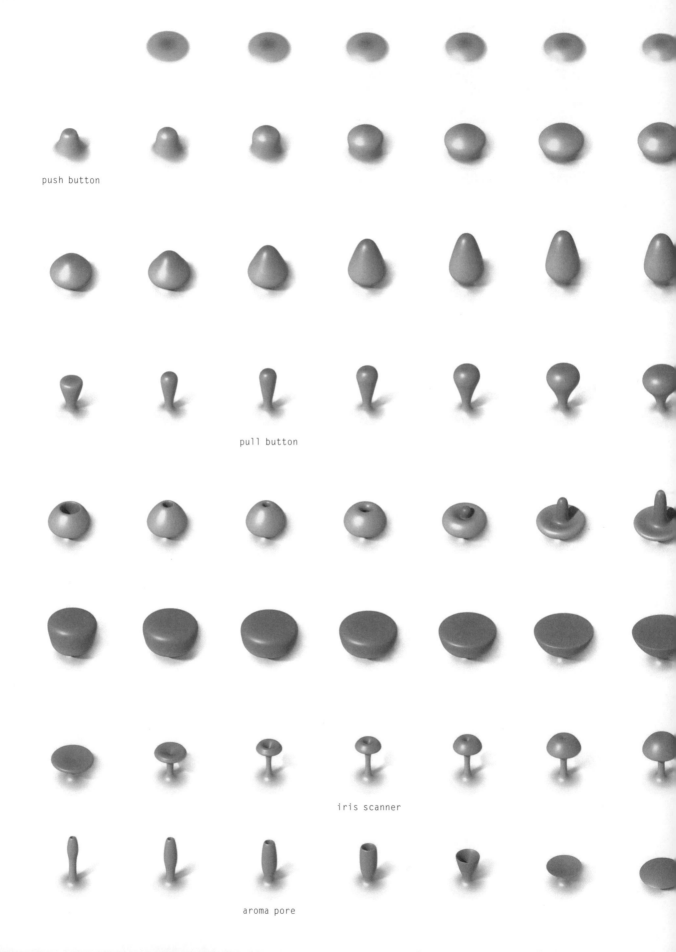

push button

pull button

iris scanner

aroma pore

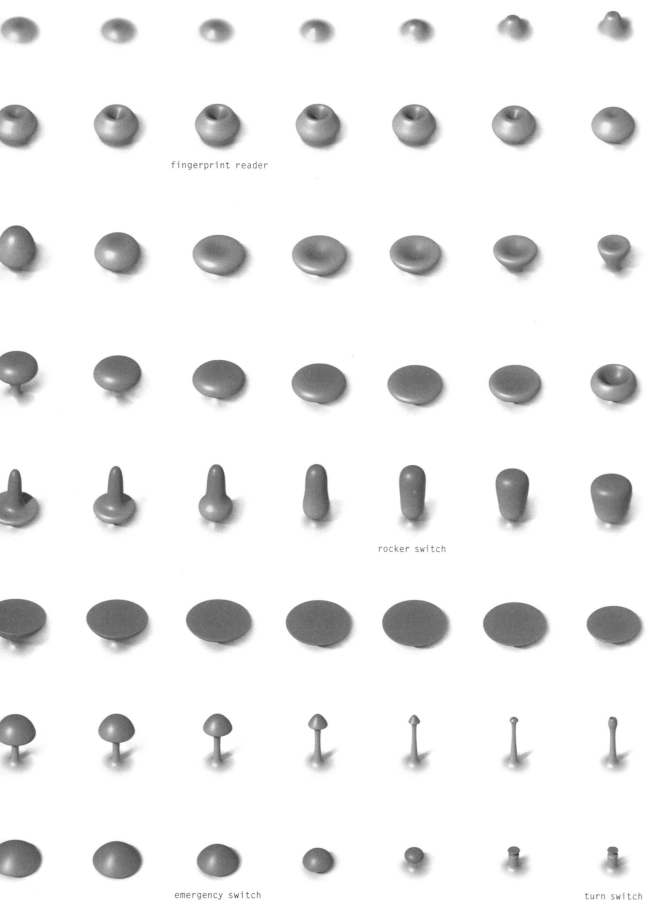

fingerprint reader

rocker switch

emergency switch

turn switch

TOOLS YOU BAKE: Baking tins produced by means of metal forming and based on a circle. The beechwood moulds on which the tins are based were originally used for metal ware such as hub caps or lampshades. Practical example: Sebastian Summa, Hrafnkell Birgisson, photographs: Jo Hany

Bessy, 0.6 Litre

Eltoga, 1.0 Litre

Sturickow, 1.3 Litre

Wiesner, 1.7 Litre

Collatz, 1.8 Litre

Stubbak, 2.0 Litre

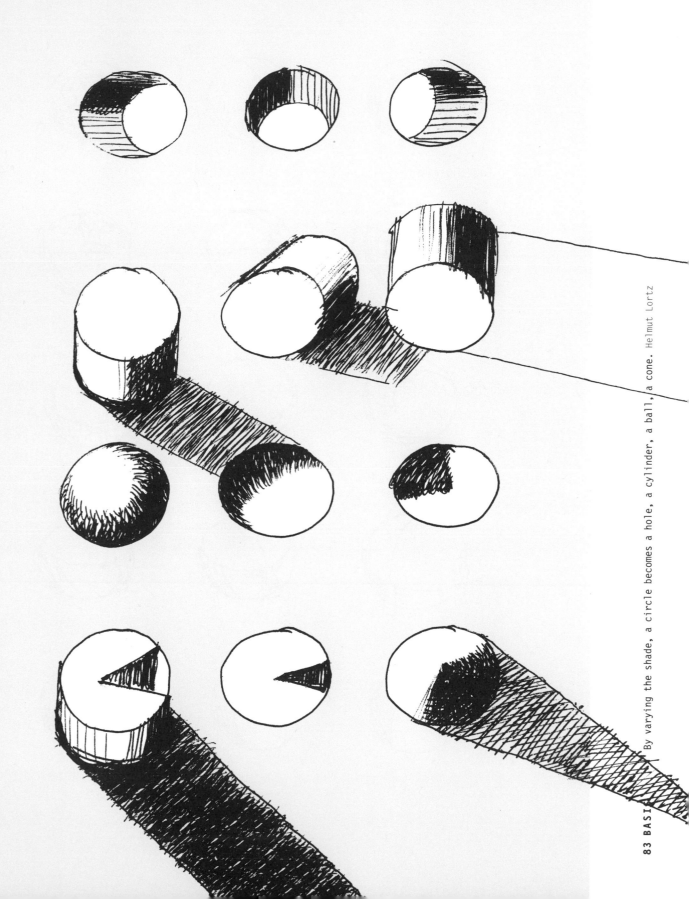

By varying the shade, a circle becomes a hole, a cylinder, a ball, a cone. Helmut Lortz

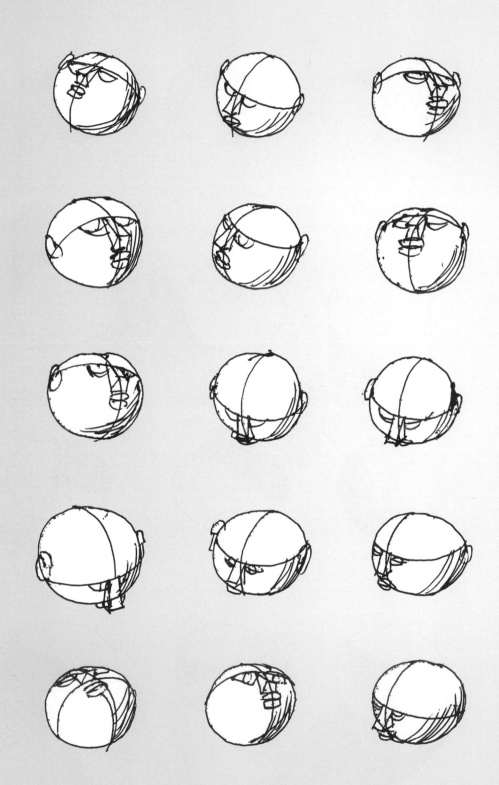

85 **BASIS** Construction of a cup. Theres Weishappel

rotation around a vertical axis

rotation and turning around a horizontal axis

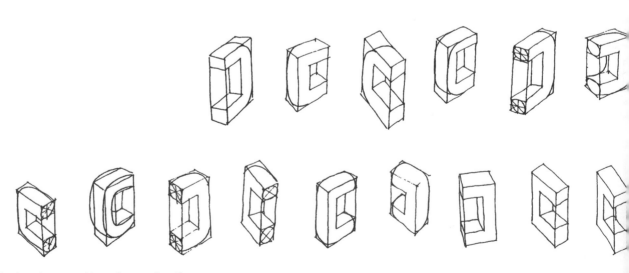

designed perspective of a cup handle

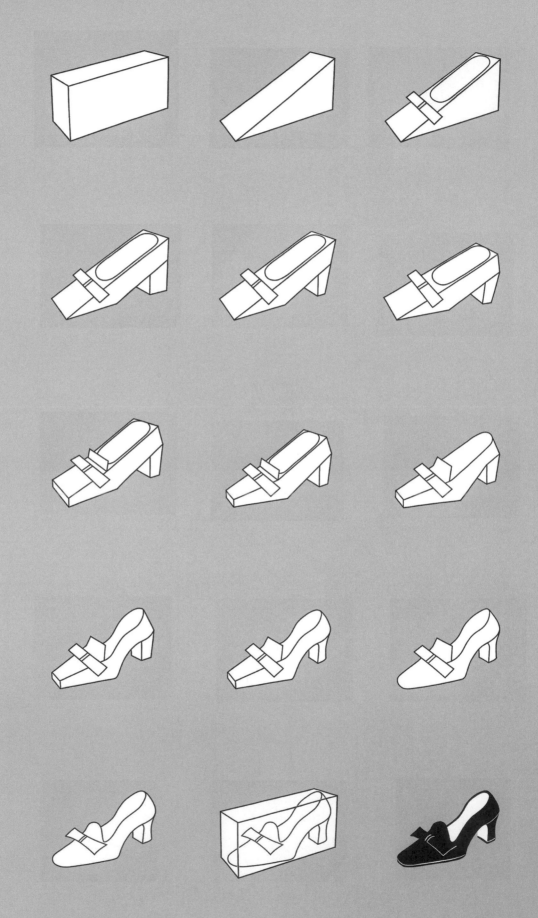

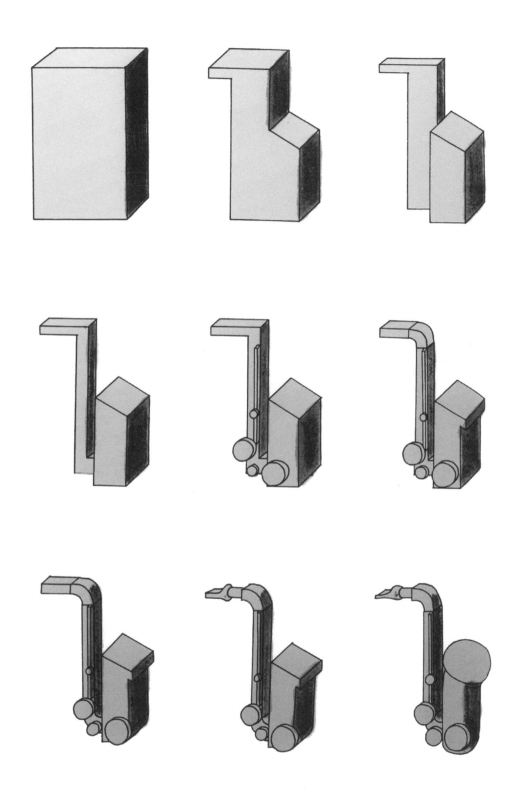

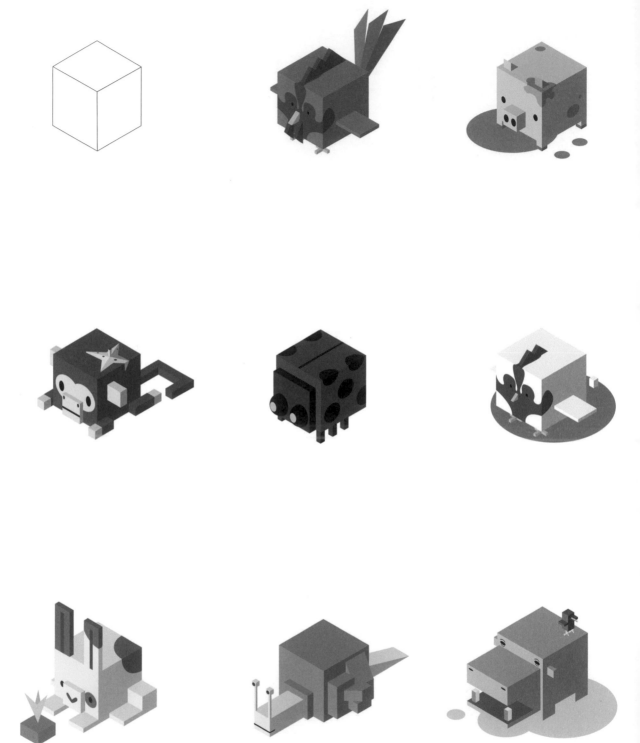

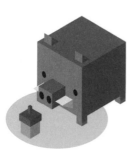

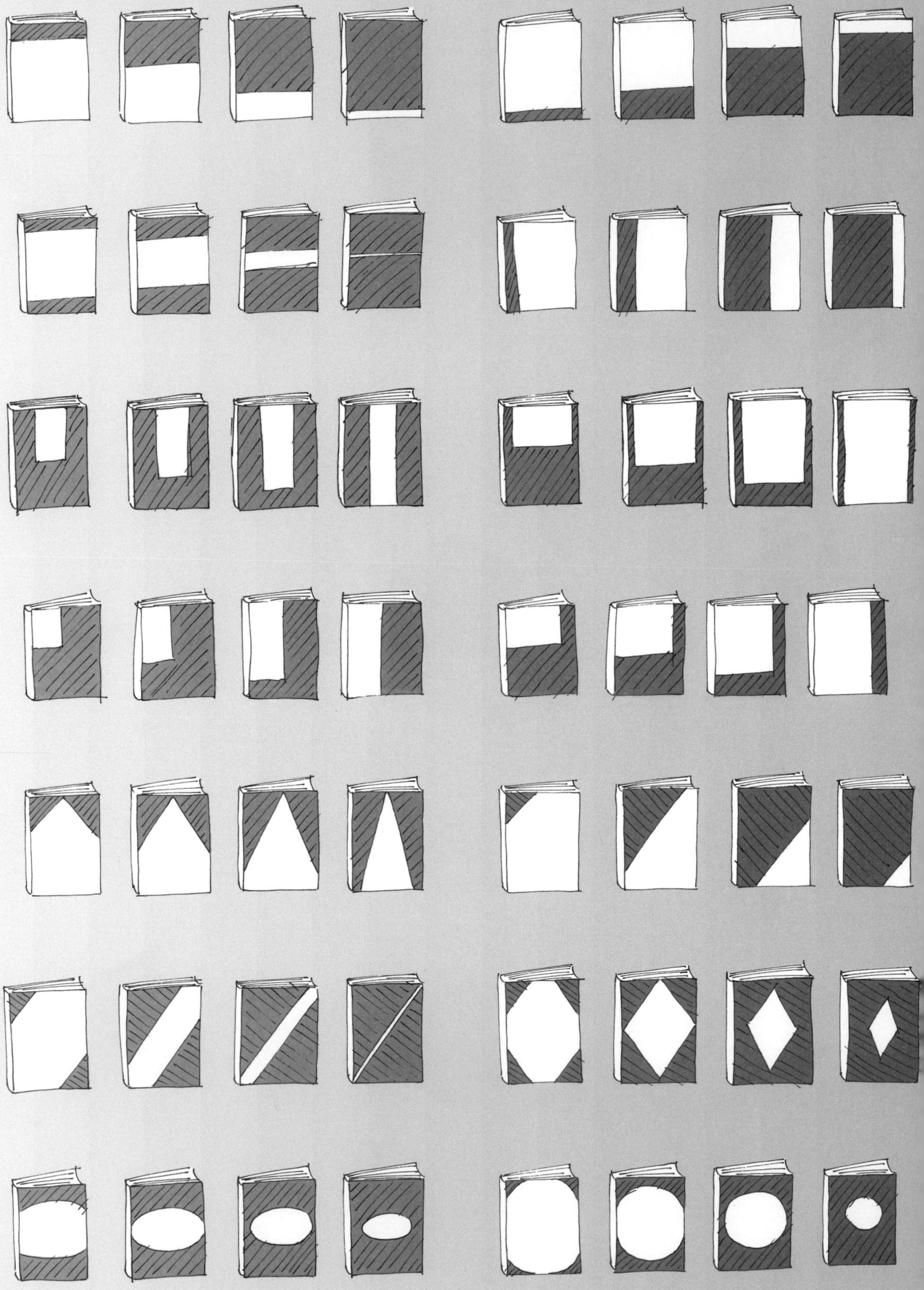

 Study of the arrangement of book covers. Armin Lindauer

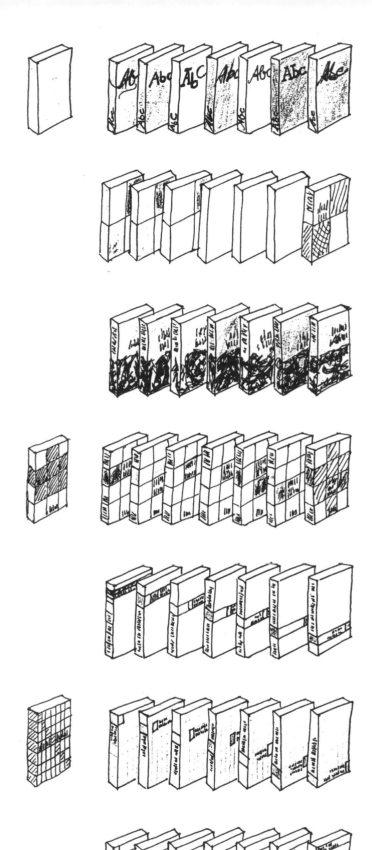

Surface segmentation constant.
Content variable.

Surface segmentation constant.
Content variable.

Position of image and text constant.
Image and text variable.

Surface segmentation is based
on a grid. Use of the grid cells
variable.

Picture element constant.
Position of the title line variable.

Size of picture element constant.
Position of the title line
variable in line increments.

Height of picture element and
writing constant.
Position variable in
opposite line increments.

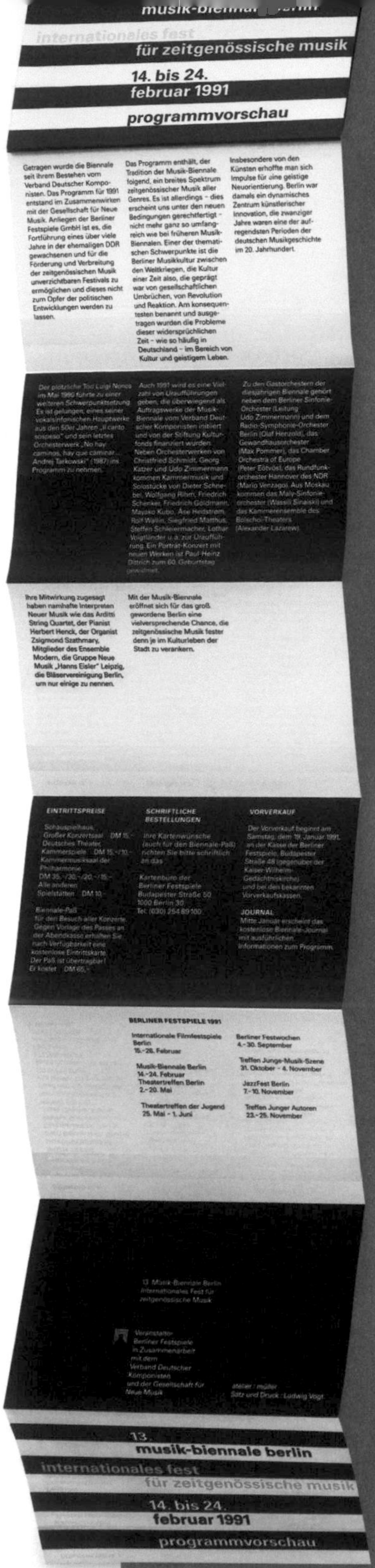

programme folder, format DIN A 6

title pages of the programme preview,
format DIN A 4

The different year's issues vary
through an additional colour
and the principle of variation of
the five lines.

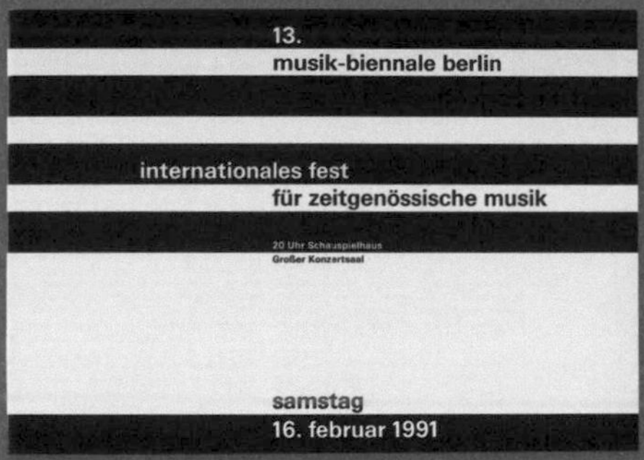

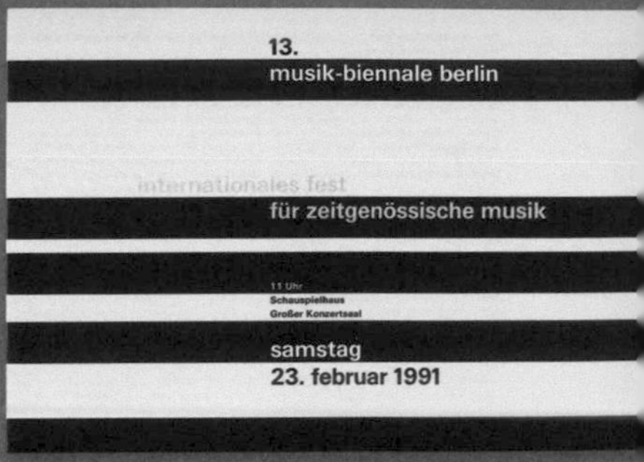

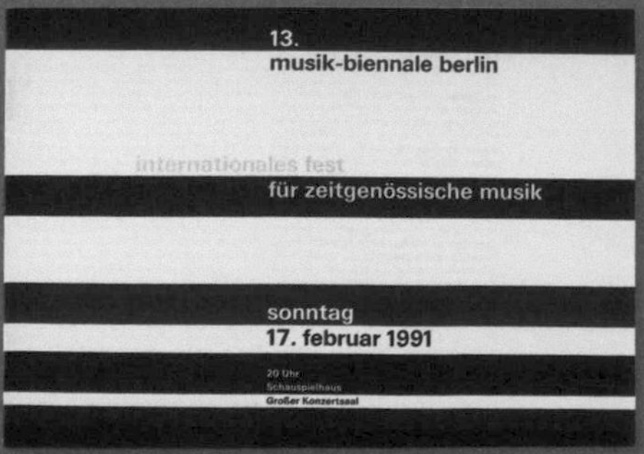

14.
musik-biennale berlin

internationales fest
für zeitgenössische musik

12. bis 21. märz
1993

13.
musik-biennale berlin

internationales fest
für zeitgenössische musik

20 Uhr Schauspielhaus
Großer Konzertsaal

samstag
16. februar 1991

13.
musik-biennale berlin

internationales fest
für zeitgenössische musik

11 Uhr
Schauspielhaus
Großer Konzertsaal

samstag
23. februar 1991

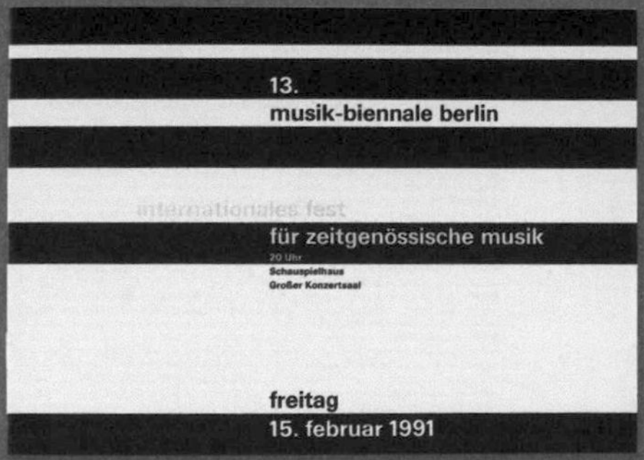

13.
musik-biennale berlin

internationales fest
für zeitgenössische musik
20 Uhr
Schauspielhaus
Großer Konzertsaal

freitag
15. februar 1991

13.
musik-biennale berlin

internationales fest
für zeitgenössische musik

11 Uhr
Schauspielhaus
Kammermusiksaal

samstag
16. februar 1991

13.
musik-biennale berlin

internationales fest
für zeitgenössische musik

sonntag
17. februar 1991

20 Uhr
Schauspielhaus
Großer Konzertsaal

13.
musik-biennale berlin

internationales fest
für zeitgenössische musik

19.30 Uhr
Schauspielhaus
Kammermusiksaal

donnerstag
21. februar 1991

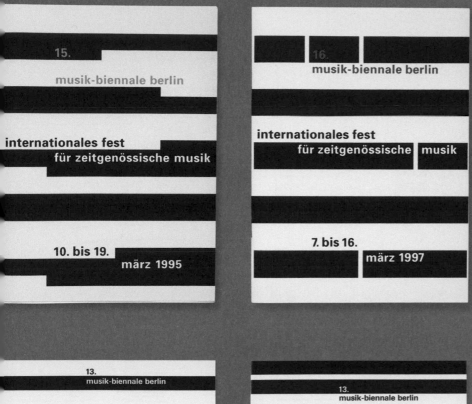

evening programmes,
format DIN A5

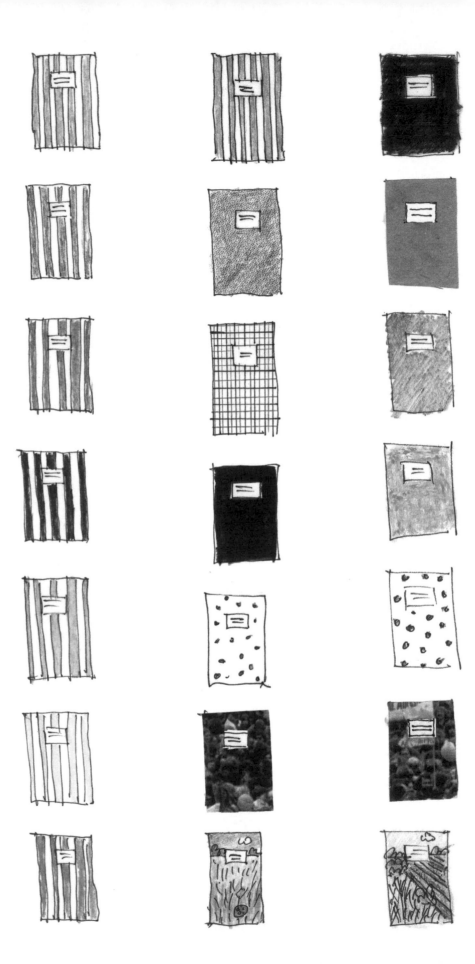

KLASSIK·JETZT!

**KLASSIK·JETZT!**

Traugott Buhre Sylvester
und andere
Goethe
**URFAUST**
Regie: Leonhard Koppelmann

Dauer: 78:51

866101

**KLASSIK·JETZT!**

Fritzi Haberlandt  Max vo
Hille Darjes  Hans-Mich
und andere
Lessing
**EMILIA GA**
Regie: Leonhard Ko

KLASSIK·JETZT!

**KLASSIK·JETZT!**

Sibylle Canonica  Dagmar Manzel
Oliver Stokowski  Jule Böwe
und andere
Goethe
**STELLA**
Regie: Leonhard Koppelmann

Dauer: 76:37 Minuten

866101

**KLASSIK·JETZT!**

Wolf-Dietrich Sprenger  Hilmar Eichhor
Winfried Glatzeder  Jutta Hoffmann
und andere
Kleist
**DER ZERBROCHNE KR**
Regie: Leonhard Koppelmann

KLASSIK·JETZT!

argon
hörbuch

**SWR**

**KLASSIK·JETZT!**

Hans-Michael Rehberg  Alexandra Henkel
Oliver Stokowski  Wolfgang Pregler
und andere
Schiller
**DIE RÄUBER**
Regie: Leonhard Koppelmann

Dauer: 75:09 Minuten

866101753

KLASSIK·JETZT!

argon
hörbuch

866101

**SWR**

KLASSIK:JETZT!

Peter Fitz   Corinna Kirchhoff
Lavinia Wilson   Ulrich Matthes
und andere

Kleist

**PRINZ FRIEDRICH VON HOMBURG**

Regie: Leonhard Koppelmann

Dauer: 79:56 Minuten

866101746

KLASSIK:JETZT!

Sandra Hüller
Walter Renneisen
und andere

Büchner

**WOYZECK**

Regie: Leonhard Koppelmann

Dauer: 70:56 Minuten

866101760

SWR

KLASSIK:JETZT!

Birgit Minichmayr   Ilja Richter
Walter Kreye   Andreas Pietschmann
und andere

Schiller

**KABALE UND LIEBE**

Regie: Leonhard Koppelmann

KLASSIK:JETZT!

Boris Aljinovic   Horst Hiemer
Hille Darjes   Carmen Birk
und andere

Lenz

**DER HOFMEISTER**
oder Vorteile der Privaterziehung

Regie: Leonhard Koppelmann

Dauer: 73:46 Minuten

866101791

KLASSIK:JETZT!

Ulrike Krumbiegel   Hilmar Thate
Philipp Hochmair   Boris Aljinovic
Burghart Klaußner

Goethe

**IPHIGENIE AUF T...**

Regie: Leonhard Koppelmann

KLASSIK:JETZT!

argon
hörbuch

mdr

**100 BASIS** Design concept: The ticket is put on characteristic fabrics. The materiality hints at the content of the plays.
Practical example: Andreas Brietzke, Maria Clara Rezende for sans serif

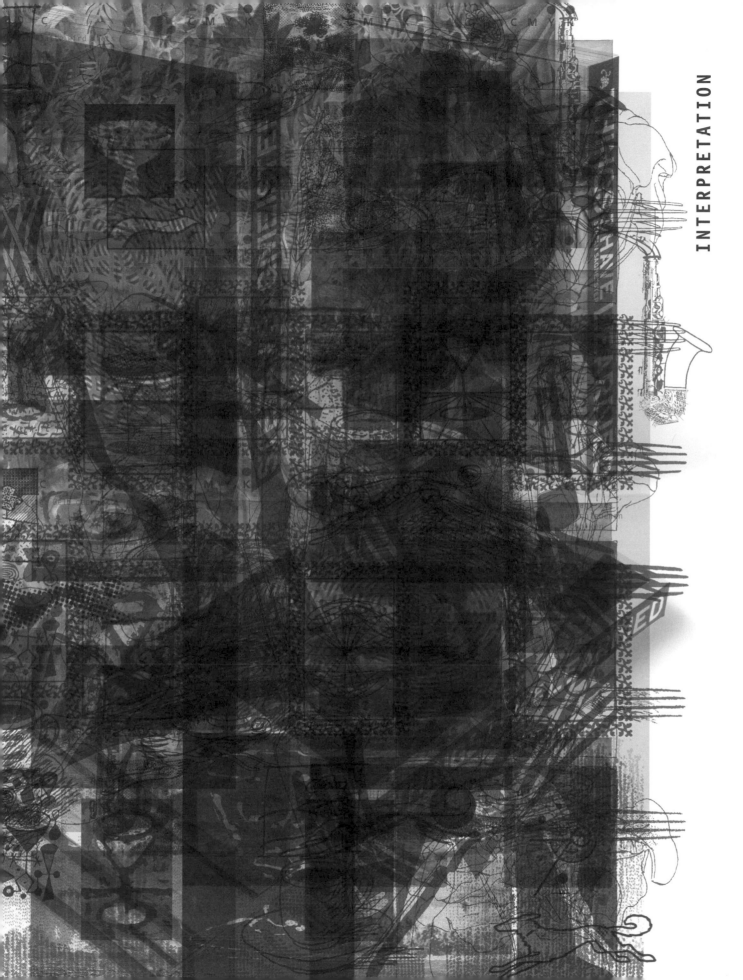

**2. INTERPRETATION**   A visual representation is always a construction of reality, even if it demands a high level of realism or reproduction fidelity. Each representation translates, interprets or explains something, subsequently becoming an interpretation that is shaped, not least, by the person behind it. That person's perception, their targeted or subconscious implementation, is therefore always part of the message. As Rudolf Arnheim put it in ART AND VISUAL PERCEPTION. THE NEW VERSION: "All reproduction is visual interpretation."[1]

In times of excessive style variations and permanent changes in style, one is tempted to say that style is a constraint. Today, more than ever, the intentional statement should play the deciding role in the choice of style or type of representation. Style should interpret and support the message.

Anything can be used as an object for various different interpretations. When testing the medium, it makes sense to select something which is simple, well-known and easily reproducible. Determining style and clarifying compositional questions from the start makes it easier to concentrate on the variation of the 'representation' parameter. In that way, its qualities and the changes it makes to the message become traceable and appraisable.

In order to become familiar with as many techniques as possible, the investigation should include a wide range of options>[108/pp.128]. The following suggestions represent only a few of the countless possibilities: line, area, halftone, structure, surface, material, light, hand drawing, construction, graphite pencil, coloured pencil, all print techniques — from linocuts to offset and collotype. Replacing commonly used materials with others, for example, replacing the porcelain of a cup with other materials like metal, wood, stone, fabric, fur and paper, etc., helps to experience the potential of the 'representation' parameter. Equally, it does not always suffice to revert to known techniques or methods — that is why it is essential to venture into the unexpected, to combine, invent and create something of your own. It is precisely that individual style, or an invented technique that can lead to unique and innovative results. The more stylistic means the designer can choose from, the more targeted he can be in communicating his message. Even these, initially only formal, investigations, which are more or less geared towards expanding visual vocabulary, show that the content-related component always becomes visible. One of the most important aims of these interpretations is to acquire a whole host of technical abilities from which we can choose when needed.

As the example of the O.R.T. OffsetReproTechnik enterprise>[pp.132–133] shows, different services can be communicated through the means of interpretation of a small landscape drawing. Thereby the different techniques and images are the reference to the service portfolio of the company. By contrast, the five thousand

pictures of a glass›¹²² are almost identical. Its representation always remains
the same in principle, but only in principle. The attentive beholder notices minimal
differences and is tempted to attach importance to them. French philosopher
Jacques Derrida argues that the meaning of a word changes every time it is uttered.
Seen from this perspective, then, serial work gains yet another dimension.

The works in the INTERPRETATION chapter are not always clearly distinguishable
from those in the following VARIATION chapter, yet we can ascertain the following:
while one chapter investigates expression by means of representational style,
the other is all about functionally redesigning the object.

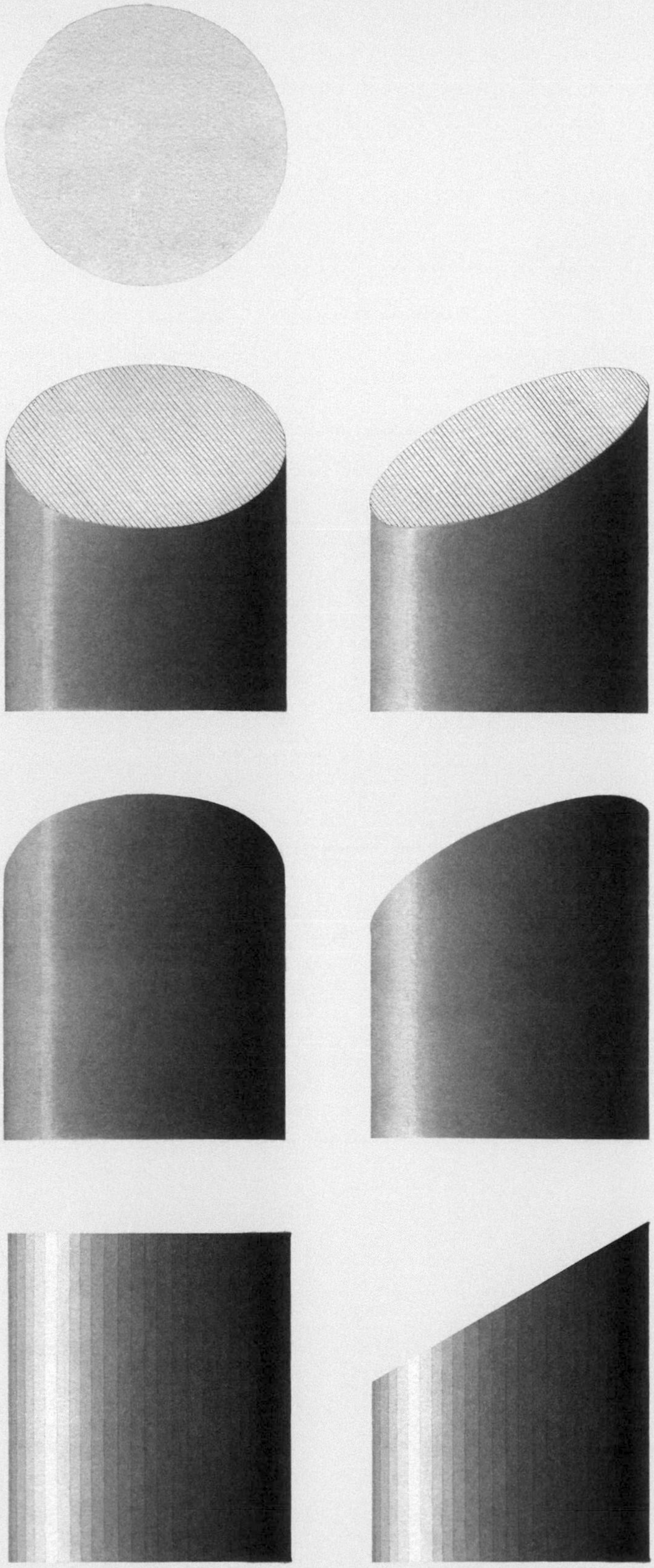

**105 INTERPRETATION** The perspective determines the interpretation of the object. After an illustration by Alexandre Meunier

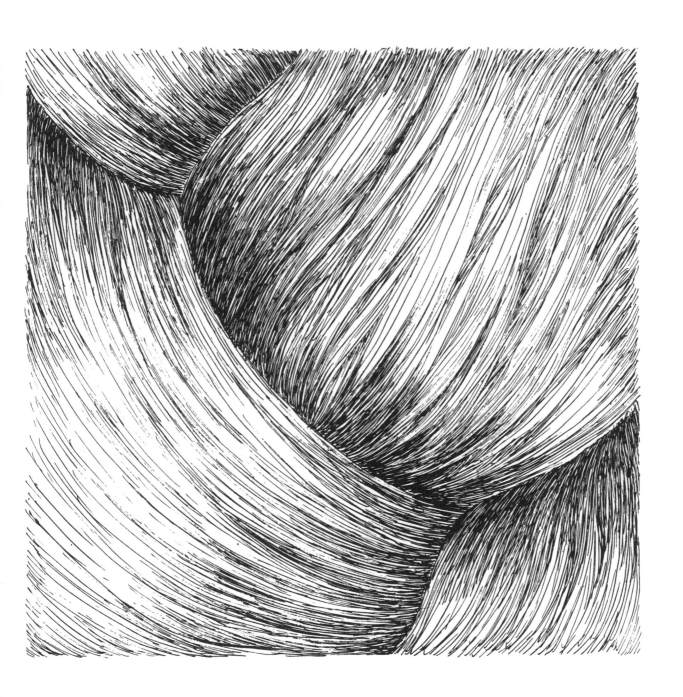

 Different hatching determines the effect of the image. Theres Weishappel

water colour with
sections left unpainted

reservage technique

drawing

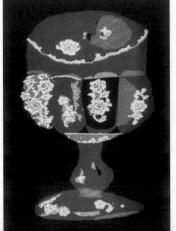

collage of lace

photograph

edges stressed

sharpened

separation of shades 1

separation of shades 2

contour

glass filter

relief

chrome

**114 INTERPRETATION** HOW TO LOOK AT THINGS THROUGH A WINE GLASS Persiflage of the 'how-to' literature of the 1930s and 1940s. References to style of art history by means of black-and-white drawings of a wine glass. Ad Reinhardt The coloured pictures are based on these models. Edward Tufte, Bonnie Scranton

Peter Paul Rubens, THE RAPE OF THE DAUGHTERS OF LEUCIPPUS, 1618; Rembrandt Harmensz van Rijn, PORTRAIT OF AGATHA BAS, 1641; **117 INTERPRETATION** Hans Baldung Grien, PORTRAIT OF A LADY, 1530.

Interpretations in the style of modern painters: Henri Rousseau, Oskar Kokoschka, Marc Chagall. Michael Ryba

line drawing

line drawing

light reflection

silhouette

ink drawing

ink drawing

Depiction of a fork in different techniques. Bardo Fiederling

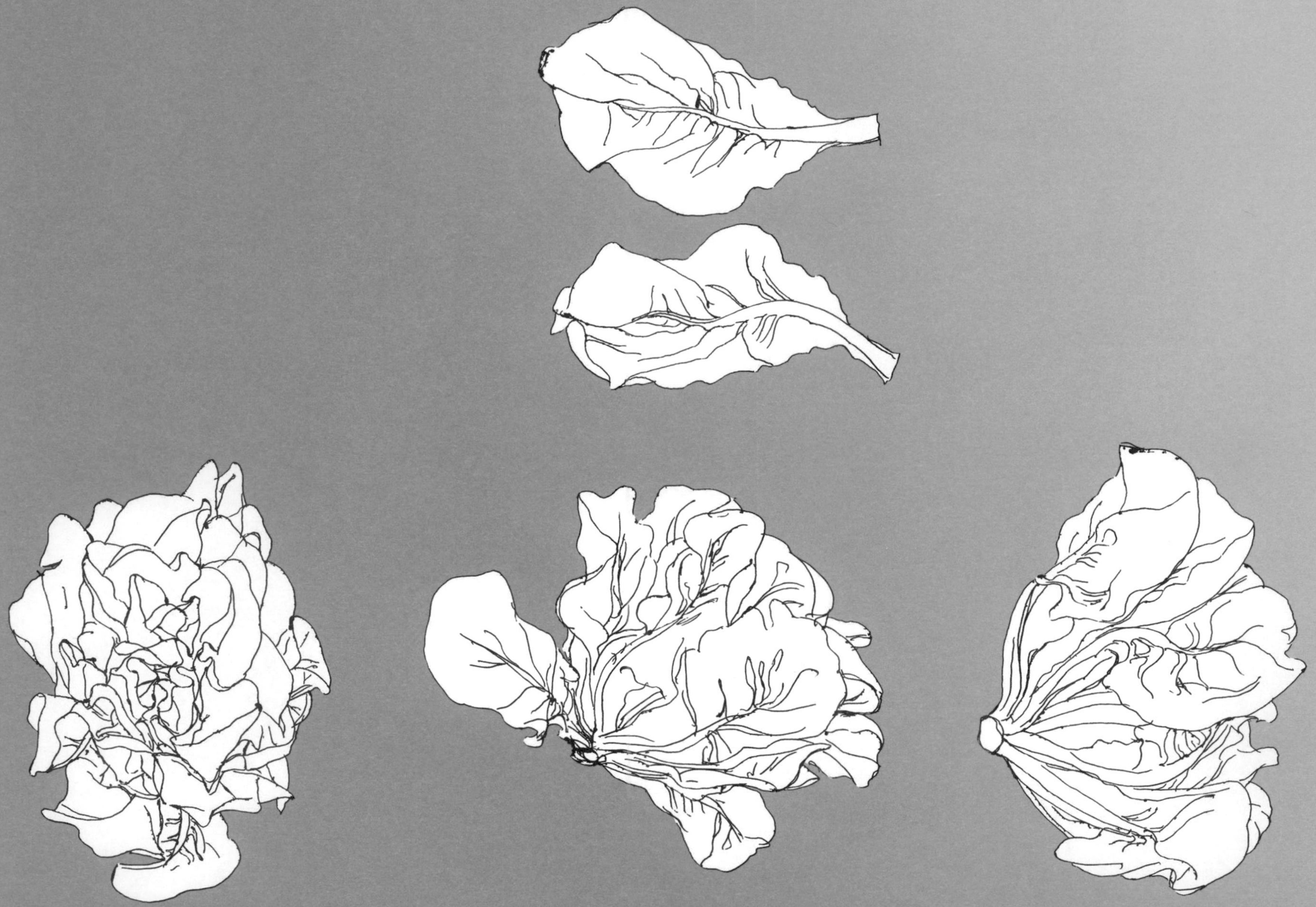

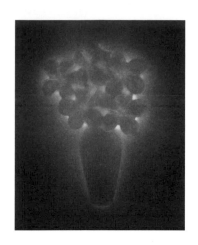

**126 INTERPRETATION** Financial statements 2001/2002 of the lighting engineering company Zumtobel. The mould is motif and cover at the same time. The business field of the company is highlighted by light effects. Practical example: Stefan Sagmeister

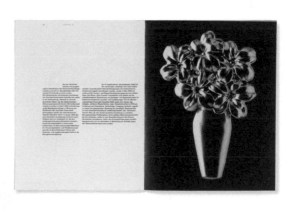

Practical example: Peter Andersen, Adolfo Best-Maugard,
Karl, Chip Kidd, Paul Rand, Rudolph Ruzicka, Elvis Swift, Triboro

Warren Chappell, William A. Dwiggins, Guy Fleming, Jonathan Hoefler, Anita

original Borzoi

Since 1915 there have been numerous interpretations of the 'Borzoi' by famous designers, such as Boris Artzybasheff, Warren Chappell, William A. Dwiggins, Chuck Gabriel, Joseph Claude Sinel, Thomas M. Cleland, José Miguel Covarrubias Duclaud.

**131 INTERPRETATION**

original image

colour markers

chalk drawing

chalk drawing

pen, scumbled

pen, scumbled

drawing, coloured

free cut forms

drawing, plane model

drawing, plane model,
shades of grey

plane model,
colour markers

drawing, plane model,
paint

contour with marker

contour with marker

colour pencil

computer drawing,
coloured by hand

digitalized drawing

digitalized drawing

computer drawing,
coloured by hand

computer drawing,
coloured by hand

computer drawing,
grey areas

computer drawing,
coloured areas

computer drawing,
coloured areas

computer drawing,
red, green blue

**OffsetReproTechnik**
Kirchner + Graser GmbH & Co
Produktions KG

O.R.T.     Charlottenstraße 95     Telefon     Telekopierer
1000 Berlin 61     **030/251 80 07**     **030/251 30 95**

---

**OffsetReproTechnik**
Kirchner + Graser GmbH & Co
Produktions KG

O.R.T.     Charlottenstraße 95     Telefon     Telekopierer
1000 Berlin 61     **030/251 80 07**     **030/251 30 95**

---

**OffsetReproTechnik**
Kirchner + Graser GmbH & Co
Produktions KG

O.R.T.     Charlottenstraße 95     Telefon     Telekopierer
1000 Berlin 61     **030/251 80 07**     **030/251 30 95**

Berlin, den

**Sparkasse der**    **Zahl**
**Stadt Berlin West**    **3 Tag**
BLZ 100 500 00    **30 Ta**
Konto-Nr. 0250010909

**Berliner Bank AG**
BLZ 100 200 00
Konto-Nr. 421 4501 500

---

**OffsetReproTechnik**
Kirchner + Graser GmbH & Co
Produktions KG

O.R.T.     Charlottenstraße 95     Telefon     Telekopierer
1000 Berlin 61     **030/251 80 07**     **030/251 30 95**

Berlin, den

---

**OffsetReproTechnik**
Kirchner + Graser GmbH & Co
Produktions KG

    Telekopierer
**030/251 30 95**

O.R.T.     Charlottenstraße 95
1000 Berlin 61     Telefon
**030/251 80 07**

---

**Digital · Repro · Technik**
Gesellschaft mbH & Co
Produktions KG

D.R.T.     Bundesplatz 3
1000 Berlin 31     Telefon
**030/853 80 39**
**2512095**

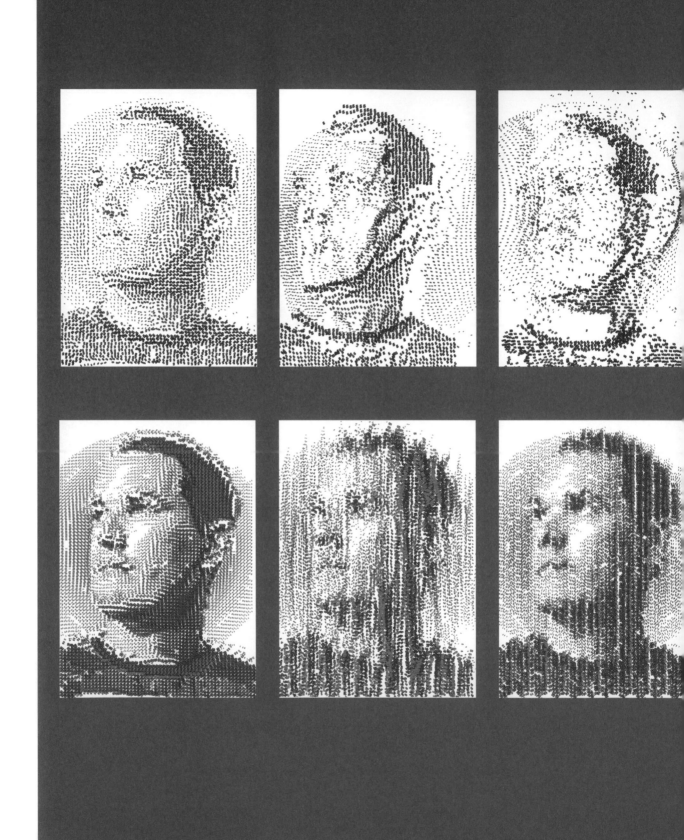

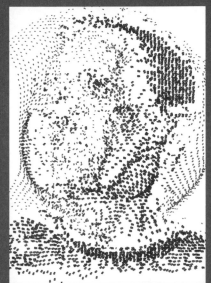

The black-and-white portrait
is imported as a pixel image
and the grey scale values of
the individual pixels are read.

Each pixel is replaced by three
letters in the colours red, green
and blue on top of each other
and rotated and shifted following
a previously defined algorithm.

First, the three coloured letters
are precisely on top of each
other.

The longer the mouse is moved over
the surfaces, the farther these
letters move away from each other.

Rotation and size of a letter
is created by the grey scale value
of the dot and the actual position
of the mouse plus a simulation
of the rotation through
mathematic functions sinus,
cosine and tangent or through
their multiplication.

The eight modes for modulation of the rotation of dots are:

1  sinus (grayscale value * mouseX * mouseY)
2  grey scale * cos(mouseX * mouseY)
3  grey scale * tan(mouseX * mouseY)
4  grey scale * tan(counter * mouseX * mouseY)
5  grey scale * sin(counter) * tan(mouseX * mouseY)
6  cos(grey scale) * sin(counter) * tan(mouseX * mouseY/10.000)
7  grey scale * sin(mouseX * mouseY)
8  sin (grey scale)

GGGRAFIK DESIGN / GÖTZ GRAMLICH / VORTRAG / DIENSTAG / 26. MÄRZ 2013 / 16 UHR / BAU ZEICHENSAAL / HOCHSCHULE MANNHEIM / PAUL-WITTSACK-STR 12 / 68163 MANNHEIM

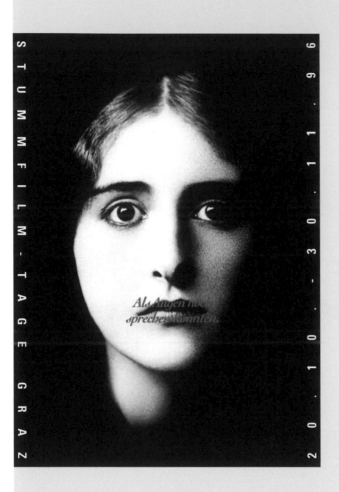

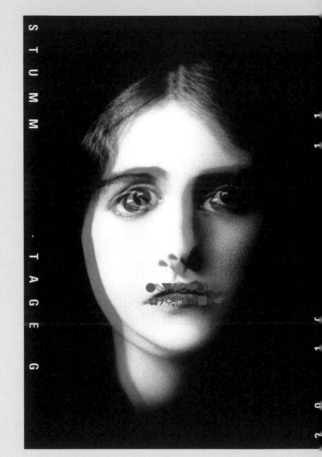

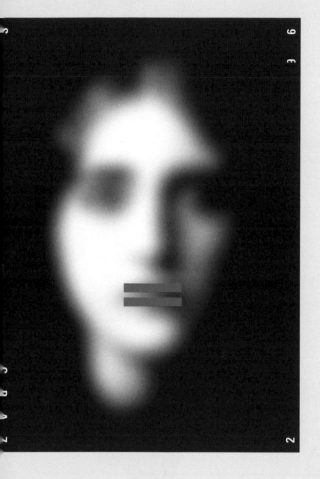

A FILM -

around 300

around 500

around 130

tailored and style dresses

around 1300

around 1600

around 1700

140 INTERPRETATION Teaching material for trainees of the women's wear sector. Drawings in the clothing style of the respective epoch are added to stamped figurines. Practical example: Betina Müller for Ott+Stein

around 1975

around 1920

around 1980

around 1850

around 1950

Laser punched slipcase for 15 brochures. Practical example: Stefan Sagmeister

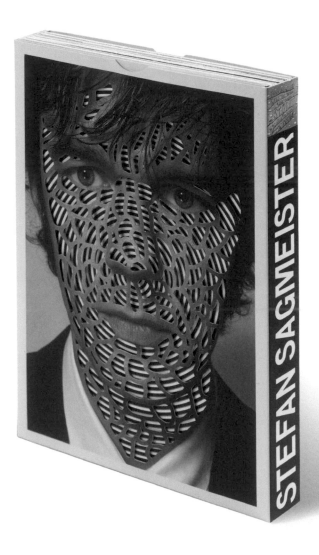

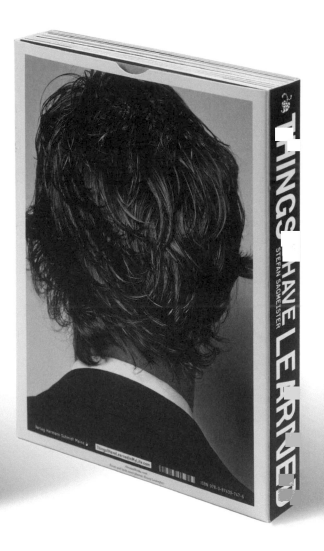

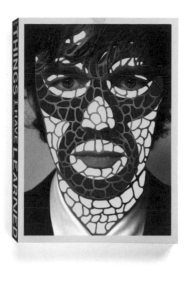

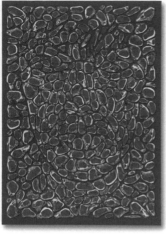
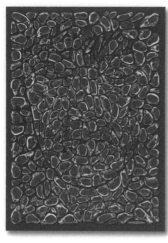

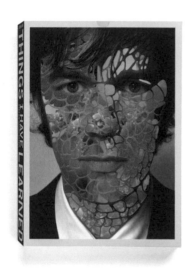

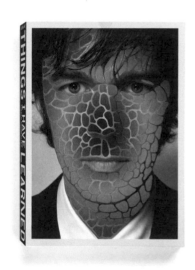

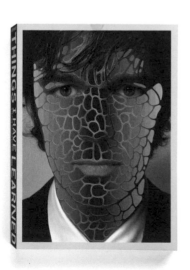

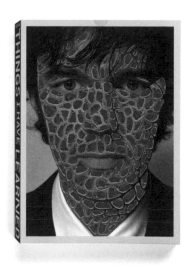

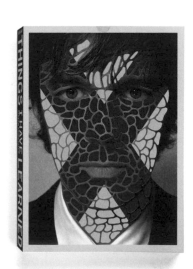

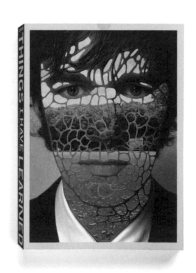

the original

soft pencil

hard pencil

colour pencil

pencil

sepia chalk drawing,
heightened with white

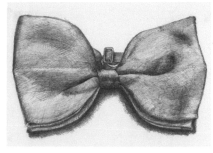

fineliner pen

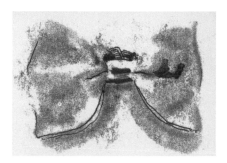

monotype

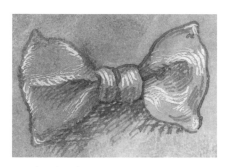

pen drawing in grey,
heightened with white

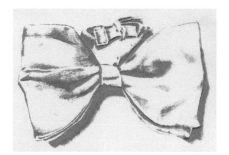

three coloured serigraph

monochrome painted

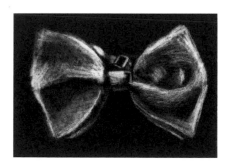

aquatinta etching

montage of
various
techniques

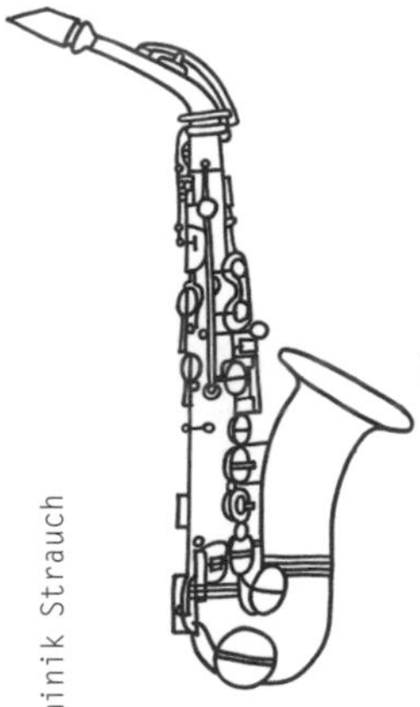

line drawing

hardened

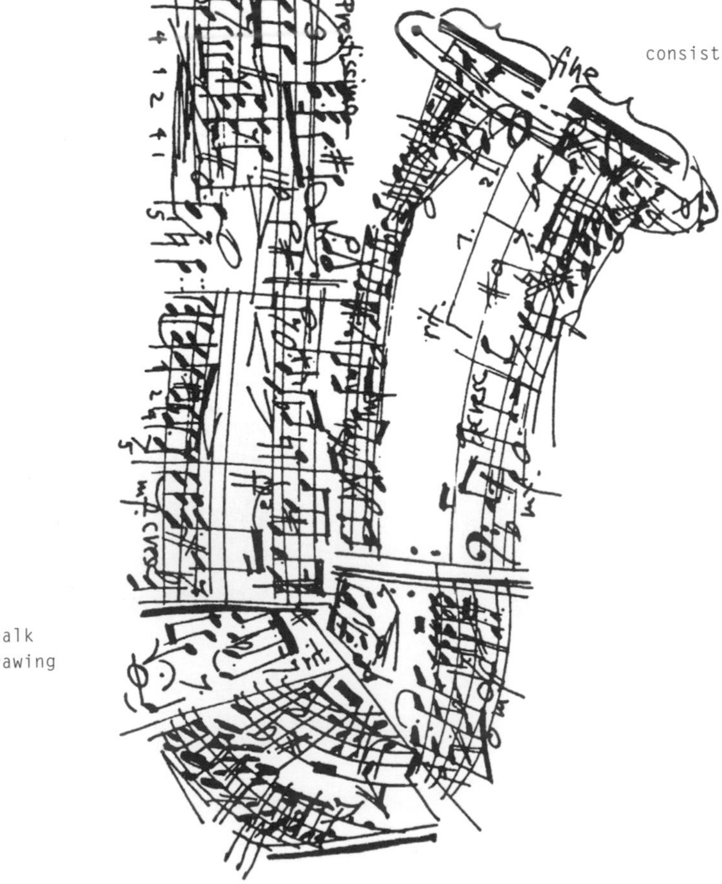

consisting of notes

chalk
drawing

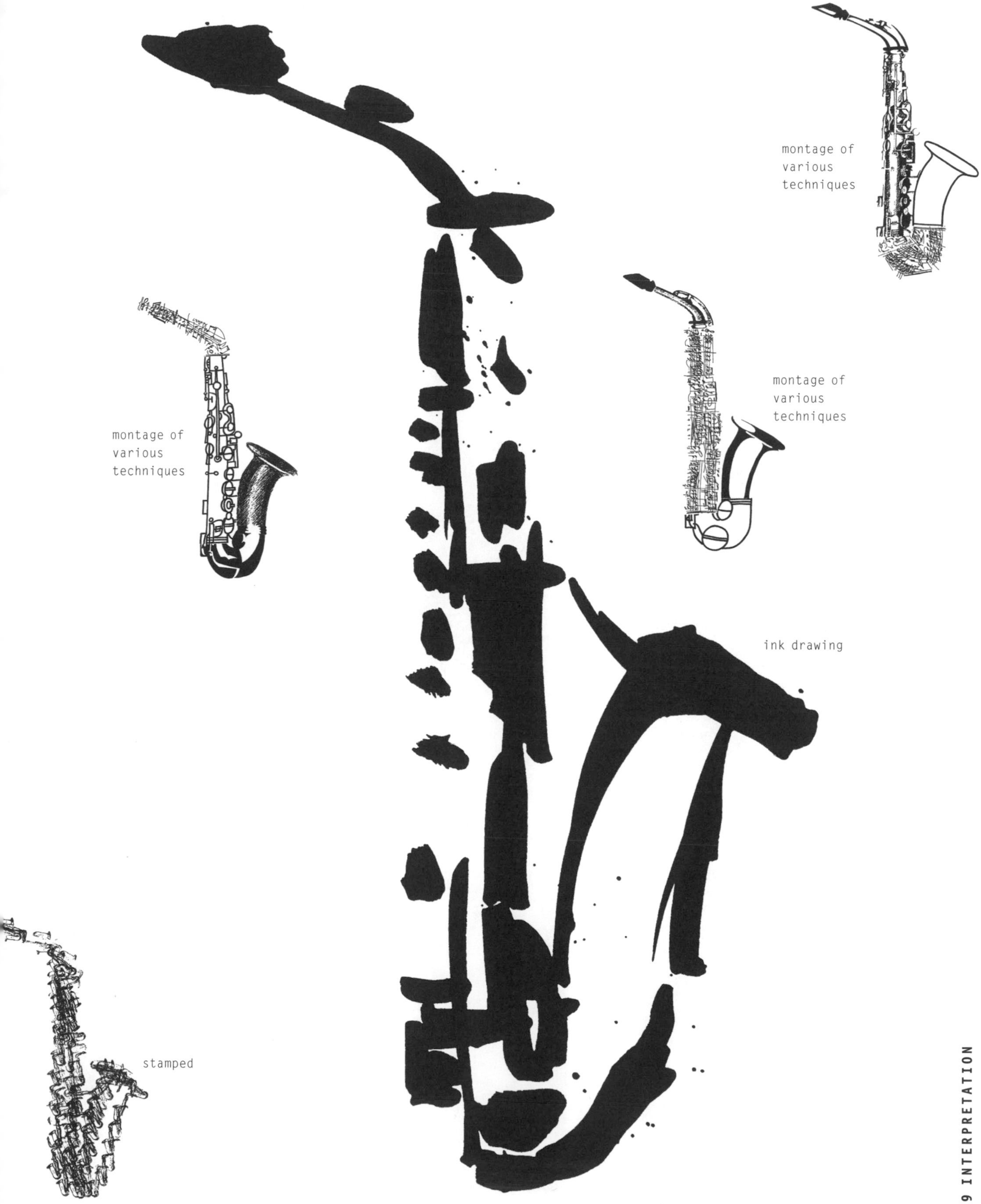

montage of
various
techniques

montage of
various
techniques

montage of
various
techniques

ink drawing

stamped

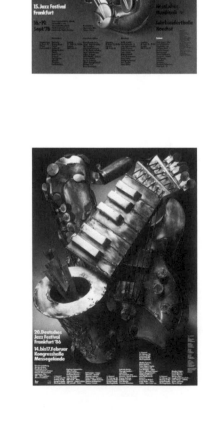

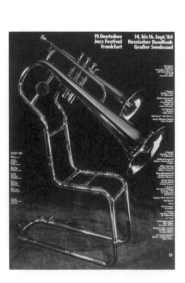

**150 INTERPRETATION** Series of posters for Frankfurt Jazz Festival. Typical instruments of jazz were taken apart, reassembled and then a photo was taken. Practical example: Günther Kieser

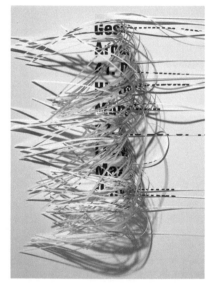

realised poster

cyan plate          magenta plate          yellow plate          black plate

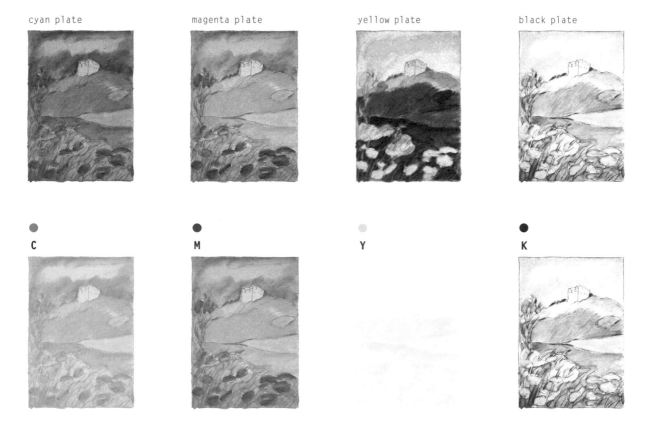

C          M          Y          K

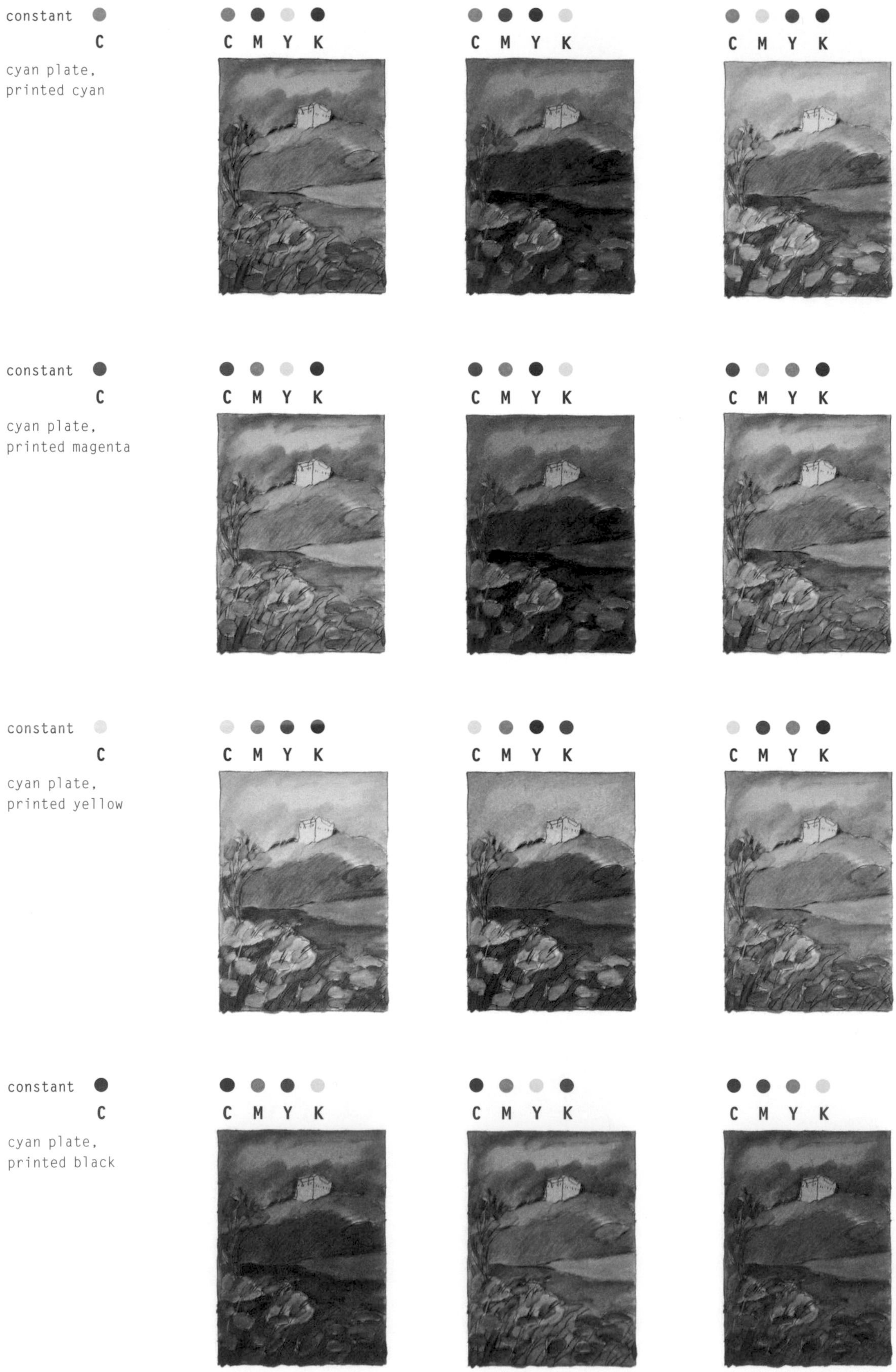

**156 INTERPRETATION** How it is done: The colour separations of a reproduced drawing are systematically varied and the four colours of printing (cyan, yellow, magenta and black) are alternated. One printing plate always prints the 'right' colour. The other three plates print with a 'wrong' colour. This leads to 24 variants of the original. Helmut Lortz

constant ● 
C
cyan plate, printed cyan

constant ● 
C
cyan plate, printed magenta

constant ● 
C
cyan plate, printed yellow

constant ● 
C
cyan plate, printed black

C M Y K

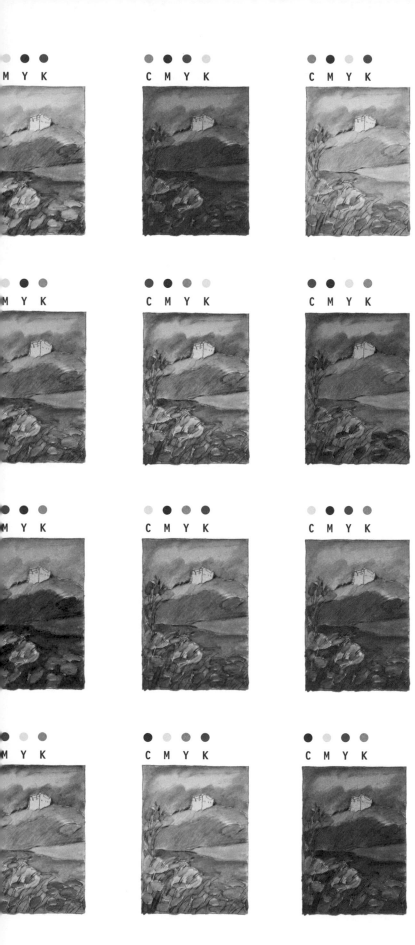

**INTERPRETATION** Systematic variation of a frequently used image from a picture database. Black-and-white separations of the colour components of a printed ad are made. Through exposure they create the different moulds for the coloured screen printing. Armin Lindauer

INTERPRETATION The images are created by means of computer graphics software; they are edited and then a photo is taken of the screen. Armin Lindauer

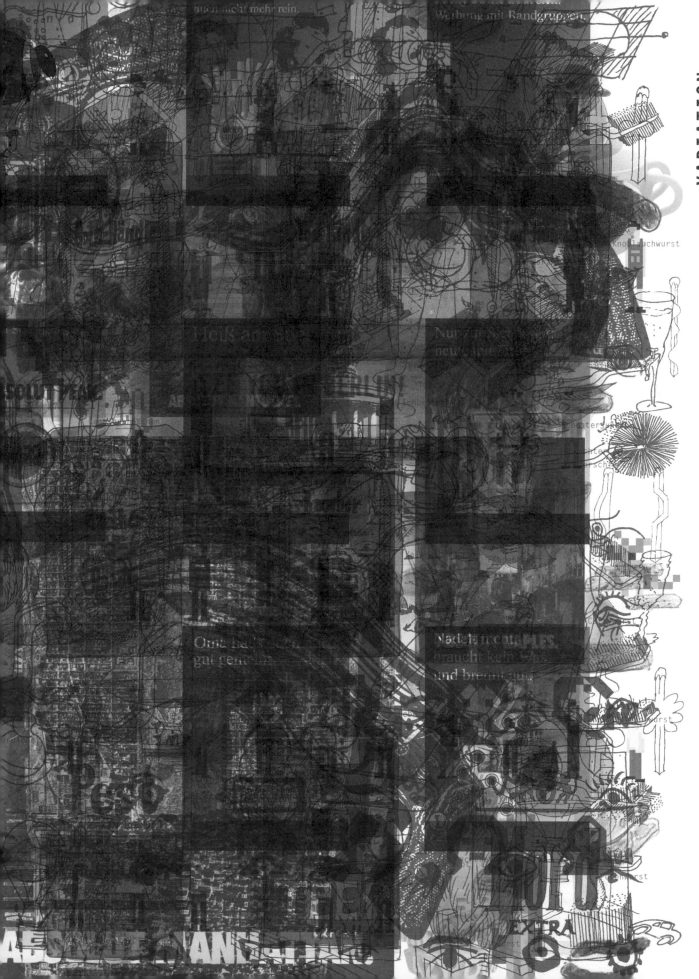

**3. VARIATION** 'Variatio delectat'— there's nothing like change! To vary, from
Latin 'variare', means "to reconfigure and thus extend a theme or an idea".
It can also imply "to render manifold, change, shift, differ, or shine in many
colours". The principle of variation in musical composition, which is characterised
by constant and variable parameters, has existed in written form since the
16th century. In music, variation means "melodic, harmonic or rhythmical
change and transformation of a theme"[1], and is by no means random, but directly
proportional to its initial form, the musical theme. Our concept of variation
intends to bring about a deliberately targeted change of the selected object, or
parts of that object, and then to modify, transform or reinvent them. What we mean
is the functional, content-related variation.

The selected object is mostly at the centre of the frame so that compositional
decisions do not have to be made. But the representational style should also
be simple and remain the same, because the rule that the simpler the representation,
the easier and quicker new ideas are noted, applies here. Composition would oppose
the quick immediate note, since the aim is to use a style that is as simple
and clear as possible. Concentrating on a single object such as a toothbrush >pp.258,
a dummy >pp.196, or a duck >pp.210 enables us to fathom out the scope of meaning and
association of the selected object. By altering functional parts such as the teat or
the handle of a dummy, new objects are created that may appear useless or funny,
absurd or novel, surprising or malicious. The object is transformed in such a way
that new possibilities emerge to handle, use and apply it.

OCTOPUZZLE >169 and the eyes by Picasso >165 show two principles that can be seen as
an early form of the aforenamed examples and which investigate the formal variations.
The interactive work OCTOPUZZLE presets the rule to always use 64 white and
64 black triangles on a quadratic basic grid of eight by eight squares. The
principle 'face' has been designed online by different people. One is astounded that
despite the fact of those restrictive preconditions so many diversified results
could be achieved. Drawn and painted eyes by Picasso which he illustrated in
multiple ways show the second example. To create this chart they were isolated from
his drawings, paintings and ceramics and reduced to their monochromatic basis and
then ordered by formal criteria. His manifold and fanciful figments vary the
principle 'eye' which remains clear — with all differences in the visual appeal.
Prepared in such a way — despite the widest range — an amazing inner coherence is
given.

Exploring known objects by means of variation stimulates the reinvention and
reinterpretation of forms and functions. The following strategies are used for this
exploration: analysis, analogy, combinatorics, segmentation, substitution,
extension, association, transformation, connection, modification and metamorphosis.

1 Renate Wahrig-Burfeind, WAHRIG. FREMDWÖRTERLEXIKON, Gütersloh, Munich 2011, p.1046.*

And that means creating amazingly new but completely useless objects. It is all about generating ideas, invention and imagination, about provocation and the targeted search for new connections. Ursula Brandstädter describes this as follows: "Basically, similarity relationships are open relationships that utilise the free space between identity and difference. [...] In cases [...] where possible similarities are sought after, a complex space for reflection emerges that introduces correspondences and analogies in relationship to a number of characteristics that had not been predefined beforehand."[2] "Many discoveries are based upon recognising analogies that nobody has ever noticed before [...], upon a shift of attention and the fusion of two reference systems."[3]

2 Ursula Brandstädter, GRUNDFRAGEN DER ÄSTHETIK, Cologne, Weimar, Vienna 2008, p. 23.*
3 Ibid., p. 56.*

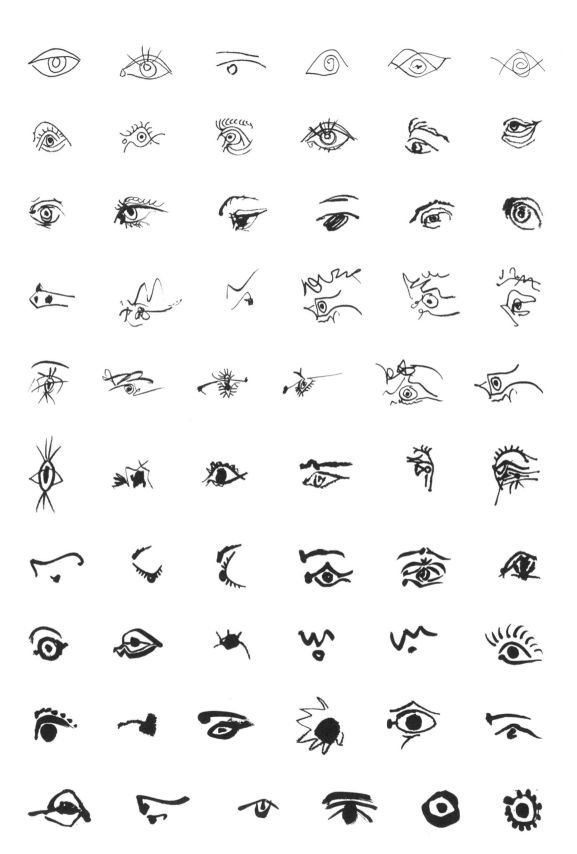

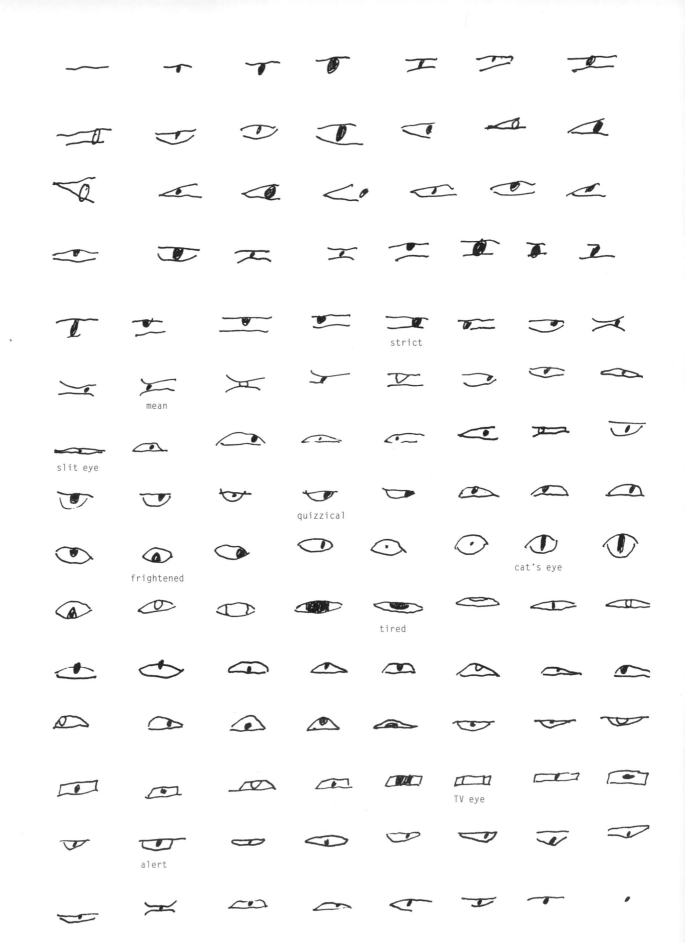

strict

mean

slit eye

quizzical

frightened

cat's eye

tired

TV eye

alert

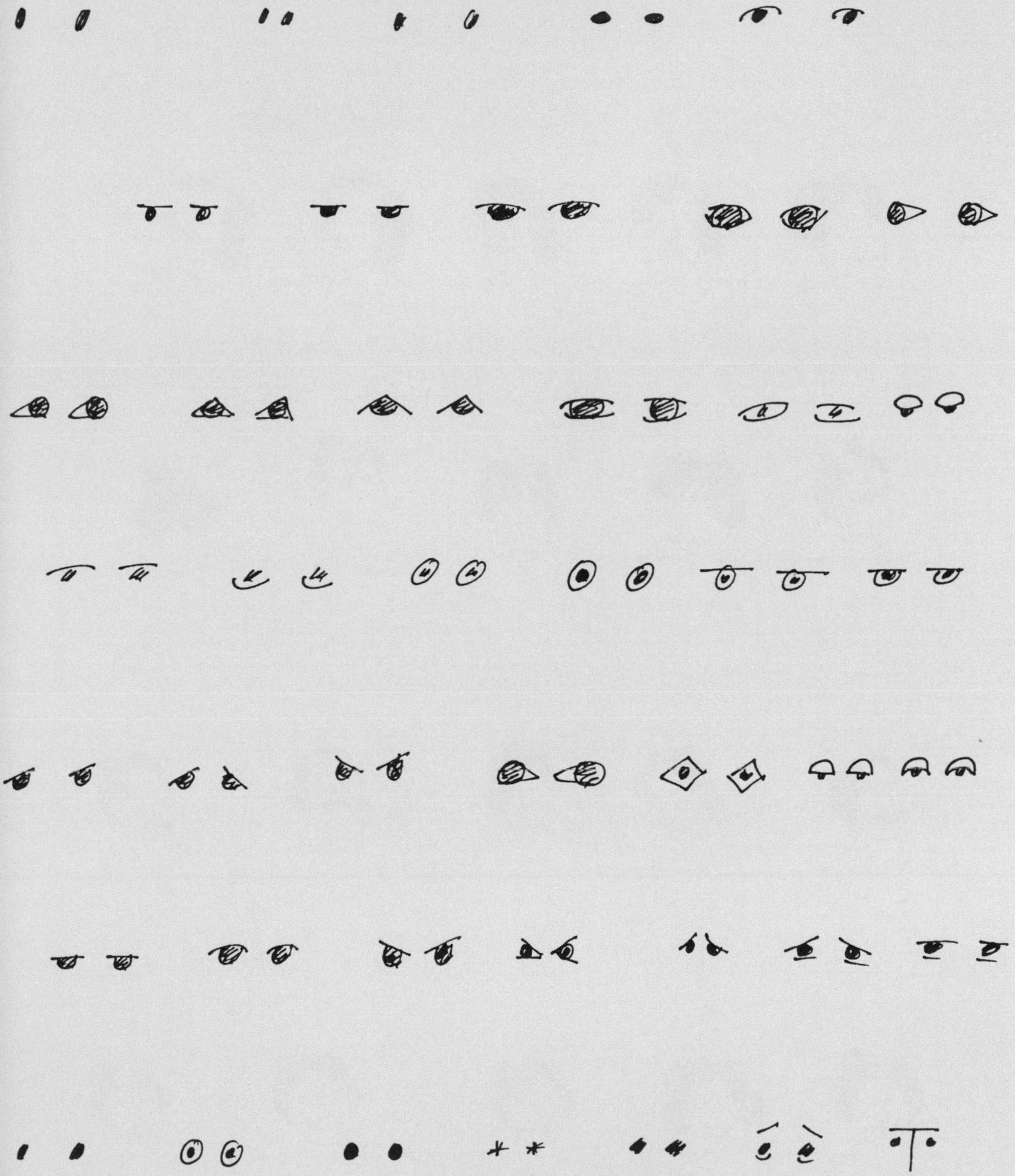

**167 VARIATION** Study of expressions of different eye shapes. Betina Müller

curious

arrogant

serious

clueless

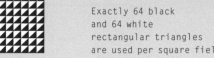

Exactly 64 black
and 64 white
rectangular triangles
are used per square field.

# spex

Das Magazin für Popkultur · www.spex.de

No.03/01 SONDER · G 6952

Sonderheft CD-ROM

## SPEX-CD-ROM
### Ausgabe März 2001

**173 VARIATION** Draft of the cover and back page for the SPEX music magazine. Embroidered elements are basically pixels too. Daniela Burger

Zeitschrift SPEX « Theorie-
arbeit von Daniela Burger ·
Studiengang Kommunika-
tionsdesign · Winter-
semester 2000 / 2001 ·
FH Potsdam · FB Design ·
Gutachter: Klaus Dufke,
Betina Müller

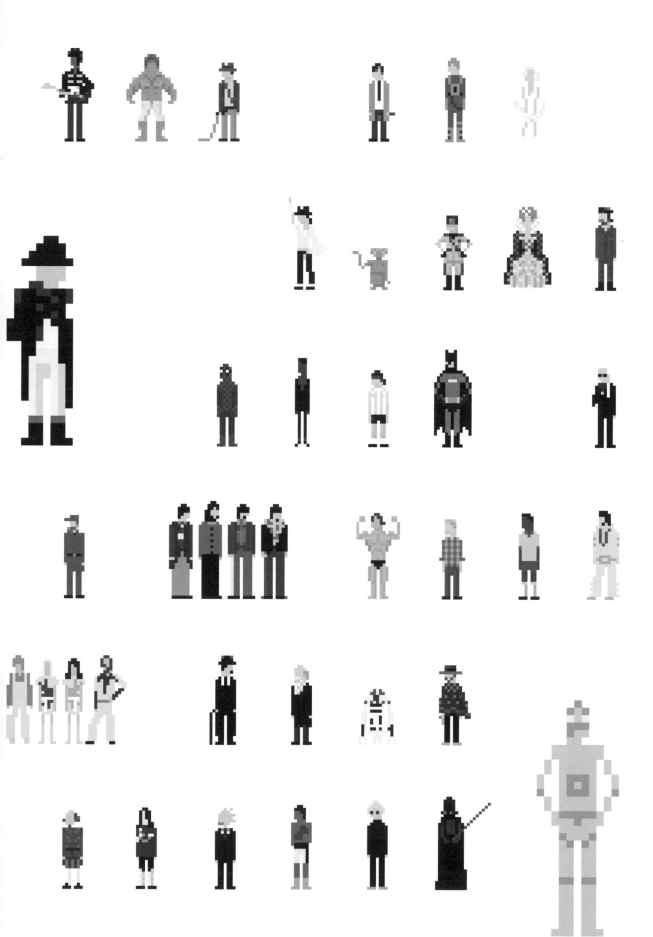

In reading direction: Jimi Hendrix, Hulk, Indiana Jones, Columbo, Luke Skywalker, Marilyn Monroe, Adam und Eva, Michael Jackson, E.T., Mussolini, Queen Elizabeth, Che Guevara, Napoleon, Spiderman, Grace Jones, Diego Maradona, Batman, Karl Lagerfeld, Fidel Castro, The Beatles, Arnold Schwarzenegger, George Lucas, Pelé, Elvis Presley, ABBA, Charlie Chaplin, Charles Darwin, R2-D2, Clint Eastwood, **175 VARIATION** Shakespeare, Michael Jackson, Albert Einstein, Mohammed Ali, Andy Warhol, Darth Vader, C-3P0. Craig Robinson

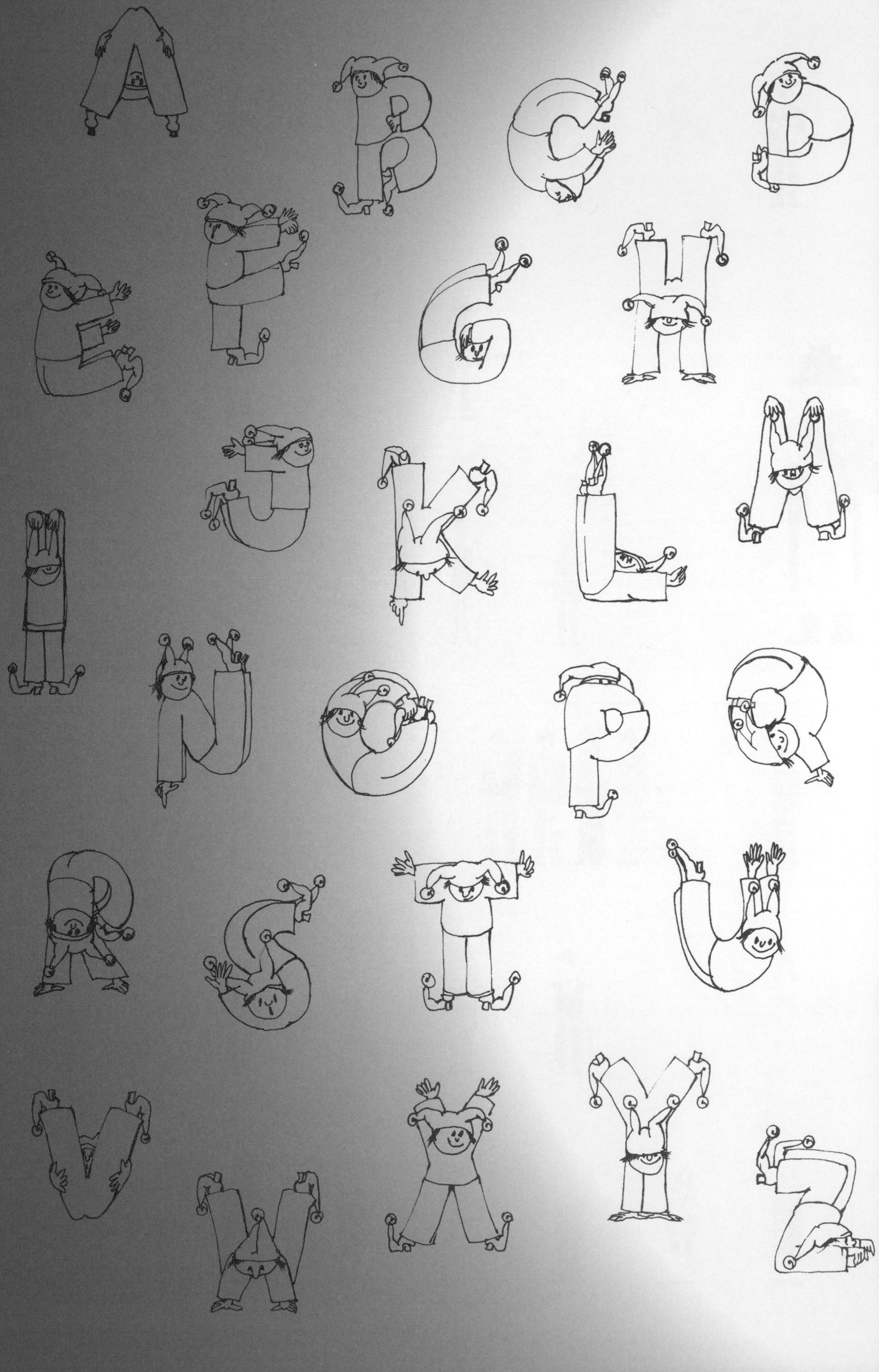

 Kasper's alphabet. Karin Cerna-Lobpreis

**178 VARIATION** Artwork for a cookbook with egg recipes. Alexandra Fragstein

back to nature trips

hunting trips

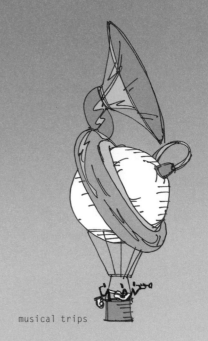

musical trips

pilgrimages

back to nature trips

**180 VARIATION** Artwork for a fictional company, advertising exclusive and extraordinary trips. Yann Ubbelohde

sports trips

painting trips

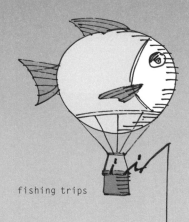

fishing trips

expeditions

gourmet trips

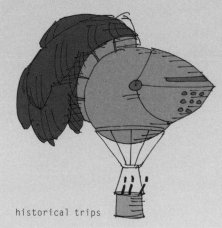

historical trips

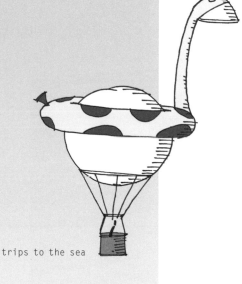

trips to the sea

honeymoons

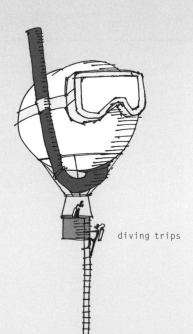

diving trips

spa trips

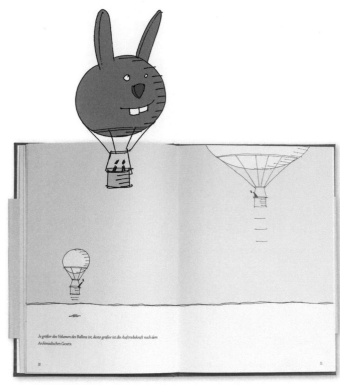

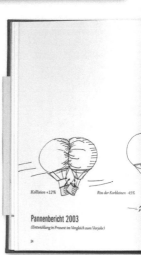

trips with children

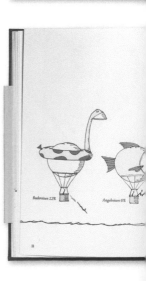

Ausblick 2004 - anhaltender Aufwind

ein innovatives Konzept

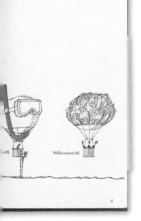

**184 VARIATION** Graphic rendering of tree types. Helmut Lortz

**187 VARIATION** Getting into shape. Graphic rendering of Christmas trees. Sabine Böing

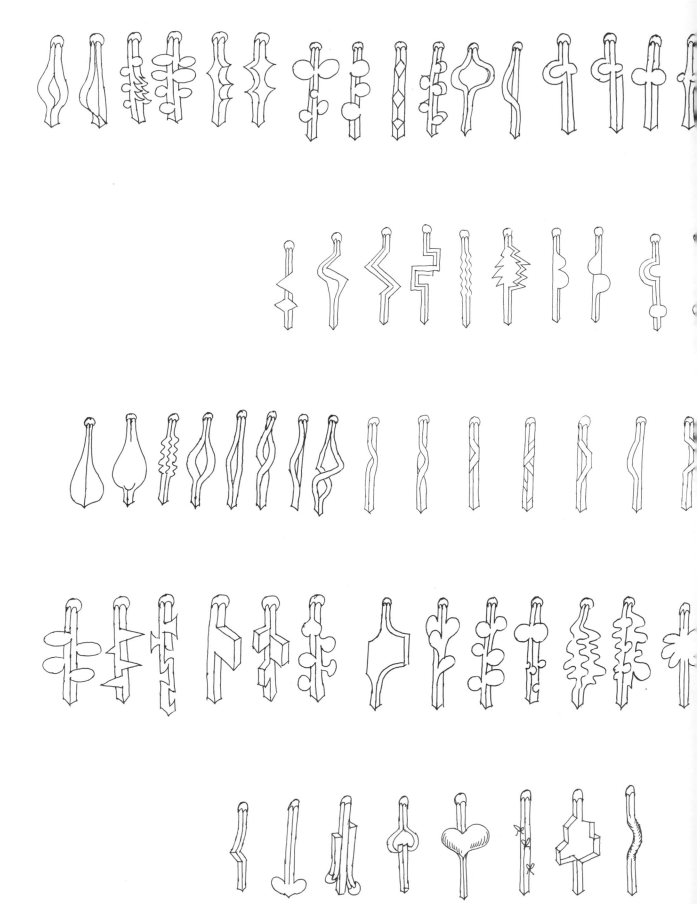

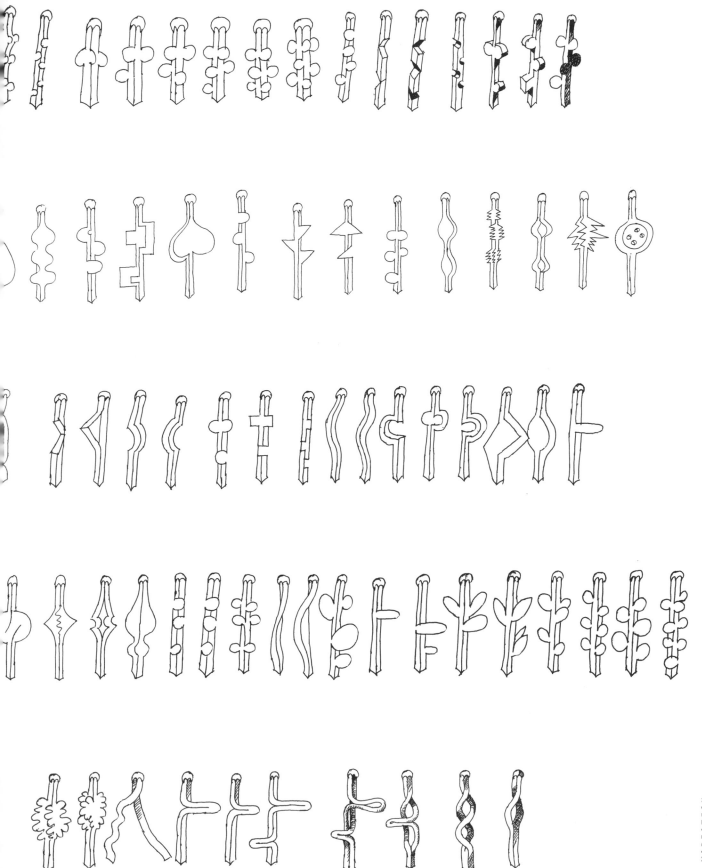

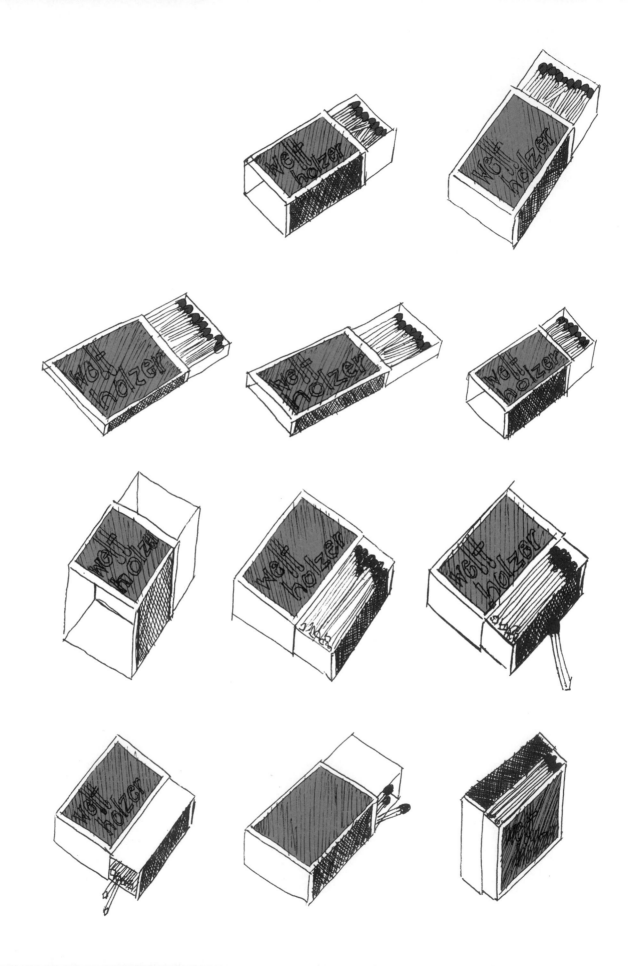

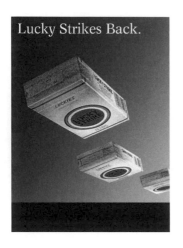

Lucky Strikes Back.

Über Satellit bekommen Sie auch nicht mehr rein.

Lucky Strike traut sich: Werbung mit Randgruppen.

Am 21.6. ist Sommeranfang.

Heiß am Stiel.

Nur zur Sicherheit: heute mit Firewall.

Oder hätten Sie lieber ein Paar Socken?

Oma hat's doch nur gut gemeint.

Nadelt nicht, braucht kein Wasser und brennt gut.

Extra für Peking: 'ne Ente.

Absolut Luckies.

Bitte nicht in diesem Ton!

Prêt-à-fumer.

Finden Sie mal eine gute Urlaubsvertretung.

Zu wissen, SIE hat es getragen...

Puzzle für Jecken!

Sie wollen den Tatort sehen? Bitte schön.

Den Rest können Sie sich ja ausmalen ...

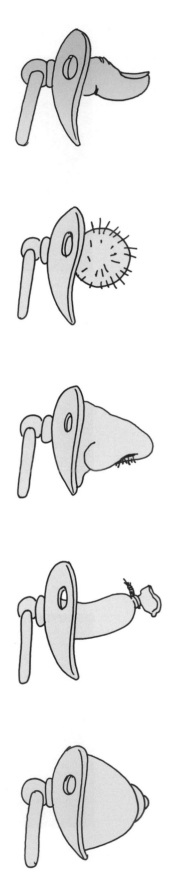

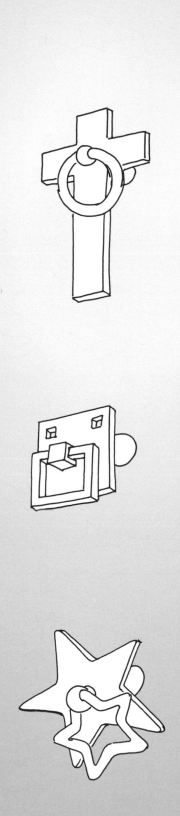

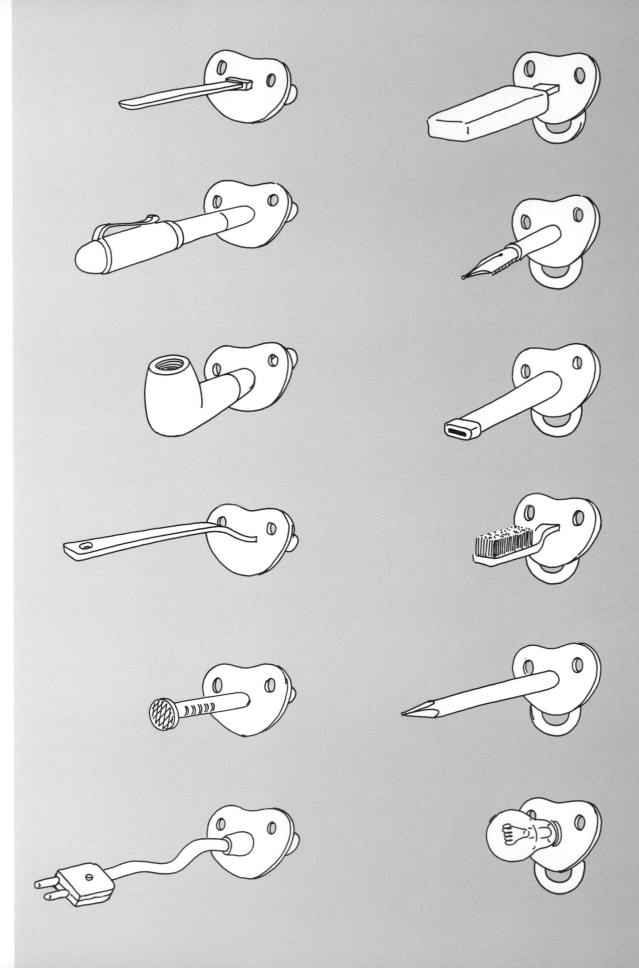

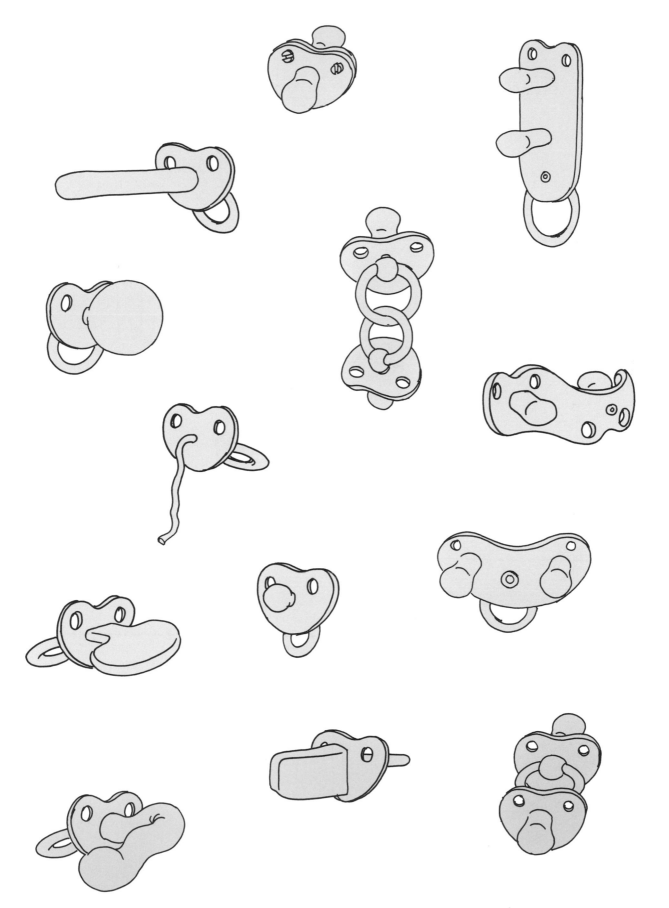

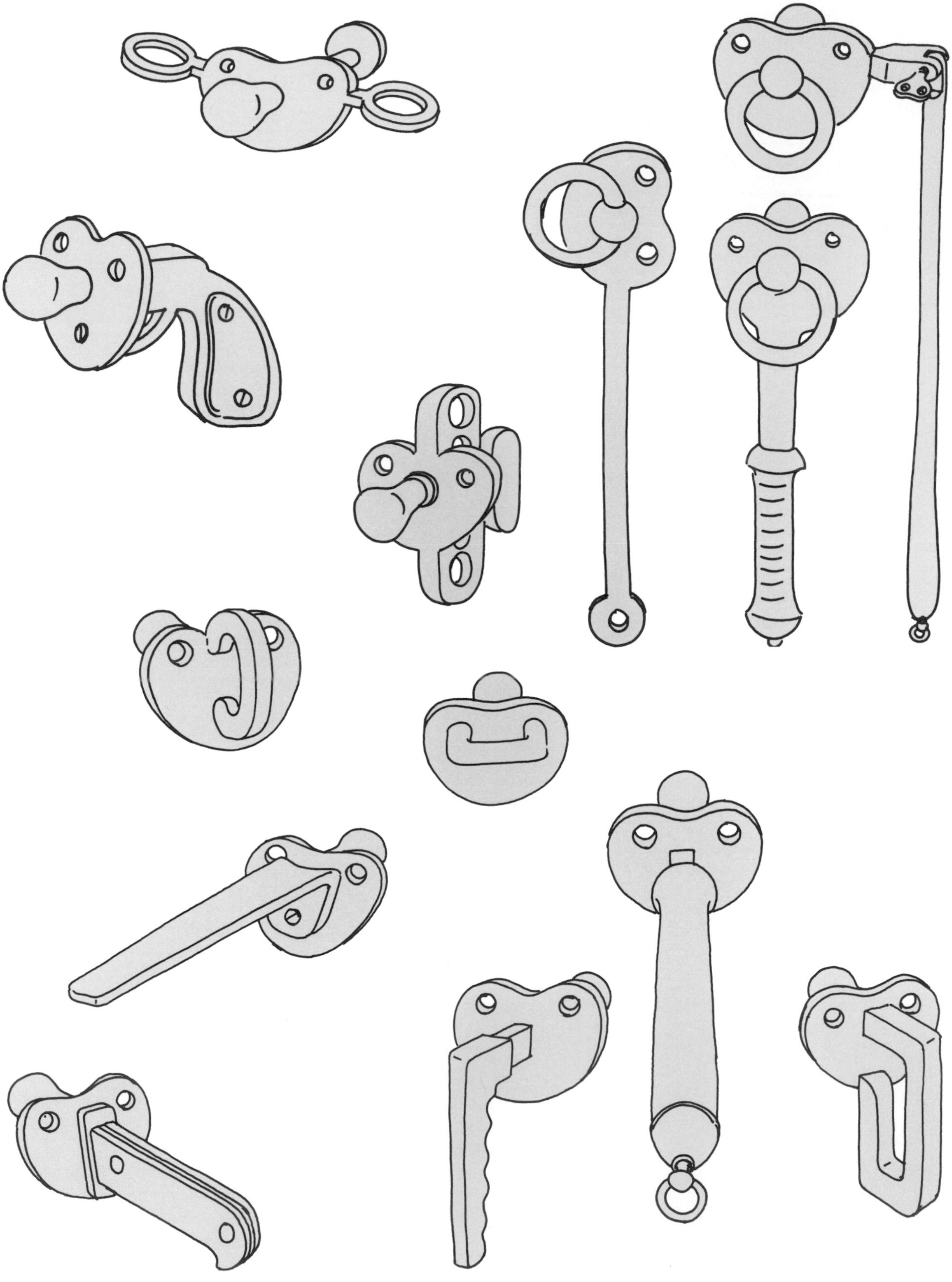

**200 VARIATION** Variations of the handle. Frank Stiebi

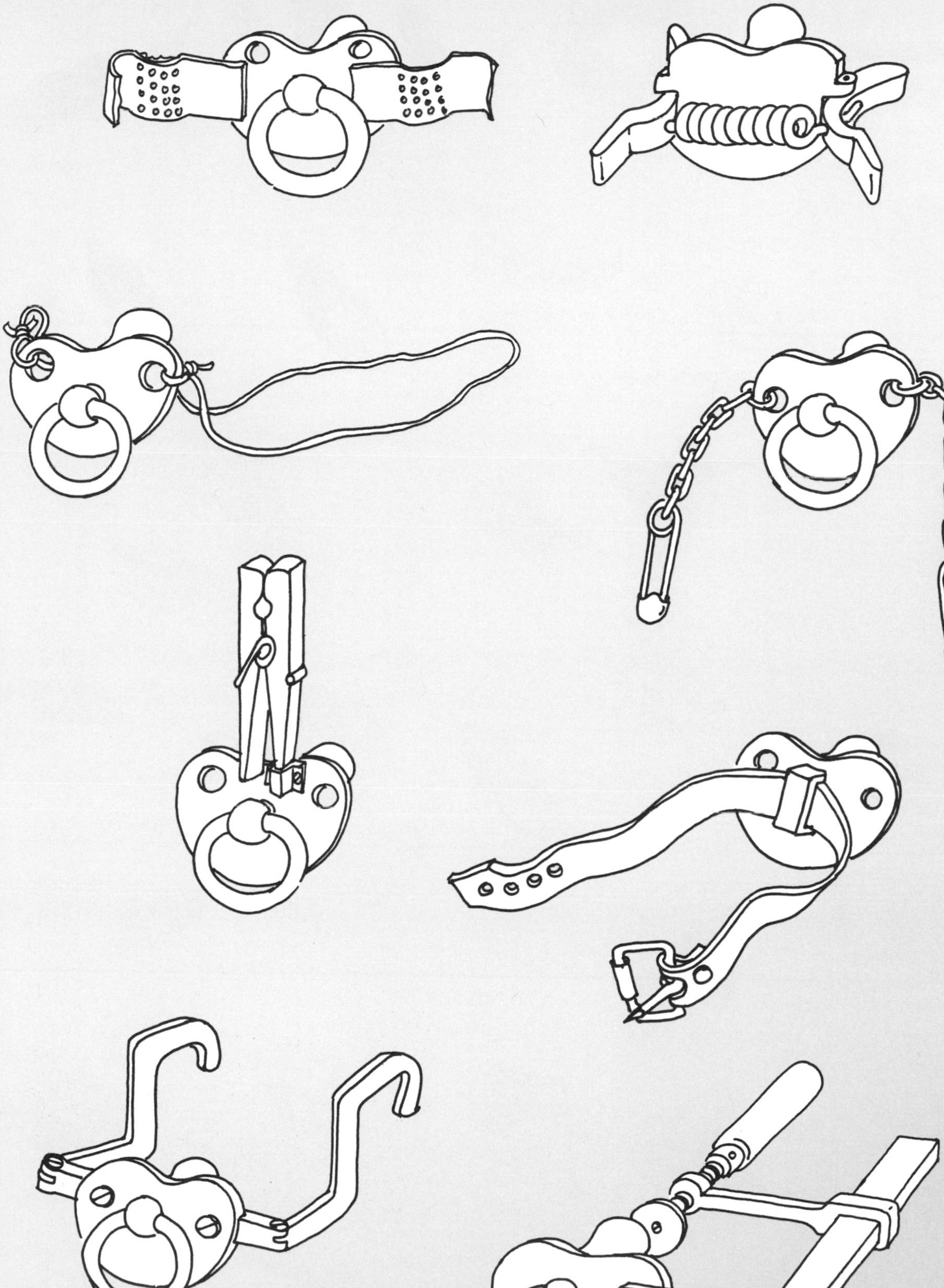

**201 VARIATION** Suggestions for fastenings.

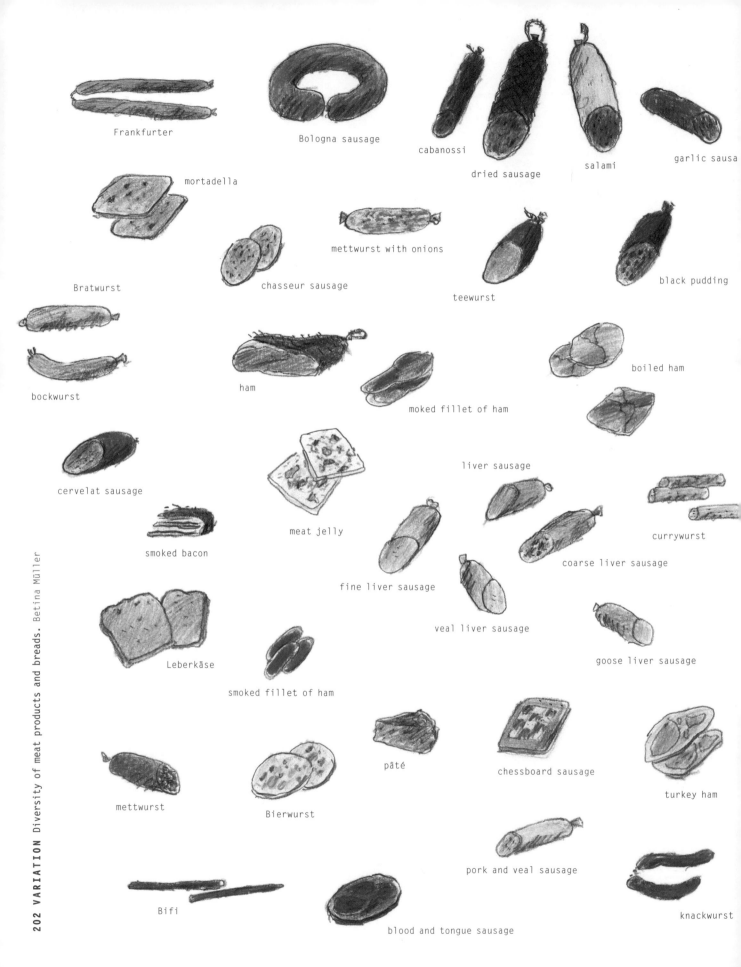

Frankfurter

Bologna sausage

cabanossi

dried sausage

salami

garlic sausa

mortadella

Bratwurst

mettwurst with onions

chasseur sausage

teewurst

black pudding

bockwurst

ham

moked fillet of ham

boiled ham

cervelat sausage

meat jelly

liver sausage

currywurst

smoked bacon

fine liver sausage

coarse liver sausage

veal liver sausage

Leberkäse

goose liver sausage

smoked fillet of ham

pâté

chessboard sausage

turkey ham

mettwurst

Bierwurst

pork and veal sausage

Bifi

blood and tongue sausage

knackwurst

whole-grain bread

toast

farm-baked bread

whole-grain toast

white rye-wheat bread

tin loaf

Steinmetz bread

french croissant

dark wheat bread

golden crust bread

croissant

puff pastry

wood-oven baked bread

stone-baked bread

raisin
bread roll

milk roll

Schusterjunge
bread roll

camping
bread roll

bread roll

army bread

Knüppel
bread roll

Schrippe
bread roll

roll

croissant

flatbread

braided yeast loaf

Kiel bread roll

caraway bread roll

white bread

baguette

party baguette

Pumpernickel

crackers

cut bread

lump bread

Schüttel bread

Hamburg
brown bread

ham sandwich

wire cup

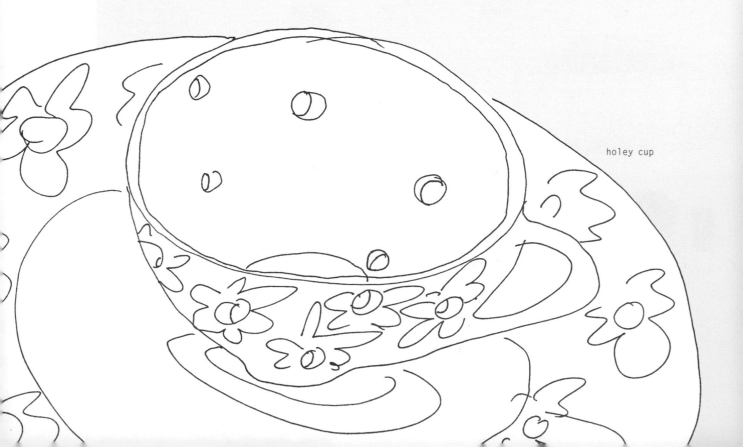

holey cup

chimney cup

submarine cup

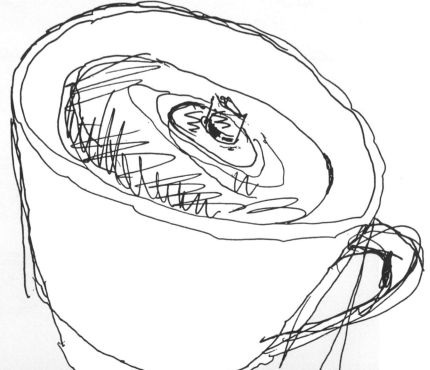

**207 VARIATION** ONE CUP A DAY is a rapid prototyping project: produce one 'real' cup within 24 hours. Bernat Cuni

Klein Bottle Cup

Low Resolution Cup

Fat Cup

Cup Cake Cup

Studded Belt Cup

Bird's Nest Cup

Rich Bitch Cup

Siamese Cup

Knitted Cup

Kryptonite Cup

Double Espresso C

Eroded Cup

Emmental Cup

Octo Cup

50 Percent Cup

Hard to Handle Cup

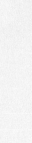

90 Degrees Cup

Fish Scales Cup

Savoy Cup

Waves Cup

Champion's Coffee Cup

Golf Ball Cup

Tub Cup

Helveticup

**VARIATION** One thousand and one ducks ... Filius Fritz Klein

duck breast

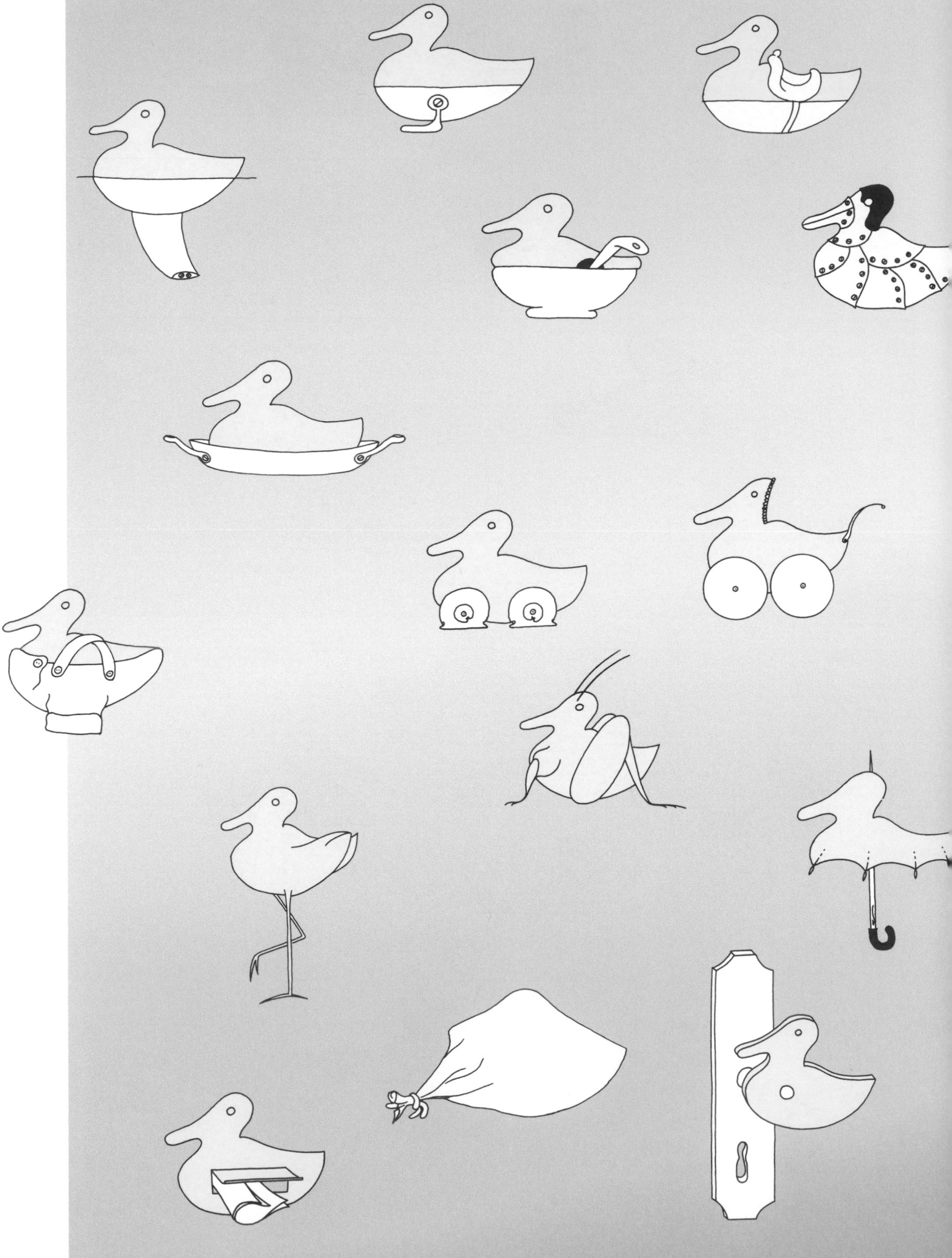

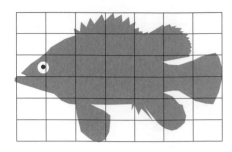

polyprion

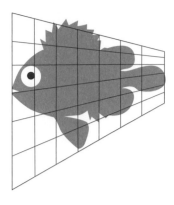

pseudopriacanthus altus

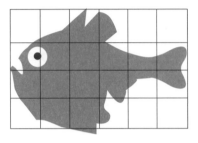

argyropelecus olfersi

sternoptyx diaphana

Fish show a basic pattern which can be altered by different mathematical operations, such as slanting and deforming, amongst others, to create new, yet similar, shapes of the same kind.

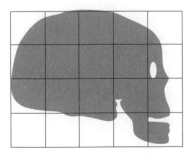

human skull

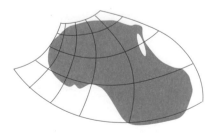

chimpanzee skull

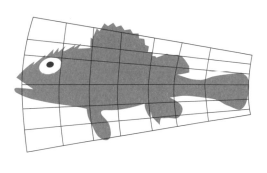

scorpaena species

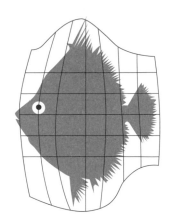

antigonia capros

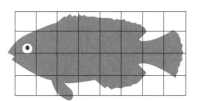

scarus species

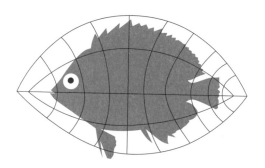

pomacanthus

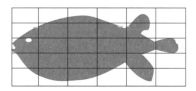

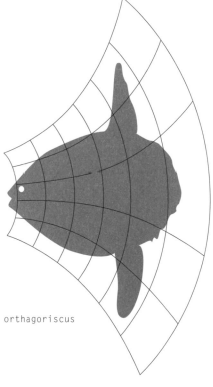

orthagoriscus

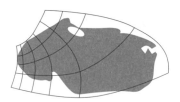

baboon skull

dog skull

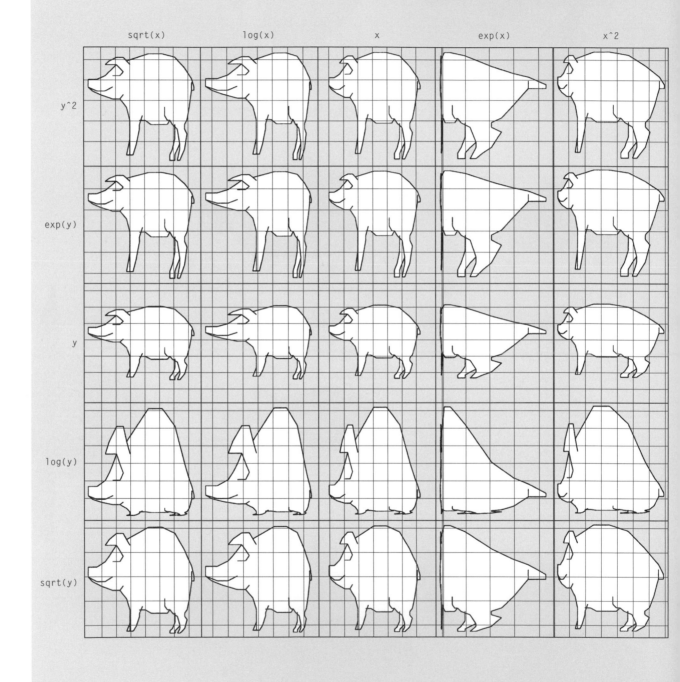

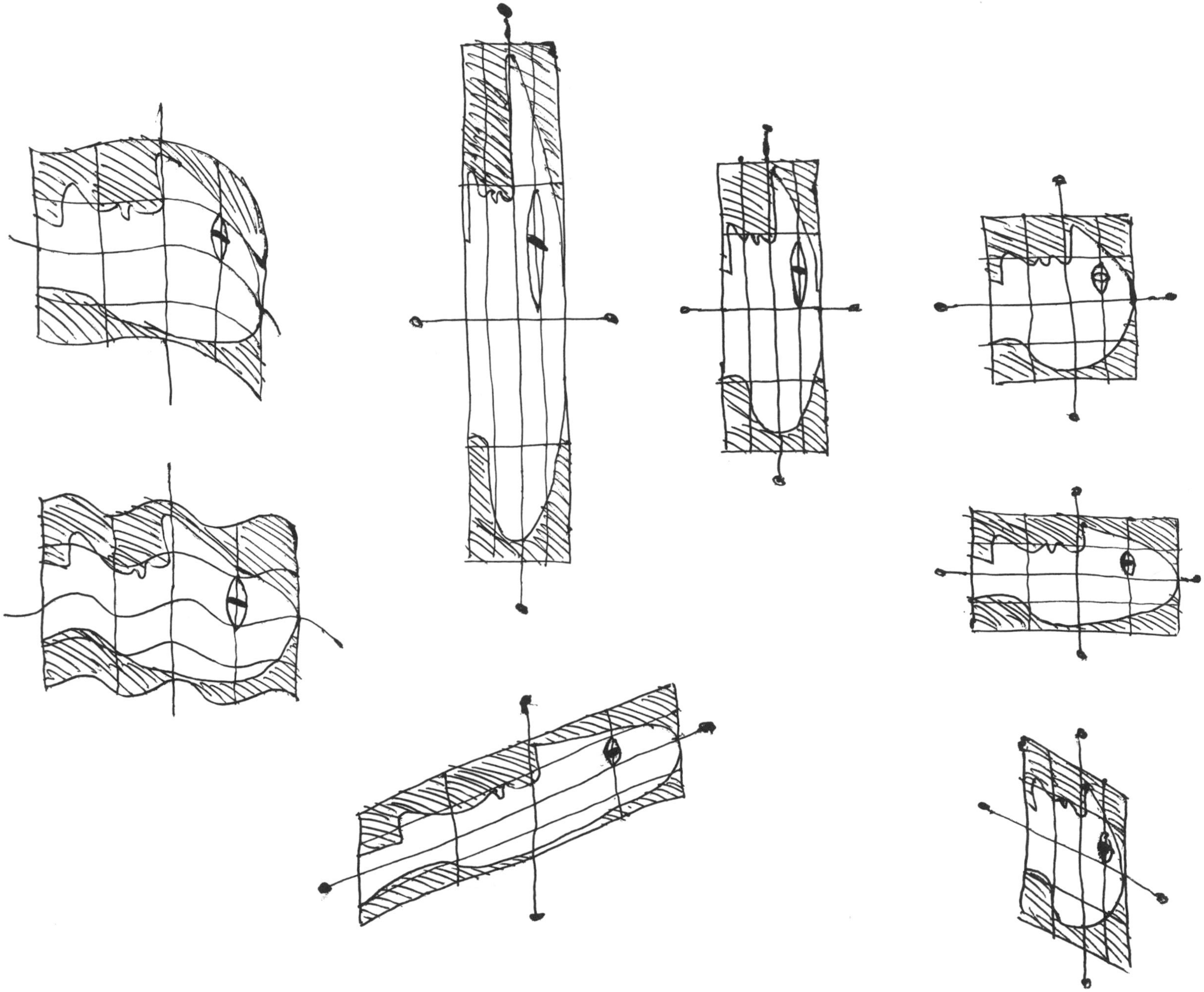

**217 VARIATION** Systematic deformation of a drawing within a coordinate system. Helmut Lortz

swallow

blackbird

greenfinch

bearded tit

robin

emperor penguin

parakeet

green headed
tanager

green woodpecker

wagtail

sparrow

pheasant

chaffinch

bullfinch

kestrel

bluetit

kingfisher

In the case of the Asian ladybird, the principle of evolution creates an enormous array of colour patterns due to genetic variation and **219 VARIATION** natural selection. Their natural population already exhibits substantial genetic diversity. *Spektrum der Wissenschaft magazine*

Karin Cerna-Lobpreis

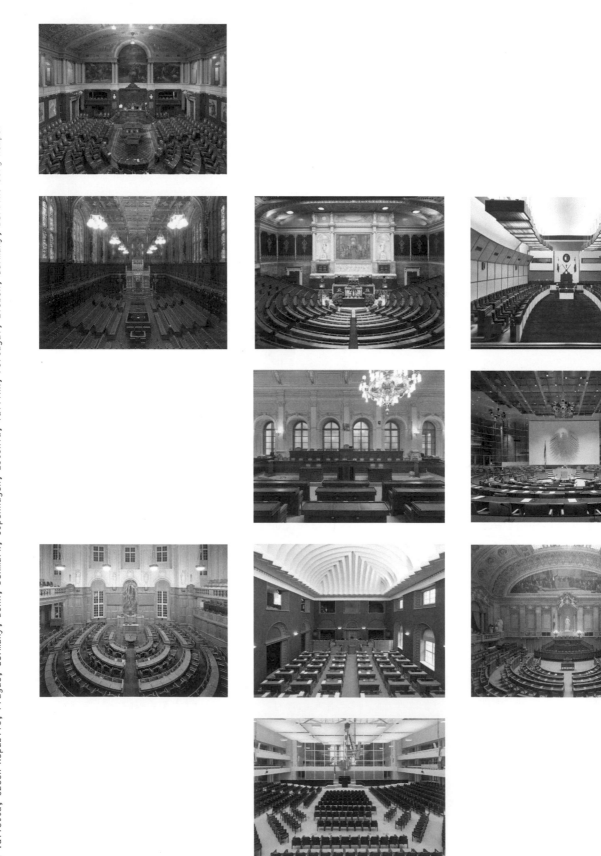

222 **VARIATION** POWER ARENAS: Assembly rooms of different countries. In reading direction: Belgium, Brussels; United Kingdom, London; France, Paris; Malta, Valletta; Czech Republic, Prague; Germany, Bonn; Denmark, Copenhagen; Estonia, Tallinn; Portugal, Lisbon; Germany, Berlin. Jörg Hempel

223 **VARIATION** In reading direction: Romania, Bucharest; Slovenia, Ljubljana; Bulgaria, Sofia; Poland, Warsaw; Hungary, Budapest; Lithuania, Vilnius.

**224 VARIATION** In reading direction: Slovenia, Ljubljana; Sweden, Stockholm; Greece, Athens; Belgium, Brussels; Luxembourg, Luxembourg; The Netherlands, The Hague; Ireland, Dublin; Italy, Rome; Romania, Bucharest. Jörg Hempel

In reading direction: France, Strasbourg, European Parliament; Austria, Vienna; Norway, Oslo; Finland, Helsinki; **225 VARIATION** Italy, Rome; Russia, Moscow; Spain, Madrid; Belgium, Brussels, European Parliament.

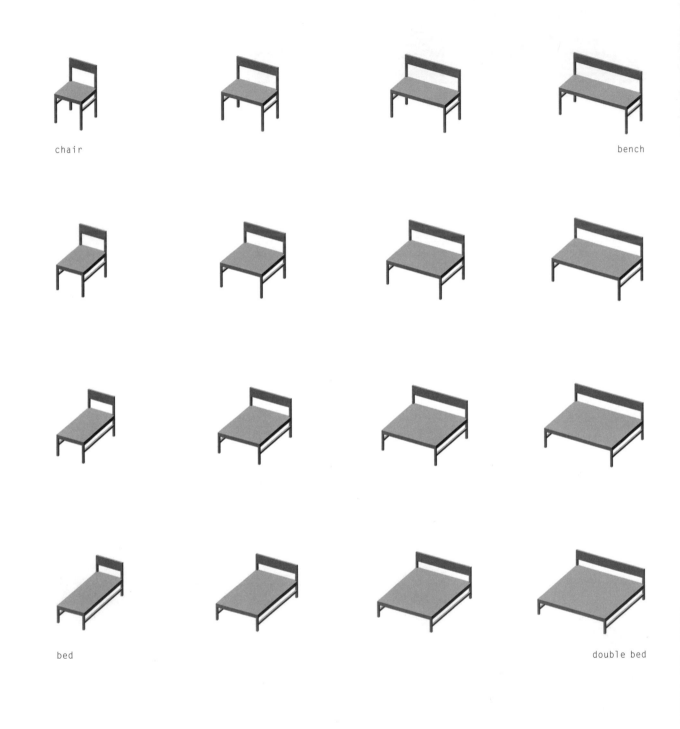

chair

bench

bed

double bed

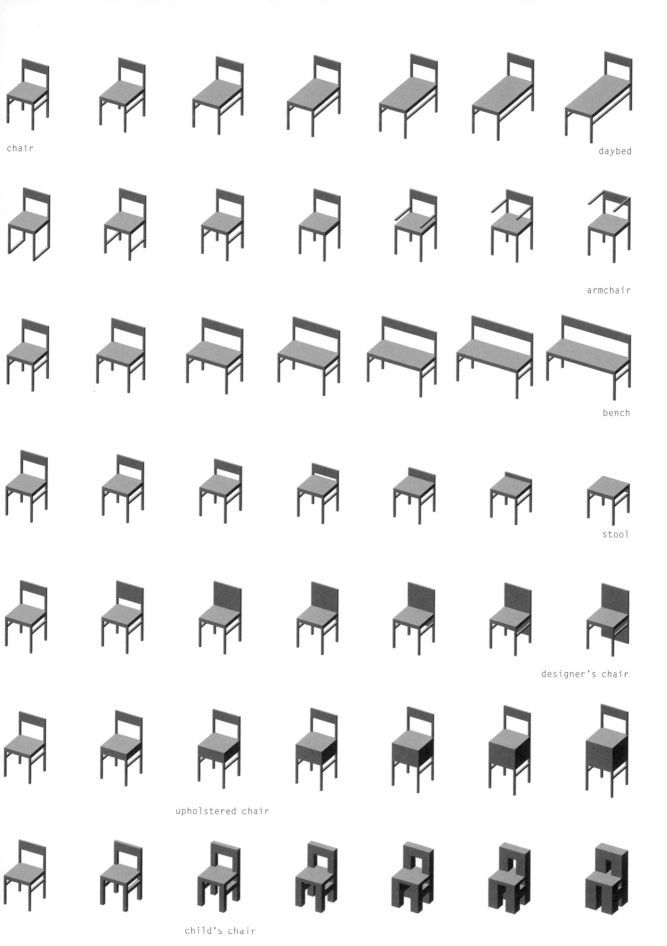

chair

daybed

armchair

bench

stool

designer's chair

upholstered chair

child's chair

 Deconstruction and recombination of an industrially manufactured table. Roman Lindebaum, Rüdiger Otte

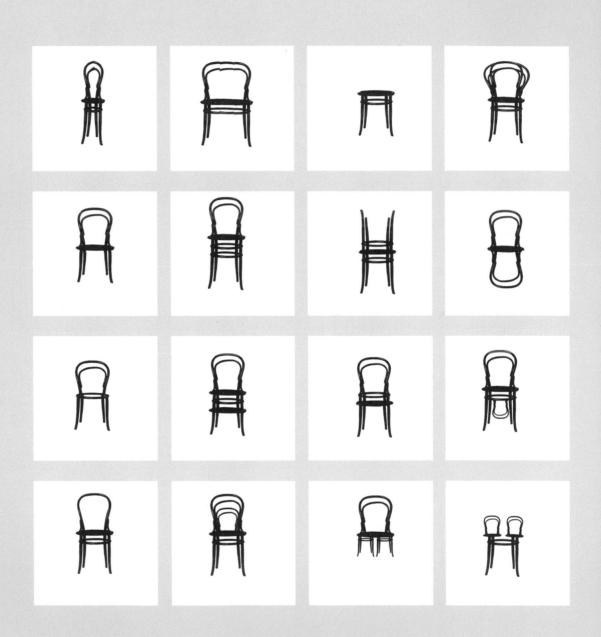

WEISSER SCHIMMEL: online computer game by an artist group in Cairo. The tautology in the title of the computer game is reflected in the **231 VARIATION** repetition of images. The white white horse is in fact the negative image of a black stallion. Practical example: Fons Hickmann

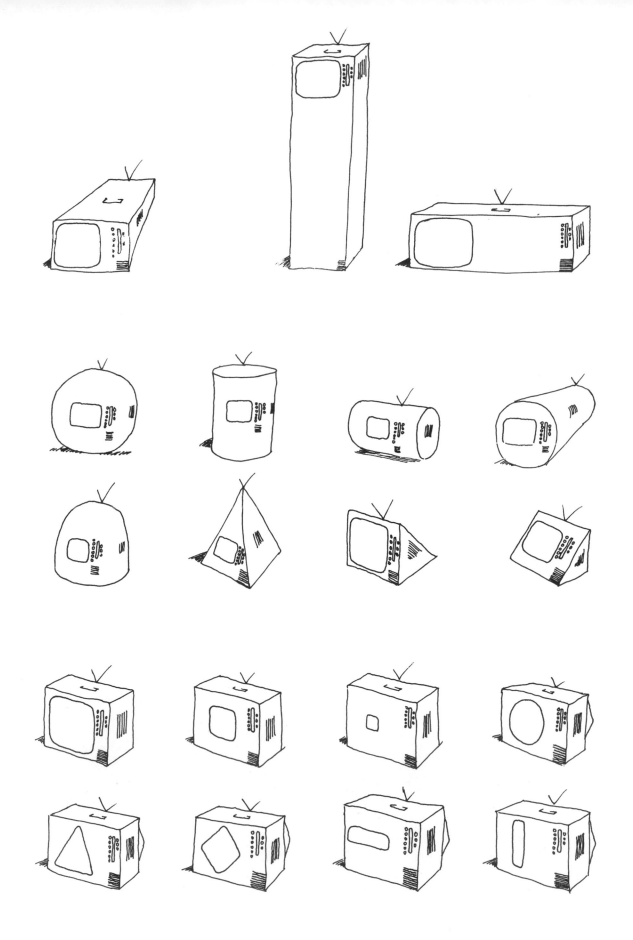

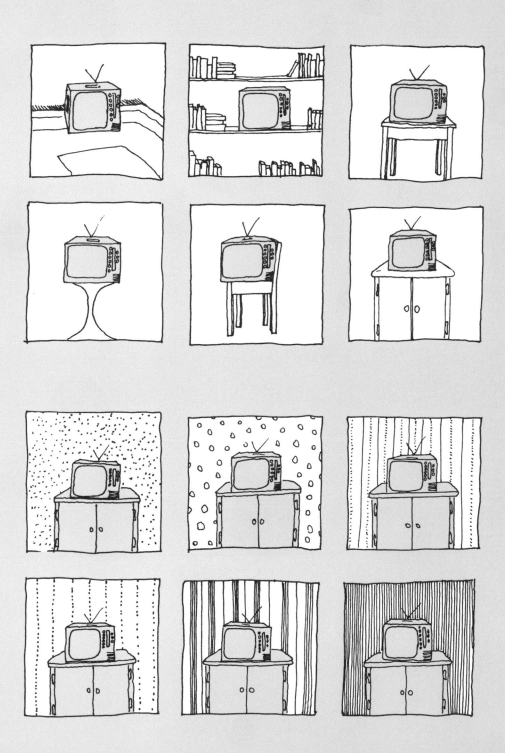

**VARIATION** The television remains the same in terms of shape and position, but the surroundings vary.

Godcat

Birdie-cat

Quiescat

Sunnycat

Aerocat

234 VARIATION The cat and its toilet: Contribution to the 'Biokats' competition. Gordon Karau

Mizó

Conceptcat

Catfish

Acropocat

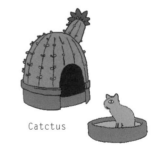

Catctus

Catska

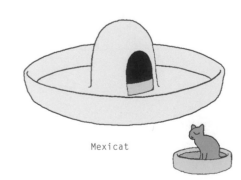

Mexicat

Mickeycat

Spacccat

Cowcat

Eastercat

Cheesecat

Historicat

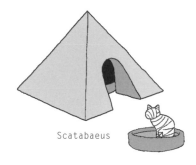
Scatabaeus

Atomicat

Catskimo

van Cat

Disco Kitten

Santacat

Ecocat

Black cat

236 VARIATION Different ways to close a suitcase and attach handles. Christian Dorn

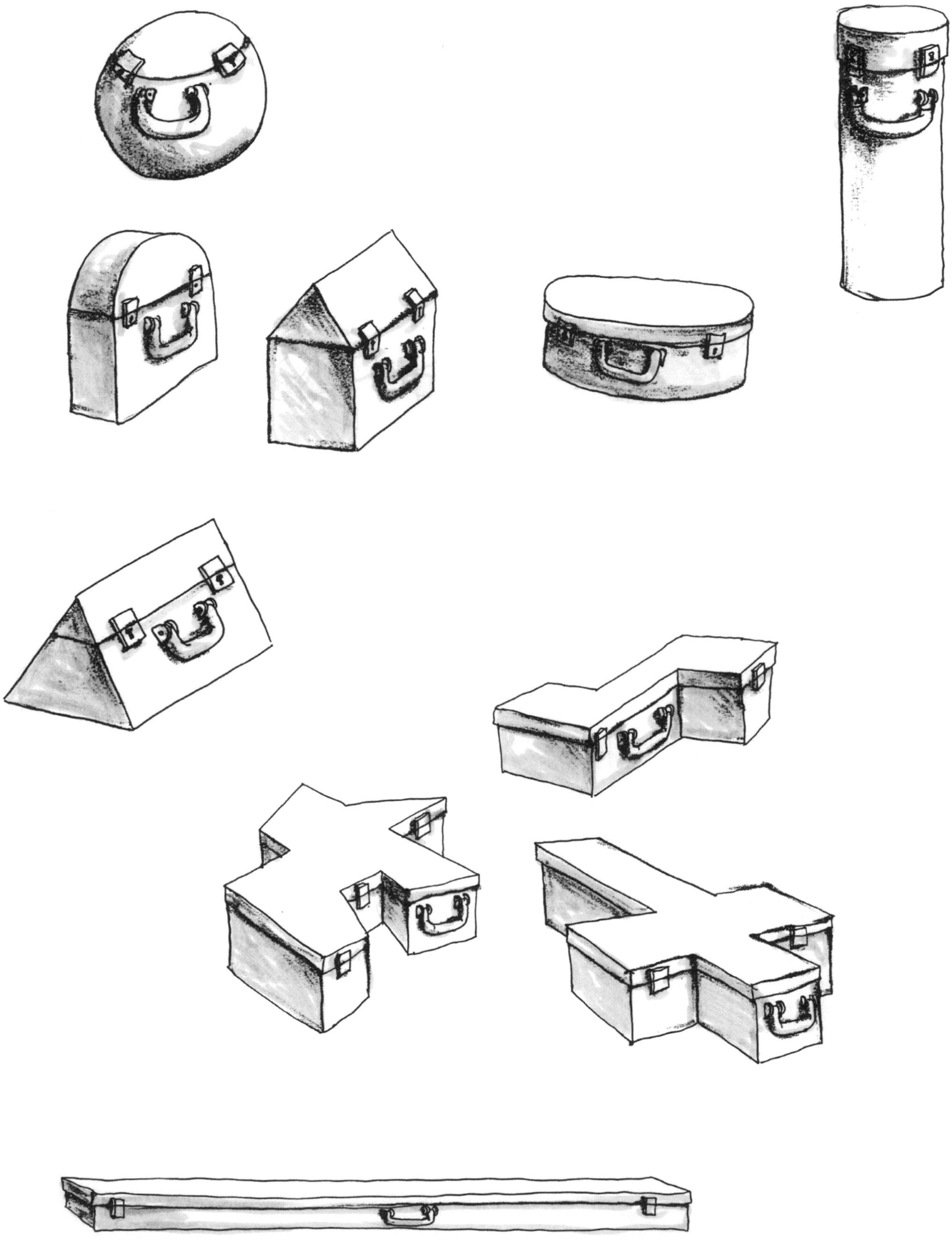

**237 VARIATION** Does the shape reveal what's inside?

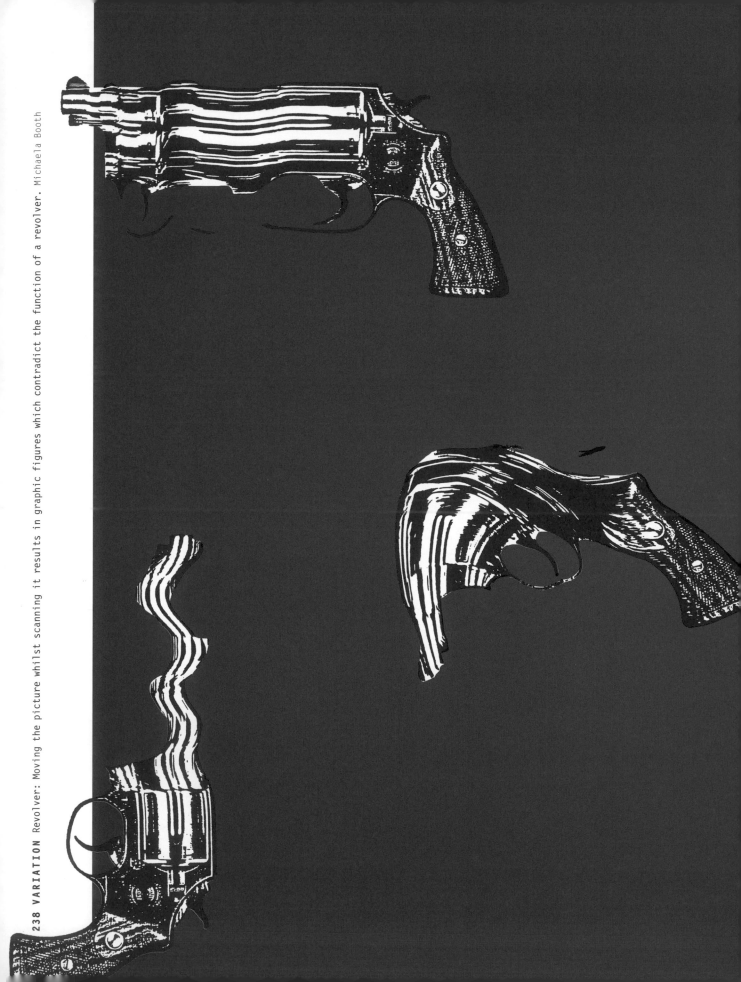

Revolver: Moving the picture whilst scanning it results in graphic figures which contradict the function of a revolver. Michaela Booth

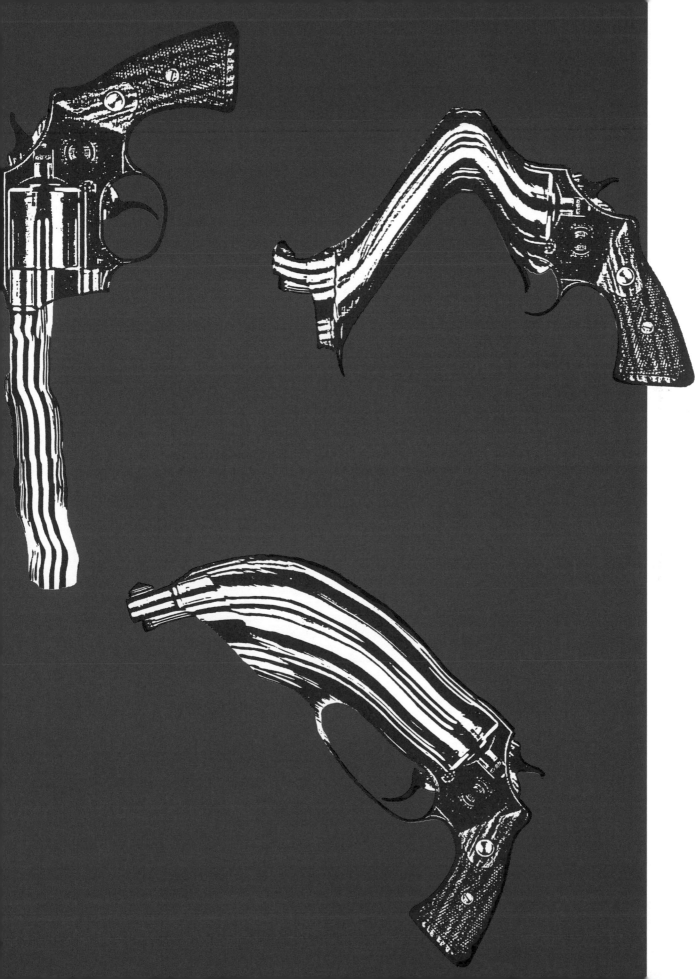

seen from inside at night

seen from inside during the day

shapes of windows and curtains

ways to open a door

doors and matching shoes

photocopied drawing

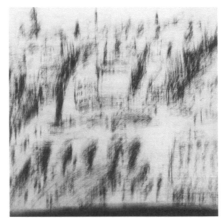

photocopy of the photocopy

re-drawn copy of the copy

copy of the re-drawn copy,
scratched

colouring the rendered copy

Some car drivers ...

... are aroused

... are cheapskates

... can't drive

... love their cars

... are snappy

... drive like a camel

... are real pigs

... run out of gas

... are a real rocket

244 VARIATION The shape of a car is an indication of its owner's style of driving. Edgar Beiger

... are anxious

... are polluters

... always have right of way

... always see red

... want to run over everything

... flee like a hunted deer

... worship their car

... are royal drivers

... are disciplined drivers

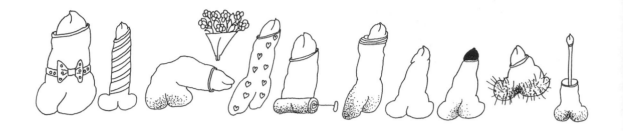

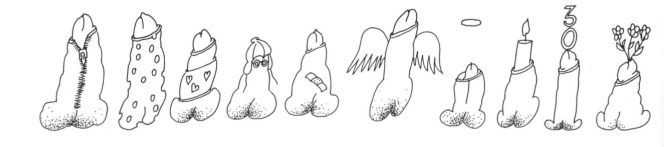

spill-over

toothache

diabetes                    run-off

longdrink                    fusel

251 **VARIATION** The glass shape corresponds to its content and to the occasion. Reinhard Binder

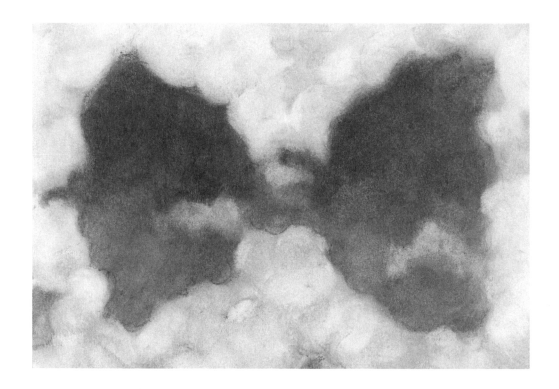

252 VARIATION The bow tie's basic shape remains the same, materials vary. Betina Müller

ABSOLUT BROOKLYN.

ABSOLUT ATHENS.

ABSOLUT PARIS.

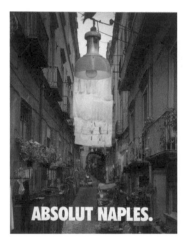

# ABSOLUT PERFECTION.

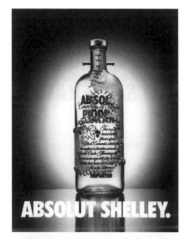

# ABSOLUT SHELLEY.

# ABSOLUT HOUDINI.

ELLEN COLTON'S DINNER PARTY WAS THE opening of the season. Her first dinner this particular year was to officially introduce Maggie, though she was already known to many of the ladies who were wearing her Miss MerMaid fashions. Among the guests was Mortimer Sheldon, a leather manufacturer from Massachusetts. He was a childless widower, his wife having died five years earlier. When his eyes first lit on Maggie, his heart beat wildly; he had found the perfect mate. Her diminutive stature, rose-gold hair and delicate feature represented the child he never had; her petite, shapely body—a pocket-Venus, he called her—made her a desirable second wife.

Mortimer had little opportunity to get close to her on that first occasion as she was surrounded most of the evening by others equally eager to welcome her. He left early, his mind a whirl with plans to make her his very own.

## THE FOLLOWING MORNING.

Maggie received a huge bouquet of roses tied with a green satin ribbon. A card was pinned to the ribbon with a diamond brooch: "Please accept this as a token of my deepest admiration," she read, astonished. The card was signed "Mortimer Sheldon" and as hard as she tried she could not remember him.

Four o'clock was the accepted time for callers and Ellen's home became the only place to be at teatime (although there were stronger libations for those who wanted them). Mortimer was the first to call that day, carrying a tremendous bouquet. When he was announced, Maggie came forward to meet him, took the flowers and asked the maid to put them in water. As she extended her hand he held it too long and kissed it greedily. Inwardly she recoiled from this unprepossessing old man. He was approaching fifty and the passing years and his unstinting devotion to business had not been kind to him. His eyes had puffy, dark bags under them, his whole being had sagged and his mouth on her hand felt loose-lipped and wet. Although he did not resemble the man in the least, a picture of Dr. Henderson flashed in Maggie's mind's eye. A few years ago, Maggie would have run from him; but now she called on her newly acquired sophistication to handle the situation.

"Mr. Sheldon,"(she withdrew her hand wishing she could wipe it off) "thank you for the flowers, but I cannot accept the gift you attached to them. She reached into a pocket of her dress and held out the diamond pin.

He pushed her hand away. "My dear, this is just a token of my affection. There is much more I will give you when we get to know each other better."

"Again I thank you," Maggie said

firmly "but believe me when I say I will not accept any gift of any kind of any of you. Flowers if you insist without. I prefer not to recieve anything."

Mortimer, delighted by her reply reserve, said, "I am very welcome my dear, anticipates me leave to treasures at your feet."

Exasperated Maggie as a way to answer when another caller was announced. She trust the brooch in his hand and moved away to greet the new comer. She managed to dodge Mortimer attentions for the rest of the afternoon and was satisfied that she had discouraged his insistence.

She had not.

Mortimer was obsessed with her extreme youth and her prettiness and came every afternoon always with flowers and once a day he had deceded but as long it...

THE FOLLOWING MORNING.
Maggie! Mortimer...
...the terrace I love your young wife...
...had his hands on her shoulder...
to draw her closer...
on her face. With a...
wrenched out of her...
hand back and slipped...
much force as she could must...
who had...
called for John and come running...
ostensibly to Maggie said but it wasn't necessary Mortimer was rubbing his...
check stung...
John first guiding Mortimer to the door was angry, but...
...with you, Morty...
leave Maggie alone!" he said.
"I wouldn't..."

ILOVE
Mortimer whined "I can do so much for her" can you understand that...
doesn't want...She has worked to become...
"She's only a child! She does not what she want. I can save her whole world," Mortimer pleaded.

John took a deep breath and said, "We've been friends for a long time, Morty and I'm so sorry to have to say must ask you to go somewhere else.

You're being rude but I'll be patient. You'll see she'll come one day. Mortimer babbled.

And no more gifts this...
Not even flowers...
John had him out of the...
time and sadness he alone, his...
Not even flowers stay away f

**ABSOLUT WELLS.**

**ABSOLUT STOKER.**

**ABSOLUT MAGNETISM.**

**ABSOLUT FAX.**

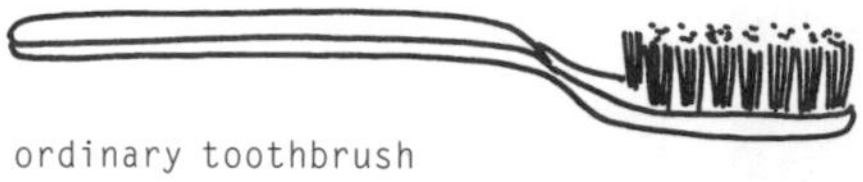

ordinary toothbrush

Double Trouble

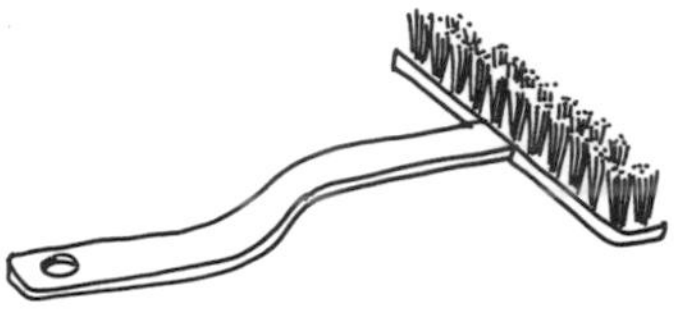

wide mouthed brush

beak brush

brush for siamese twins

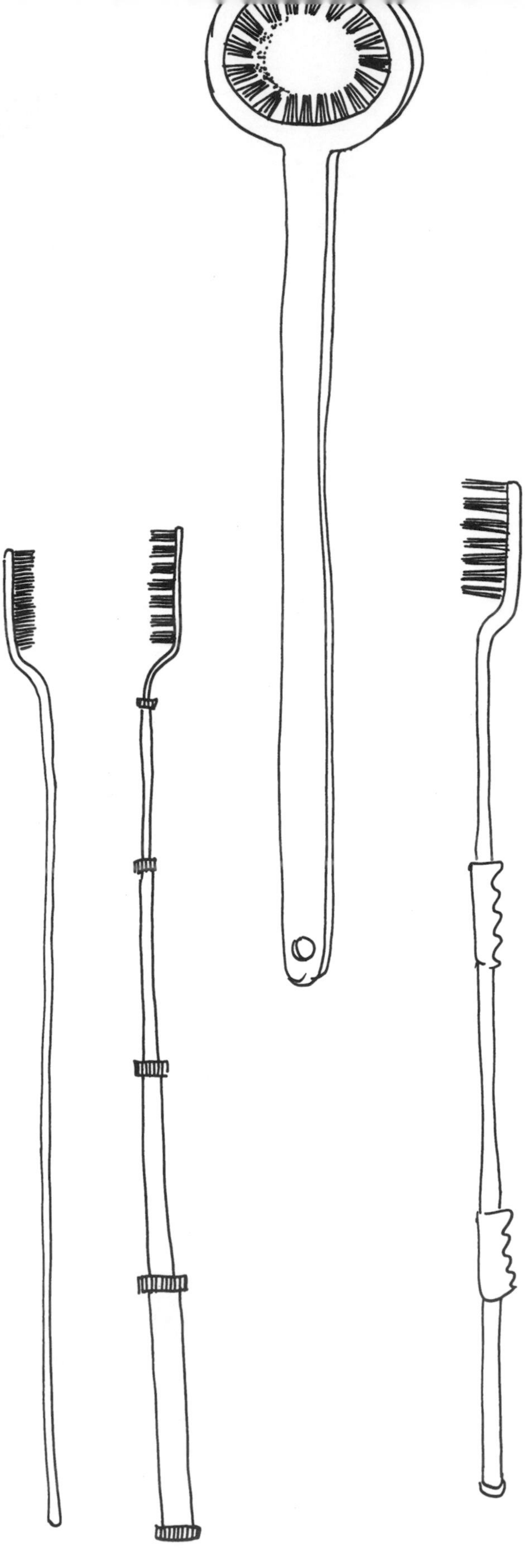

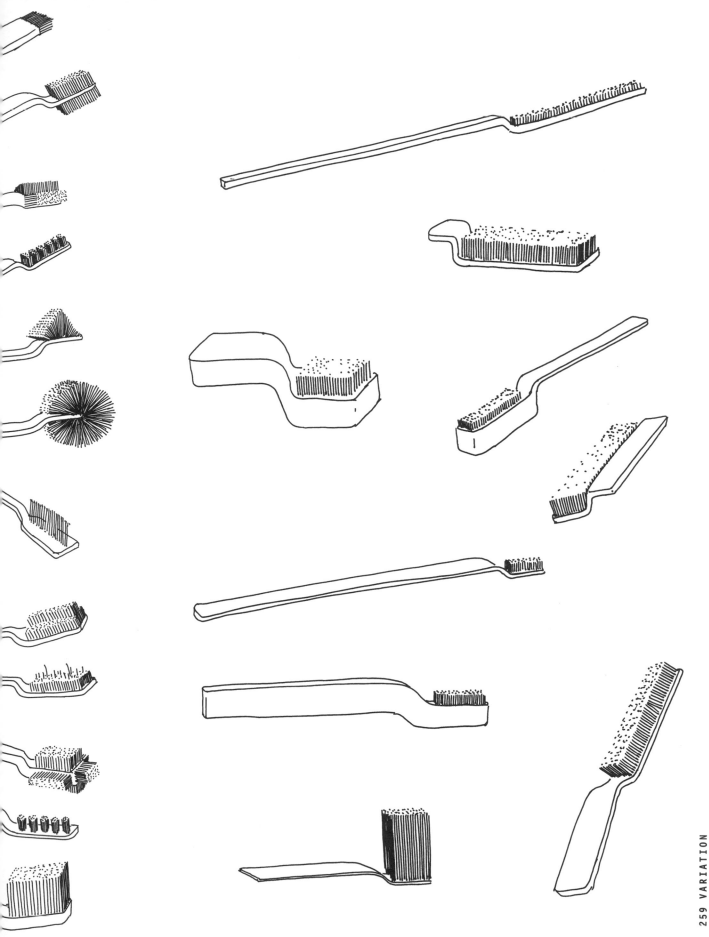

a toothbrush for every type:

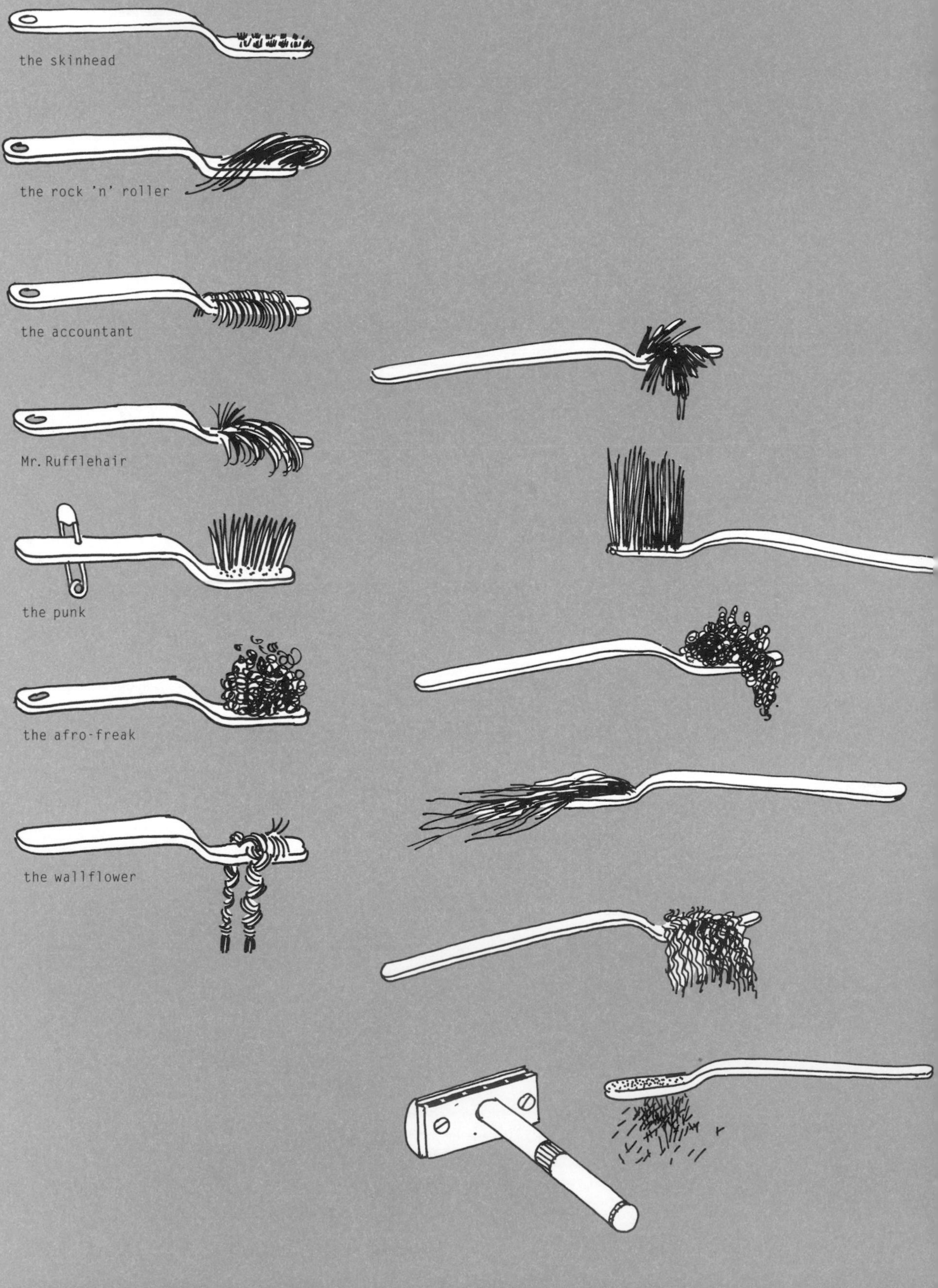

the skinhead

the rock 'n' roller

the accountant

Mr. Rufflehair

the punk

the afro-freak

the wallflower

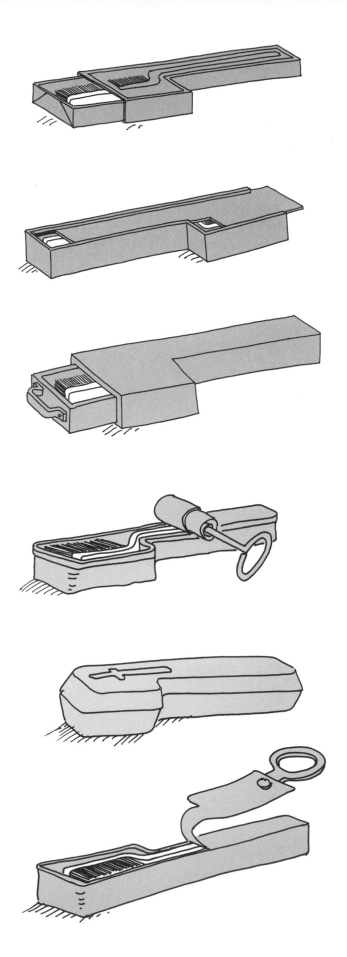

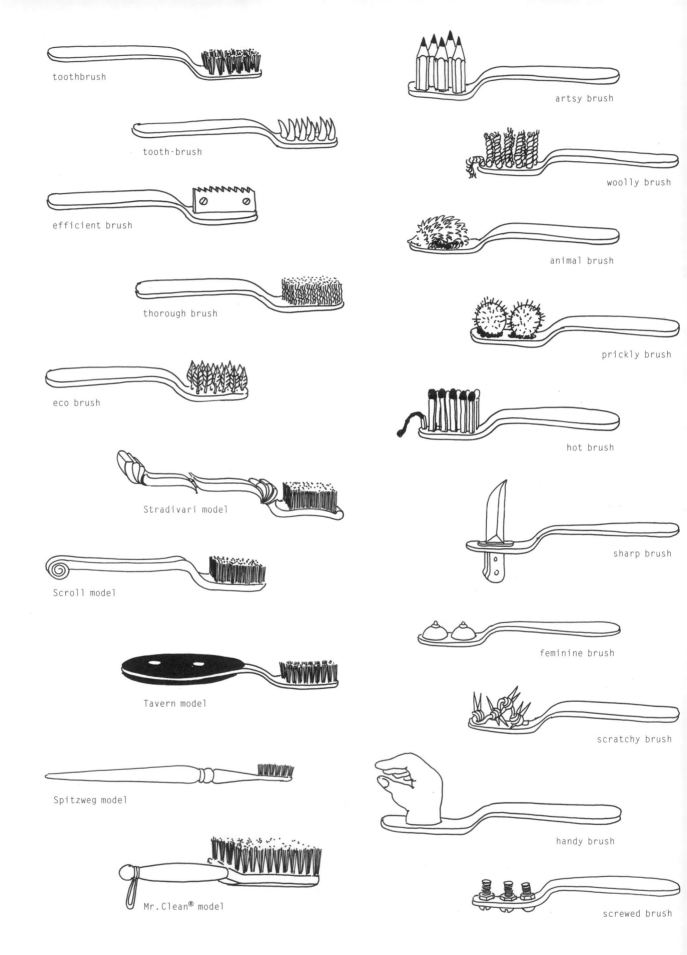

toothbrush

tooth-brush

efficient brush

thorough brush

eco brush

Stradivari model

Scroll model

Tavern model

Spitzweg model

Mr. Clean® model

artsy brush

woolly brush

animal brush

prickly brush

hot brush

sharp brush

feminine brush

scratchy brush

handy brush

screwed brush

spontaneity brush,
the eat-and-brush model

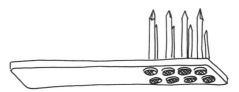

nailed brush for fakirs

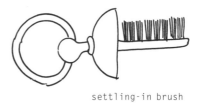

settling-in brush

boy scouts brush

exact brush with calculator

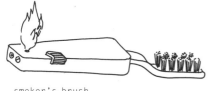

smoker's brush

bright brush with lighting

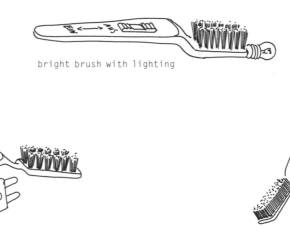

electrical brushes

anti-theft brush

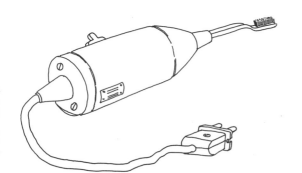

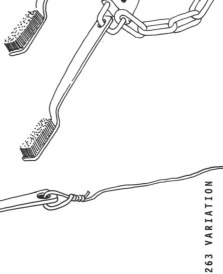

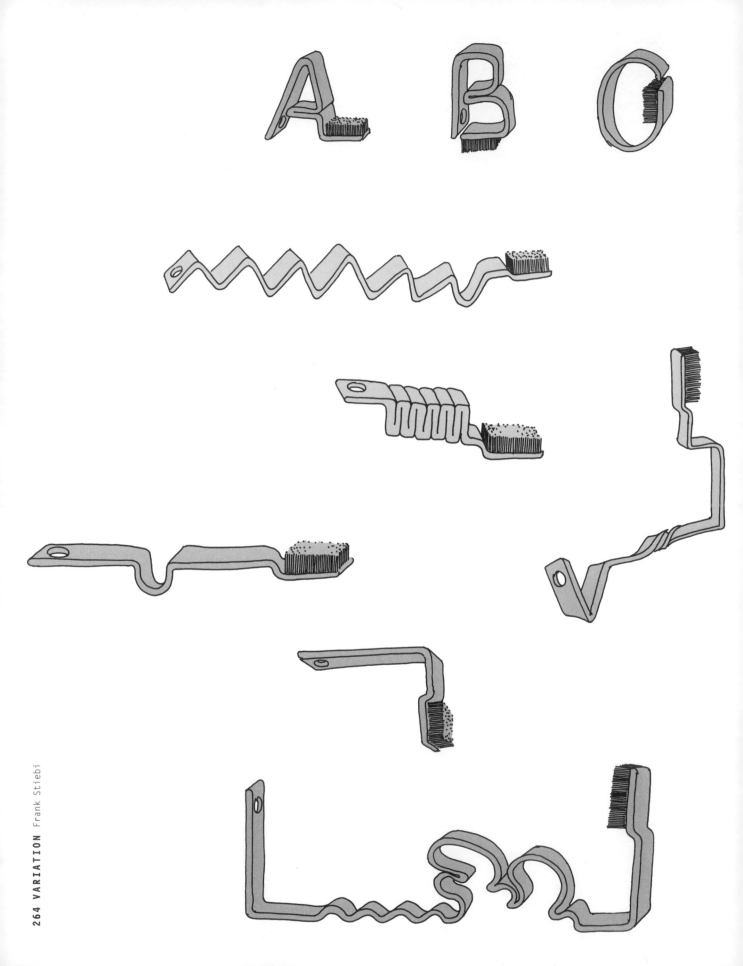

Toyball

Nail Brush

Key Beard

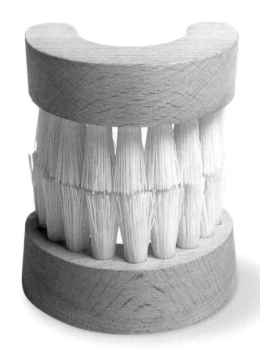

Tooth Brush

Quickie
potato brush

Fruit Nest

Propeller

**266 VARIATION** THE IMAGINARY MUSEUM: Variations of a brush, developed in collaboration with workshops of the Blindenanstalt Berlin (Berlin Institute for the Blind). Practical example: Vogt+Weizenegger together with Shin and Tomoko Azumi. Veronika Becker. Berit Burester. Elder Ferreiro Monteiro. Marti Guixe. Peter Hils. Jörg Hundertpfund. Tim Parson. Jörg Hundertpfund. Tim Parson. Manuel Tavora. Mats Theselius. Niels Engelbrecht.

Limpo
eraser

Brushhanger

Mushroom
door stopper

Diva

Daruma

Et voilá

Egg Nest

Braille
keyboard brush

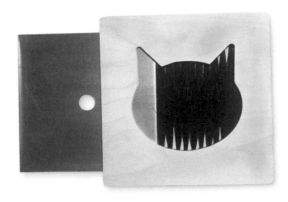

Catdoor

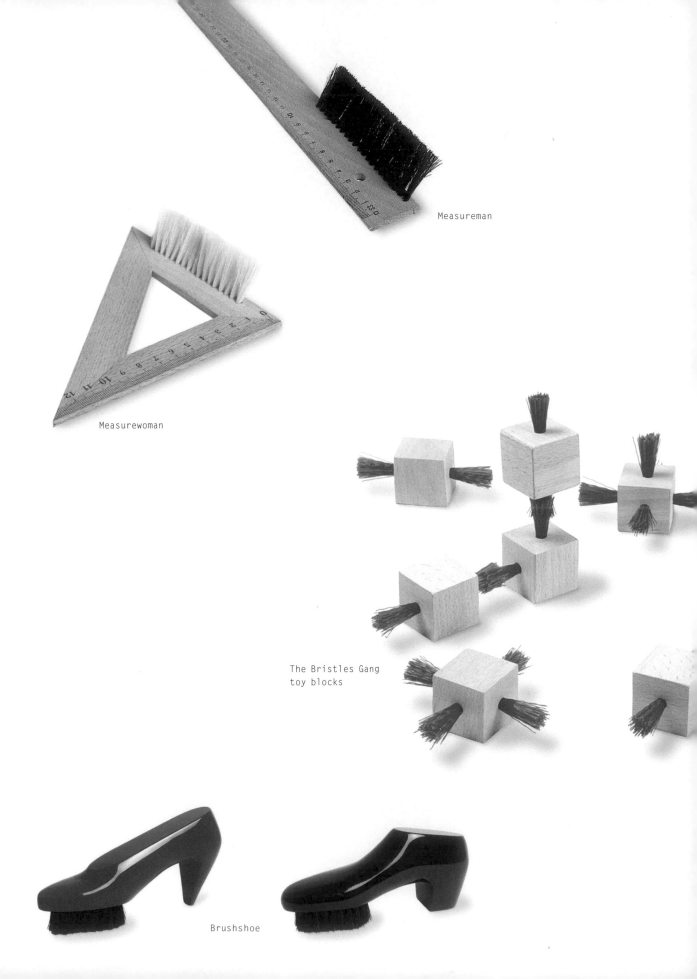

Measureman

Measurewoman

The Bristles Gang
toy blocks

Brushshoe

The Savior
back scrubber

Dustbrother

Bebox
jewel case

Bristle-light
lamp

SEE YOU IN BERLIN!

Brandenburg Gate Brush

**4. RELATION**  Having analysed the parameters of a single pictorial symbol in the previous chapters, we are now going to add a second symbol. We call the relationship between those two symbols 'relation' when the outer appearance of the signs retreats behind their relationship. The philosophical school of thought that is concerned with this phenomenon is known as relativism: it is "the epistemological theory according to which one can only recognise relations between objects, but not the objects themselves"[1].

Almost all combinations are conceivable as a pair of symbols. Again, this will first require keeping one symbol constant, while systematically varying the other. Ideally, this style of representation should remain simple. Composition in the sense of an aesthetic arrangement plays a lesser role here. These restrictive preconditions facilitate the systematic declination of possible constellations. While one of the symbols is kept constant, the parameters e.g. location, size, colour, movement, and many more, of the other symbol will change. Pictorial symbols for area or space such as the picture borders[>284], edge of the picture, and the horizon line[>pp.276], etc. can be used as a second symbol. The change in the relations of the figures to each other can be observed particularly well here. The next step involves swapping the constant and the changing object.

As an example, the positioning of 'arrow and square'[>274] shows how the simplest of elements can evoke diverse meanings, depending on their arrangement. At first, spatial aspects emerge, such as: in, in front of, behind, and through, etc., but if we introduce a second arrow, relations are expressed as well, such as: with, together, next to, against, etc. The famous symbol pair consisting of a heart and arrow[>308] is used here to express emotional relationships. Yet it would suffice to only slightly change the size and arrangement of the symbols in order to convey many different love affairs. This work probably draws its wonderfully charming and persuasive powers from the contrast between the simplicity of the representation and the dimension of the emotional message.

Furthermore, a linguistic element can be introduced as a second symbol, for instance, a word, expression, or sentence. Pictorial and linguistic symbols are placed in relation to each other. One especially fine combination is the print of a tiger with an additional syllable[>338-339]. This syllable-picture combination is especially funny when we can tell that picture and word do not really complement one another.

Traceability is also a crucial aspect of these investigations, which is impeded if a third object, or more, are introduced. By comparing similar constellations, the beginning of actions and sequences already emerge. These will be dealt with in more detail in the next chapter.

1 Bibliographisches Institut (ed.), DUDEN. FREMDWÖRTERBUCH, Mannheim, Vienna, Zurich 1982, p. 660.*

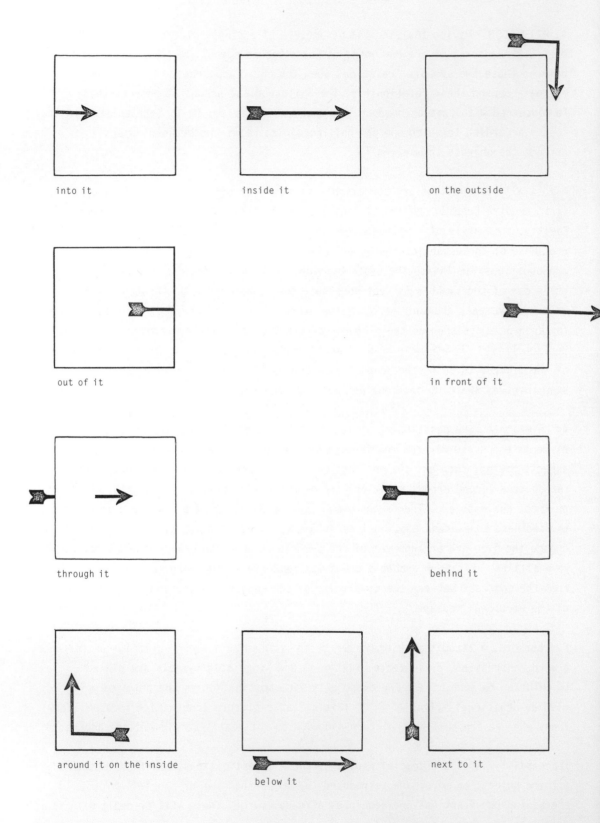

into it

inside it

on the outside

out of it

in front of it

through it

behind it

around it on the inside

below it

next to it

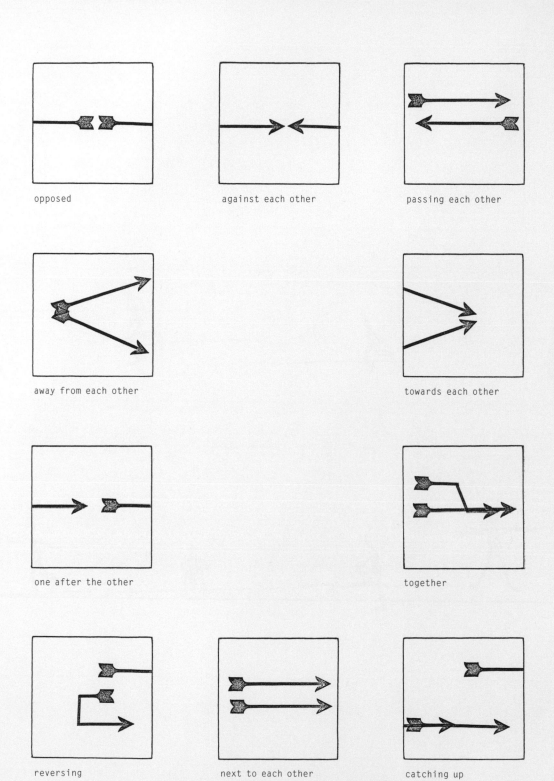

opposed

against each other

passing each other

away from each other

towards each other

one after the other

together

reversing

next to each other

catching up

foreground | middleground 1 | middleground 2 | background

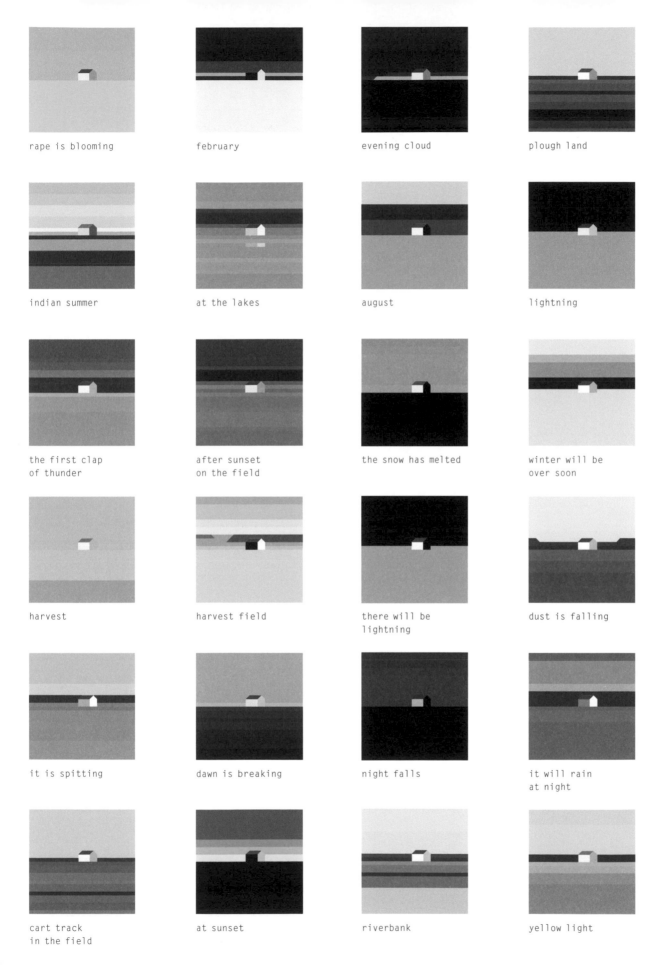

rape is blooming

february

evening cloud

plough land

indian summer

at the lakes

august

lightning

the first clap
of thunder

after sunset
on the field

the snow has melted

winter will be
over soon

harvest

harvest field

there will be
lightning

dust is falling

it is spitting

dawn is breaking

night falls

it will rain
at night

cart track
in the field

at sunset

riverbank

yellow light

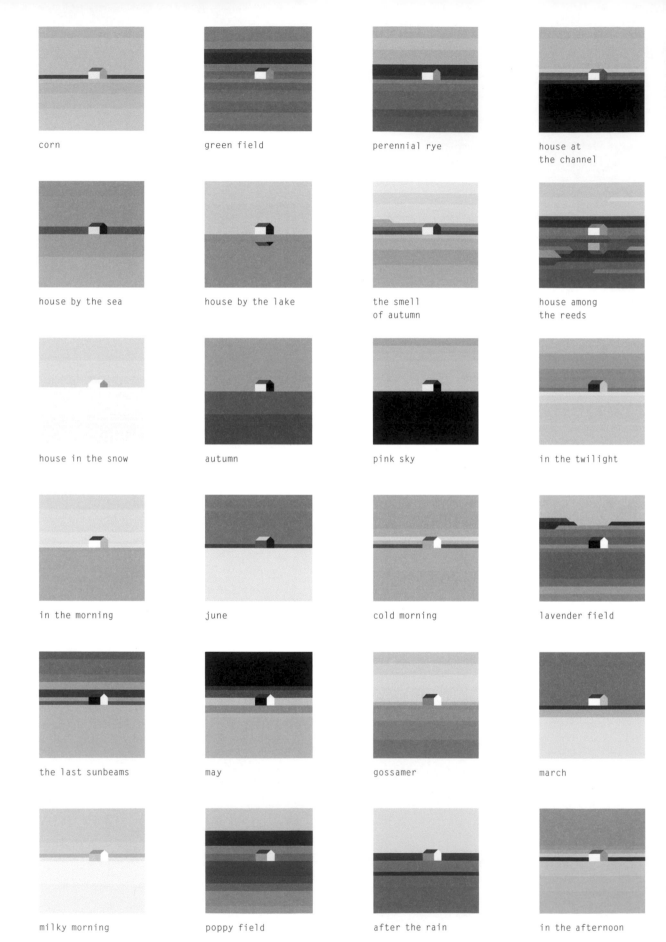

corn

green field

perennial rye

house at
the channel

house by the sea

house by the lake

the smell
of autumn

house among
the reeds

house in the snow

autumn

pink sky

in the twilight

in the morning

june

cold morning

lavender field

the last sunbeams

may

gossamer

march

milky morning

poppy field

after the rain

in the afternoon

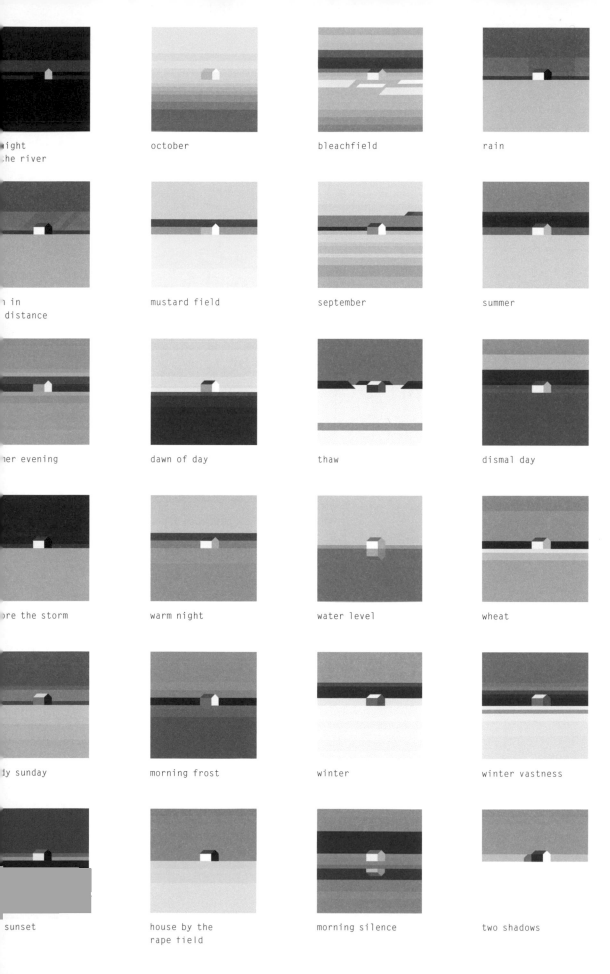

ight
he river

october

bleachfield

rain

in
distance

mustard field

september

summer

her evening

dawn of day

thaw

dismal day

ore the storm

warm night

water level

wheat

dy sunday

morning frost

winter

winter vastness

sunset

house by the
rape field

morning silence

two shadows

**284 RELATION** The female figure and the format remain the same. Different backgrounds, new objects and interactions with the format create a plethora of messages. Helmut Lortz

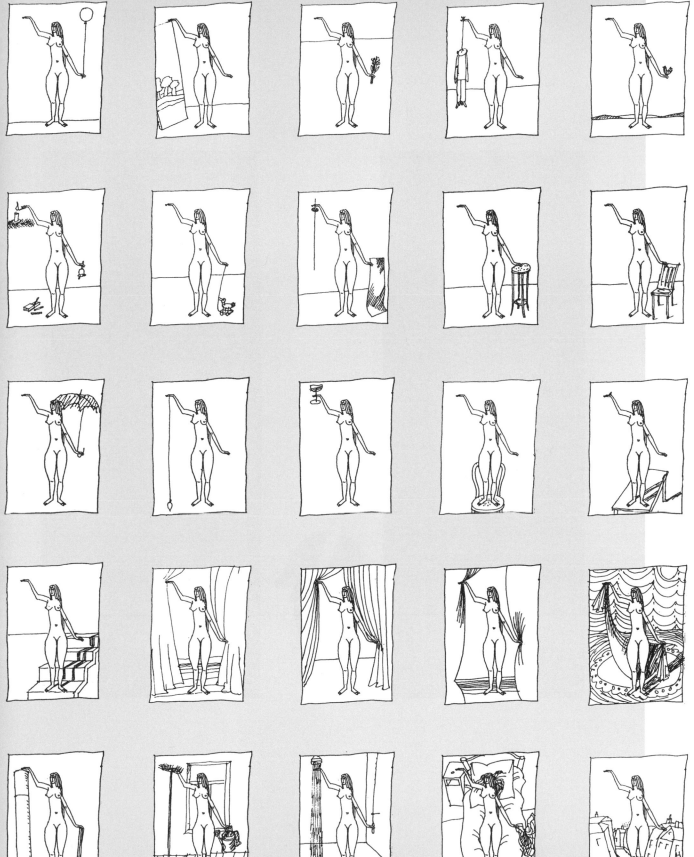

Share and shape of the black surface modify space, thereby altering the message. Dominik Strauch

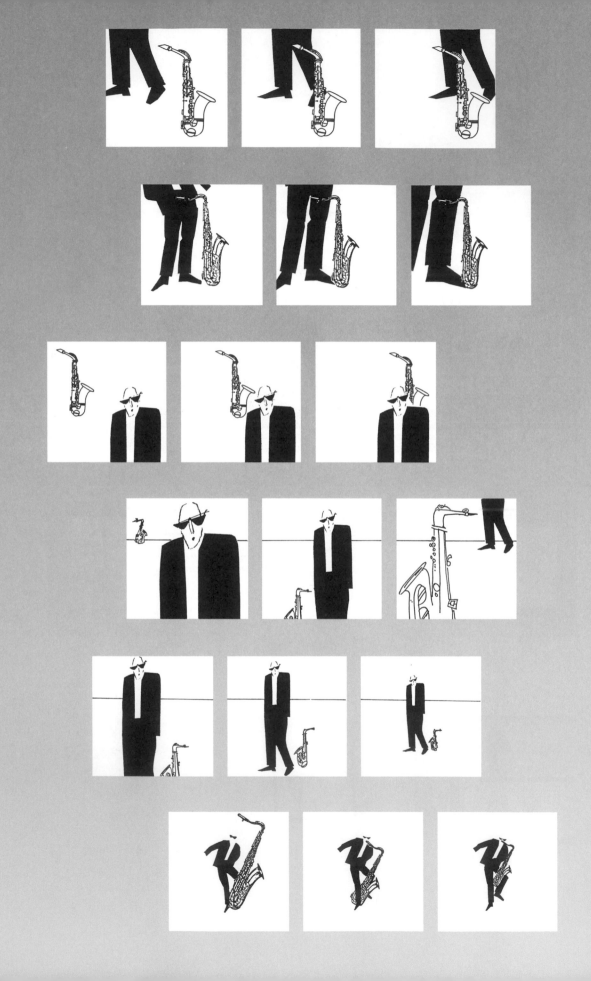

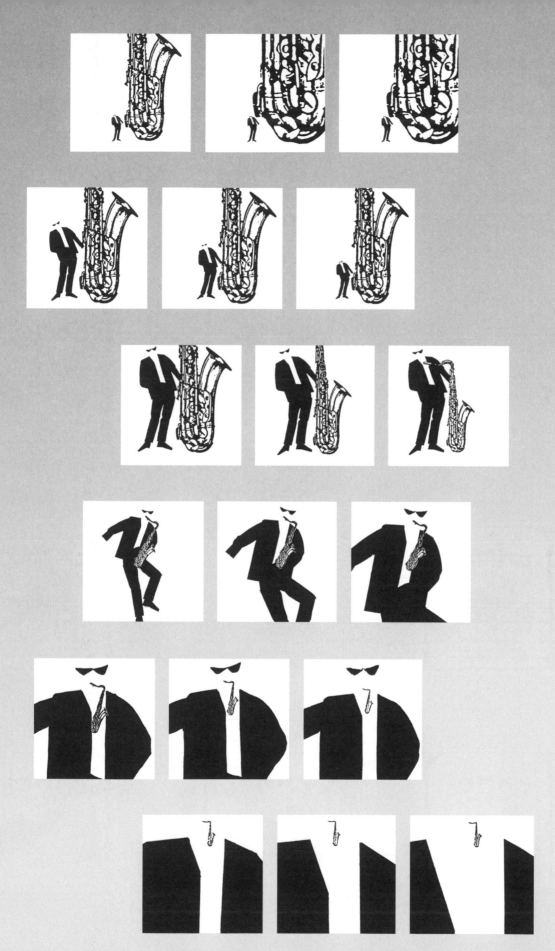

Zu den 19 Zigaretten bekommen Sie diese hübsche Schachtel ganz umsonst dazu.

REINE GESCHMACKSSACHE.

Für unsere australischen Freunde.

REINE GESCHMACKSSACHE.

Urlaubsvertretung.

REINE GESCHMACKSSACHE.

Das Größte.

REINE GESCHMACKSSACHE.

Best of Camel

REINE GESCHMACKSSACHE.

296 RELATION The 212 bones of the human skeleton are reassembled by means of the programming language Java Script. Frank Rausch

sorted according to their surface area (vertically and horizontally)

to their height (vertically and horizontally)

to their width (vertically and horizontally)

to their aspect ratio (vertically and horizontally)

to their aspect ratio (vertically)

Bones rotating around the vertical
line, then sorted according to
their aspect ratio, ascending towards
the outside.

to their width (vertically)

Bones rotating around the vertical
line, then sorted according
to their width, ascending towards
the outside.

to their width (horizontally)

Bones rotating around the
horizontal line, then sorted
according to their width,
ascending towards the outside.

to their expansion (without prior rotation)

Without prior erection of the bones
according to their expansion (=base),
ascending towards the outside.

to their width (vertically)

Bones rotating around the vertical line,
then sorted according to their width,
descending towards the outside.

in a spiral

flush with the top

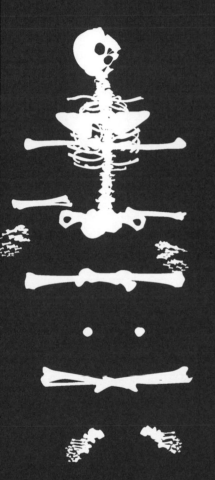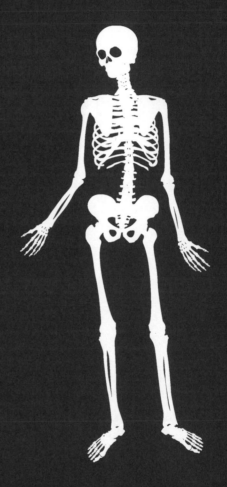

horizontally

vertically

flush with the bottom

**300 RELATION** Everyday objects are isolated and develop new ‘relations’. Theres Weishappel

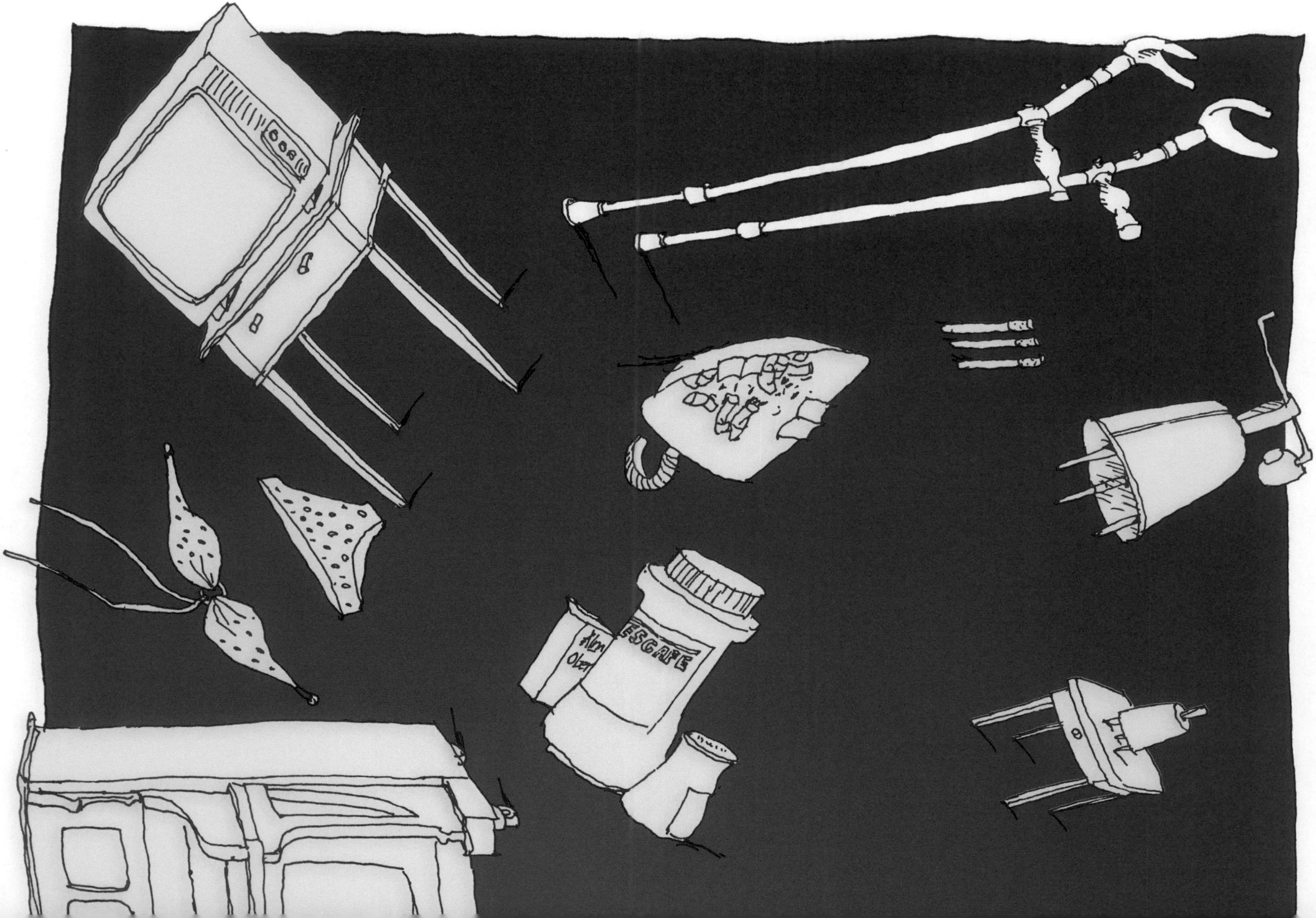

**302 RELATION** Through interaction with the environment or the advertise-
of a sales campaign for household appliances reveal their function. Practical

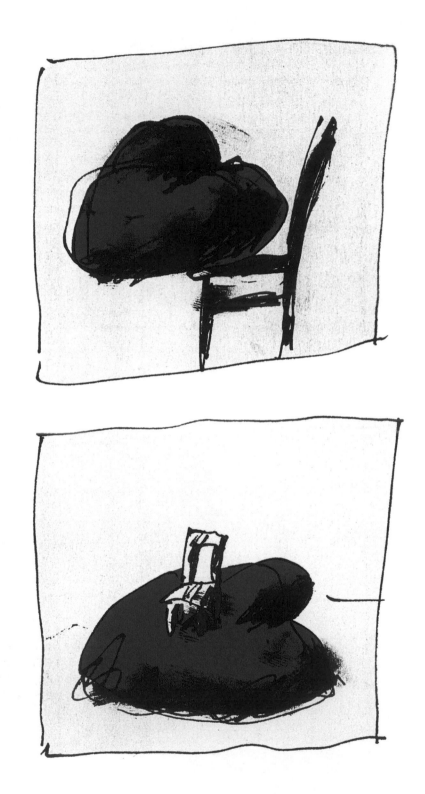

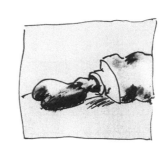

protect

throw away

burn

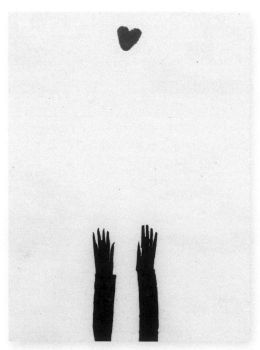

unattainable

infatuation

brief encounter

perfect love

unlucky in love

hardend to love

unexpected love

modern love

experienced
in love

grand passion

young love

too young to love

easy to love

stinging pain in the heart

open heart

It lies at my heart.

It lies heavy on my heart.

I have a heavy heart.

burning heart

football crazy

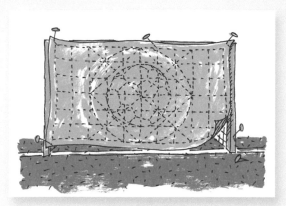

assist with a template

hand of God

football rules

cut ball

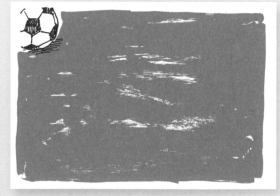

corner

art(ificial) turf

the holy turf

light ball

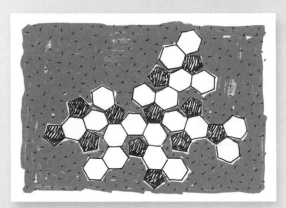

flat ball

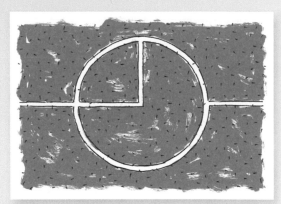

halftime

Nailed it!

tie

picture perfect pass

threadstring

pin

buttons

padlock

clothes pin

patch

safety pin

screw

paper clip

zip

scotch tape

rope

clamp

seam

staple

nail

**317 RELATION** Round and angular feel very connected. Dorothea Szeinhof

Immer voll ist auch langweilig.

100% unserer Raucher haben ihren eigenen Kopf.

Das Runde muss in das Eckige!

Endlich mal Werbung mit Inhalten.

Erinnern Sie sich? So dick sah Ihr Depot auch mal aus.

Im unteren Bild haben wir 19 Fehler versteckt.

Sorry England, 17 sind einer zu viel.

Endlich gibt es sie. Die Cigarette davor.

Weniger ist leer.

**Gute Zeiten, schlechte Zeiten.**

**Nehmen Sie sich einen Drachen zur Frau. Dann haben Sie immer Feuer.**

# Drei Stengel für Charly.

**Es gibt Jobs, die wollen alle haben.**

# Dick und Doof.

**Neu: das XL-Menü von Lucky Strike.**

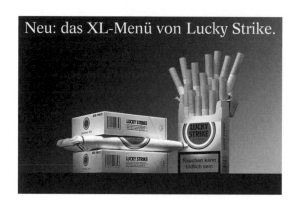

**Streng dich an, Weihnachtsmann. Wunsch ist Wunsch.**

**Möchten Sie erst einen Vokal kaufen oder gleich lösen?**

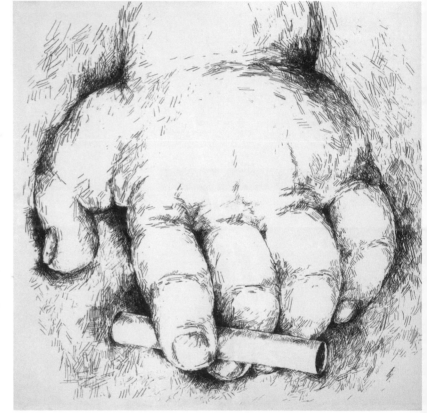

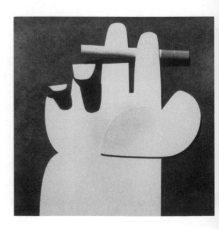

cold coffee

decaffeinated coffee

black coffee

strong coffee

weak coffee

Proportion, set-up and materials reflect the coffee's quality. Hans-Peter Schmidt

**321 RELATION**

western

disaster film

whodunit

science fiction film

romance

adventure film

erotic film

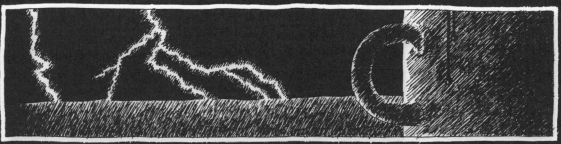

horror film

advertising spot

cut

AN ALUMNI EXHIBITION CELEBRATING COOPER UNION'S 125th ANNIVERSARY

*Milton Glaser*

The Houghton
Gallery
Cooper Union
Seven East
Seventh Street
New York, NY
10003
September 6-28,
1984

325 **RELATION** Poster for an exhibition at the Cooper Union design school. Practical example

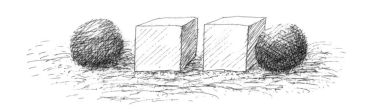

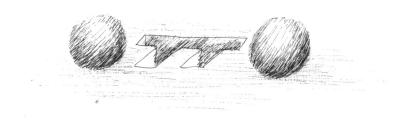

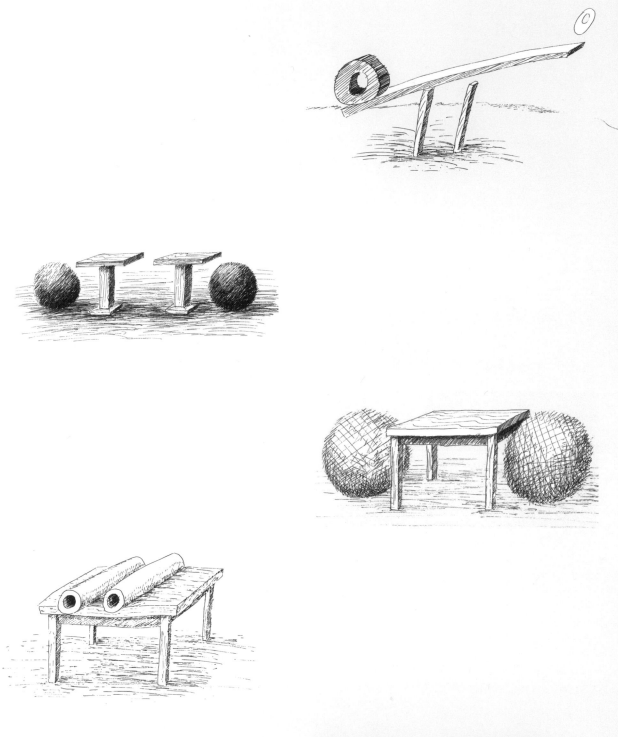
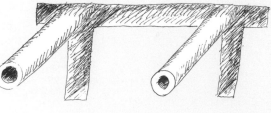

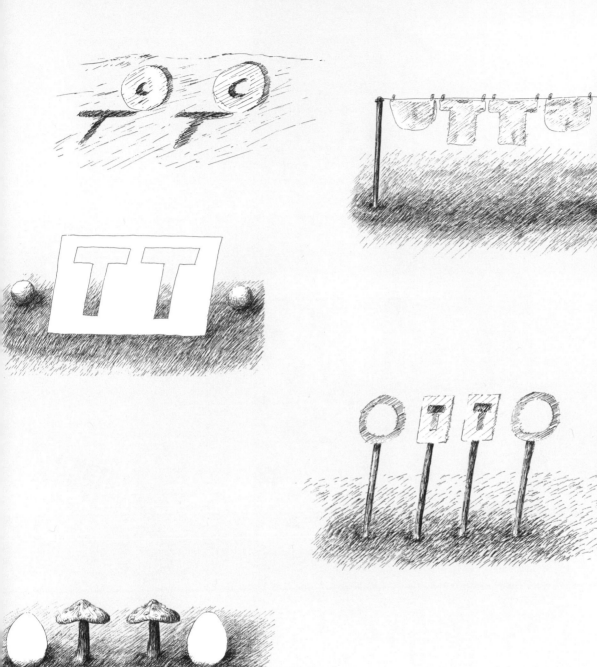

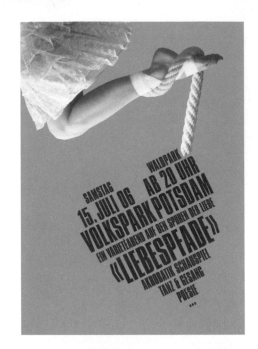

# 5 JAHRE VOLKSPARK
## SOMMERSAISON ERÖFFNUNG
### FEIERN IM WIESENPARK: 14.00 BIS 17.00 UHR
## TUSCH ... POTSDAMS GROESSTE
# KAFFEETAFEL
**KAFFEE & KUCHEN, LIVEMUSIK, GROSSE SCHATZSUCHE
GEBURTSTAGSTHEATER UND KINDERVARIETÉ**
## MONTAG 1. MAI 06

WEITERE INFORMATIONEN UNTER DER TELEFONNUMMER 0331.2 71 98-0
ODER IM INTERNET UNTER WWW.VOLKSPARK-POTSDAM.DE

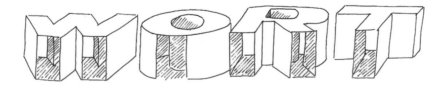

**335 RELATION** Relationships between words and images. Hans-Peter Schmidt

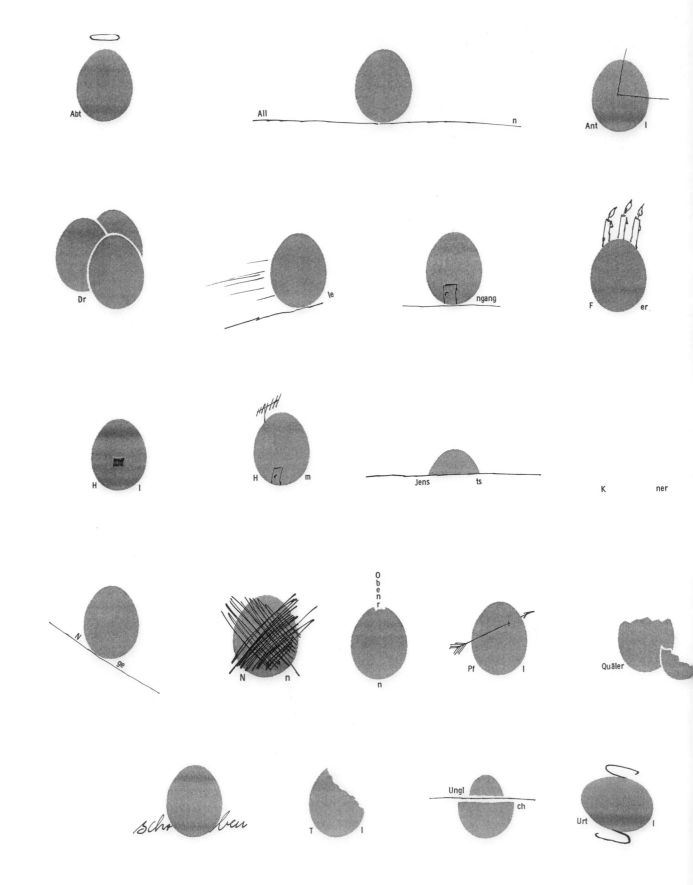

Abt

All                                                                                          n

Ant                                              l

Dr

le

ngang

F                            er

H              l

H              m

Jens                    ts

K                    ner

N        ge

N            n

O
b
e
n
r

n

Pf              l

Quäler

schr      ben

T        l

Ungl
ch

Urt          l

B ____ de

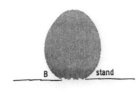

B ____ stand

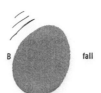

B ____ fall

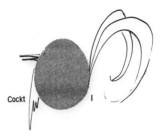

Cockt ____ I

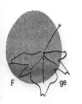

F ____ ge

G ____ l

Gl ____ chung

Gr ____ s

H ____ rat

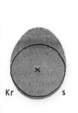

Kr ____ s

L ____ ter

L ____ er

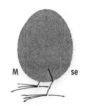

M ____ se

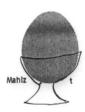

Mahlz ____ t

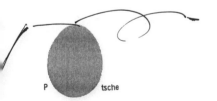

P ____ tsche

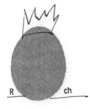

R ____ ch

R ____ se

Sch ____ ss

W ____ n

Z ____ ger

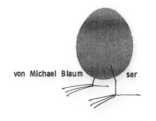

von Michael Blaum ____ ser

HAS

NÖ

HEF

AR

BÖSAR

LIS

GAR

GESCHÄF

GEWAL

KÜNF

SCHMÄCH

PRE

HE

WICH

LE

ERO

WÜ

EPILEP

SPAS

SEMIO

POLI

EINDEU

METHO

LÄS

MU

VERNÜNF

EINFÄL

LUS

PHLEGMA

THEORE

WUCH

ZO

HEU

GUTMÜ

MONARSCHIE

monarchy

ANARSCHIST

EINMARSCHIEREN

PATRIARSCH

DARSCHSTELLUNG

DIE ARSCHE VON NOAH

ARSCHIVIST

ARSCHIMED

ARSCHLOCH

ARSCHEOLOG

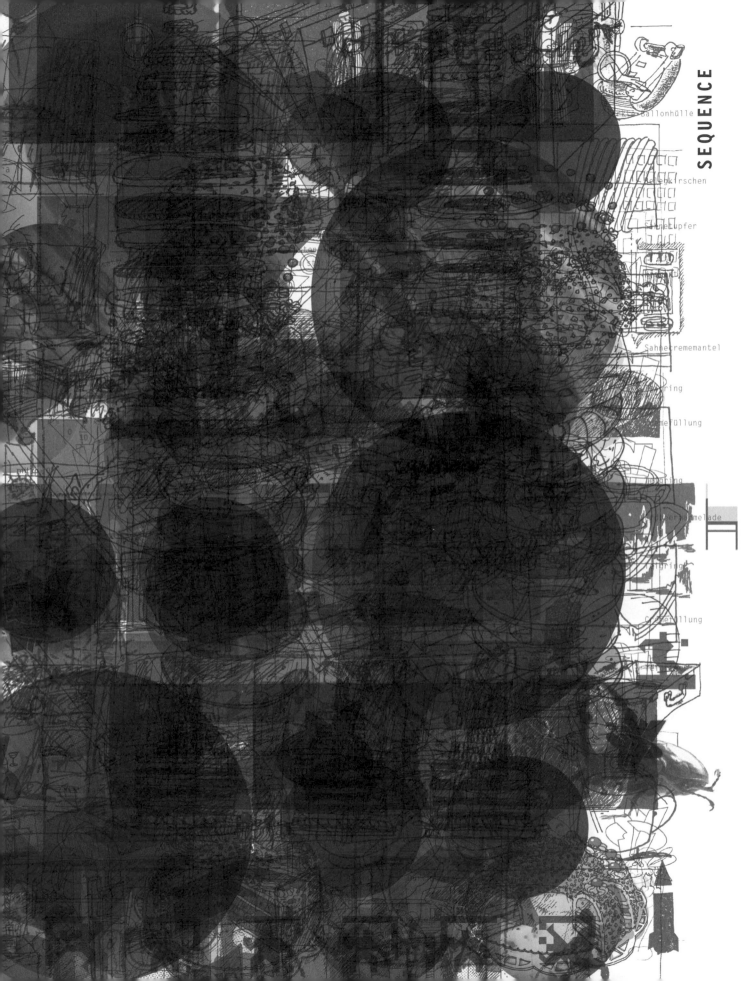

**5. SEQUENCE**   When rows, variations or relations are transformed into a process or narrative, or when a row, series or a chain of individual pictures are related to one another in terms of time, content or form, then we call it a sequence. Many different expressions such as picture sequence, picture story, picture narrative, cartoon, graphic novel or storyboard mean more or less the same thing, and their boundaries are naturally fluid.

Which constants can we establish in picture sequences? Firstly, it is the time-dependent factor, which is expressed in the manifold interdependent relationships between single pictures. Secondly, a coherent pictorial style would probably be useful, as this facilitates 'readability', which is precisely why drastic changes in style are rather uncommon. Any further constants are difficult to identify and rather depend on tradition and personal style. It is evident, then, that formal requirements have to remain vague to make way for a scope for development that is determined by the complex interplay of content, form and time.

We have long been familiar with picture sequences that tell stories or narrate history. The TELEPHOS FRIEZE [about 200-150 BC] on the inside of the Pergamon altar in Berlin is an early example. It tells the chronological life story of Telephos, a hero of Greek mythology. A further early example is the relief of TRAJAN'S COLUMN [113 AD] in Rom. The frieze on the column spirals upwards from base to capital in 23 turns, reaching a length of 200 metres. It portrays scenes from the victorious military campaigns that the Romans waged against the Dacians. Ever since the Middle Ages, stories from the Bible have been depicted in Christian churches by means of picture sequences. One famous example is the ISENHEIM ALTARPIECE [approx. 1506-1515], which illustrates the course of the ecclesiastical year on the wings of its altar. One set of open wings shows the crucifixion, another shows the annunciation, incarnation and resurrection of Christ. Hence, picture sequences have long served as a method of turning the temporal content of individual pictures into an easily comprehensible story through juxtaposition or by placing the images opposite each other.

The comic originates from the English comic strip, literally meaning "comical strip", which refers to its originally amusing content. Normally, these pictures are graphics with additional direct speech that sometimes, but rarely exclusively, contains a narrative text. Comics have developed a multitude of graphic figures for different kinds of narratives: speech bubbles containing direct speech, streaks or speed lines to convey the impression of speed, words imitating sound effects for noises or exclamations that are depicted in large letters, huge punctuation marks such as ellipses and question marks that are supposed to express speechlessness, perplexity or confusion. Smaller symbols or pictures in speech bubbles, such as a skull, fist or thunderclouds, depict moods such as bad temper or anger. Words imitating sounds such as fizz, crack, thud or crash, are an invention of the comic. Wilhelm Busch was an early comic pioneer whose picture stories are accompanied by funny verses that already use countless novel words, such as pluck, puff, helter-skelter, ouch!, Abracadabra!, and so on.

The 'graphic novel' is a comic in the form of a book that tells more complex, elaborate stories. Its thematic content chiefly addresses adult readers. In German, it is referred to as a graphic or illustrated novel, picture novel, comic novel or graphic literature. These names, however, have failed to gain wide popularity.

The storyboard[386-387] is chiefly used by the film industry and can be translated into German very aptly as 'Szenenbuch'. As opposed to the comic, a storyboard is usually less elaborate. It is the graphic implementation of a script or of individual scenes outlining the story and settings of the camera. Pictures that depict one single film scene are called sequences.

Other forms of picture sequences include the flipbook, the photographic series, the representation of a series of movements[376], instruction manuals, construction manuals[370-371] etc. The latter does not tell a story, but rather provides instructions or explains a procedure. What all sequences have in common is that they consider the relationship between the preceding and the following picture. As such the context plays a major role in the interpretation.

The enormous potential of picture sequences becomes all the more evident when compared to corresponding linguistic or written descriptions of the same procedure. Anyone who has tried to explain how to tie shoelaces or a tie, without actually showing how it works, has to admit that sequential representations do a much better job.

**347 SEQUENCE** Cubes falling through a flat surface. After a figure from Edward Tufte. concept: Armin Lindauer, programming: Marek Slipek

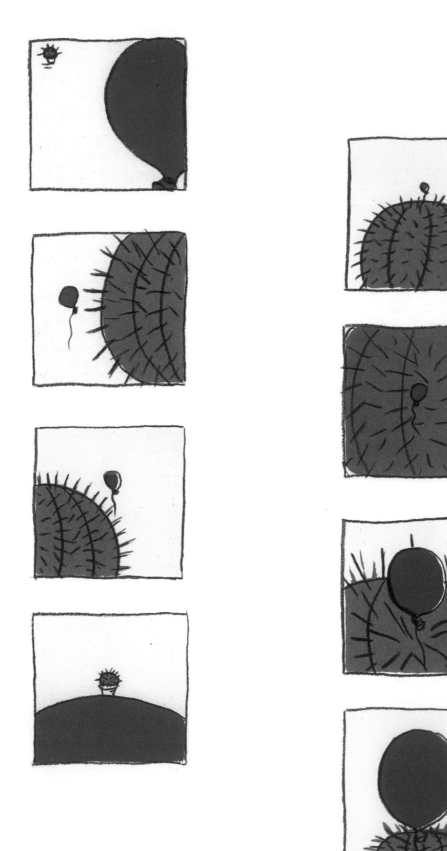

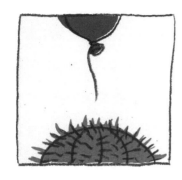

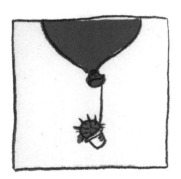

Every image consists of
exactly 64 black and
64 white rectangular triangles.

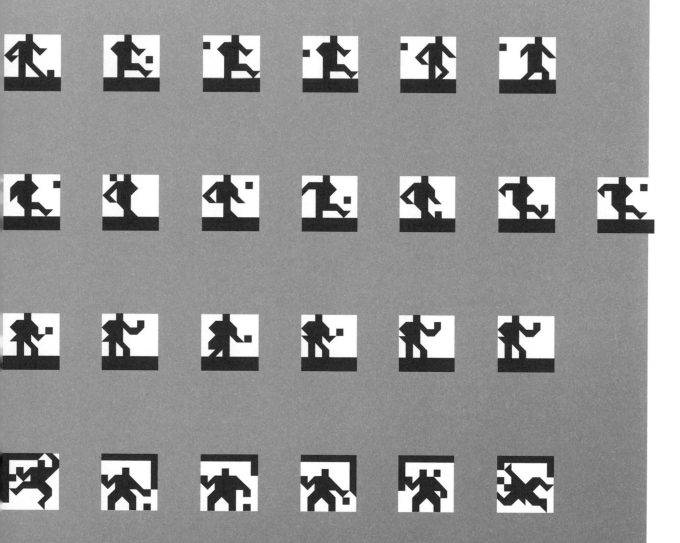

358 **SEQUENCE** The stamped symbols 'man' and 'rocket' narrate the story of war. Lutz Olaf Walter

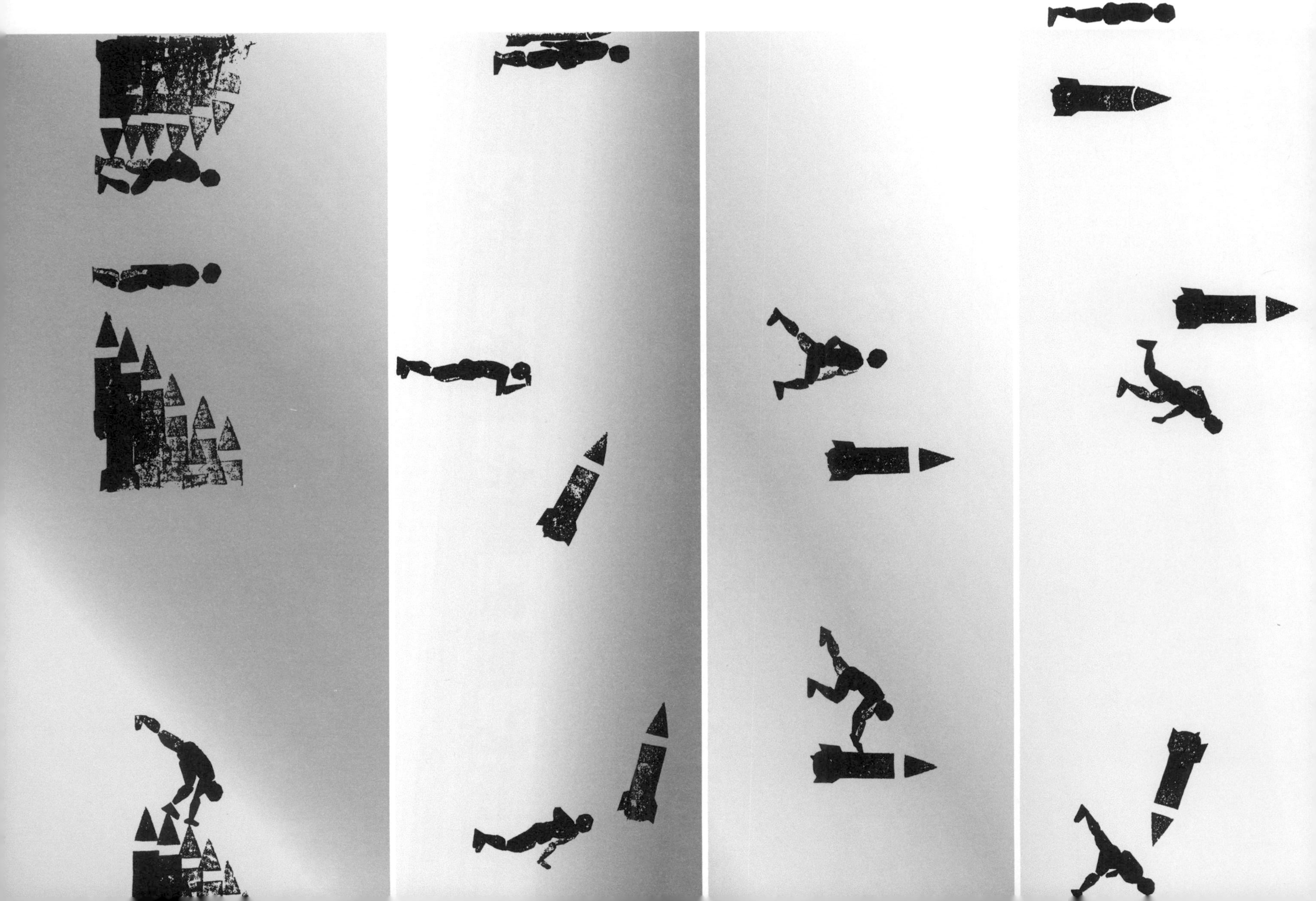

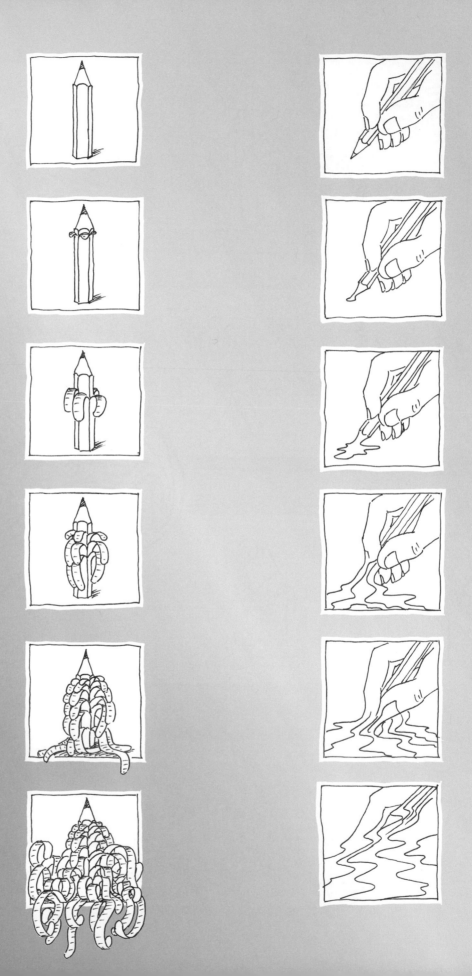

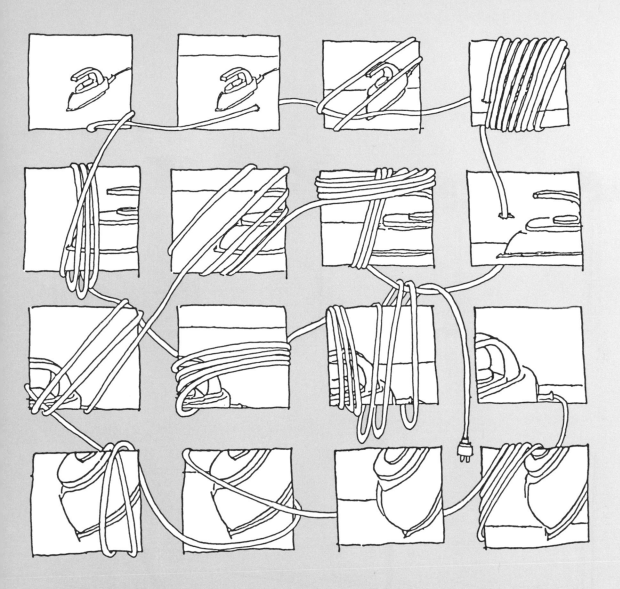

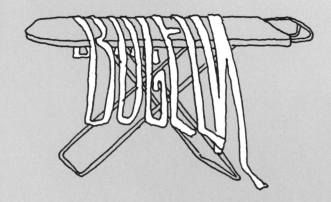

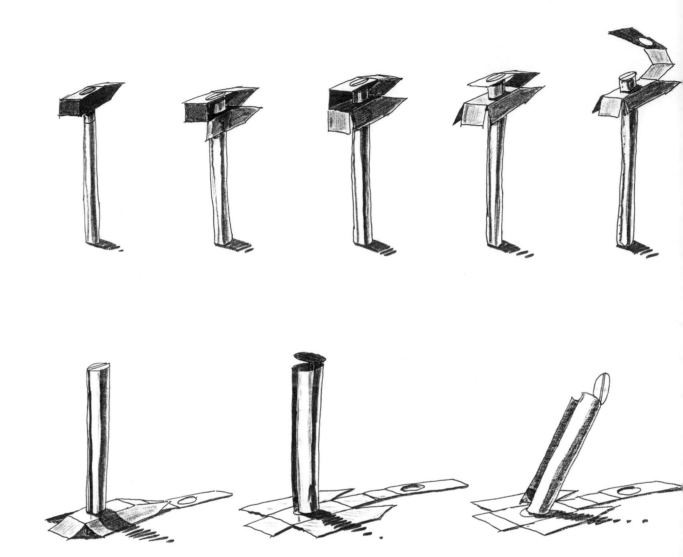

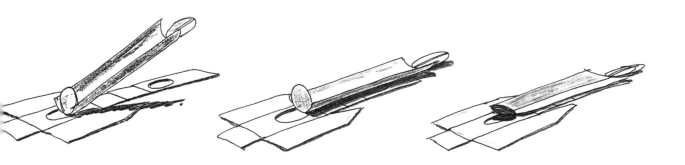

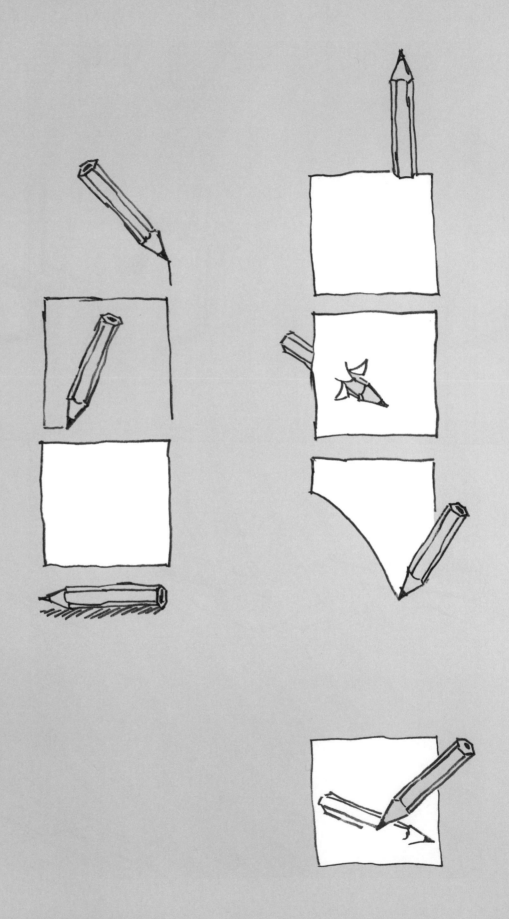

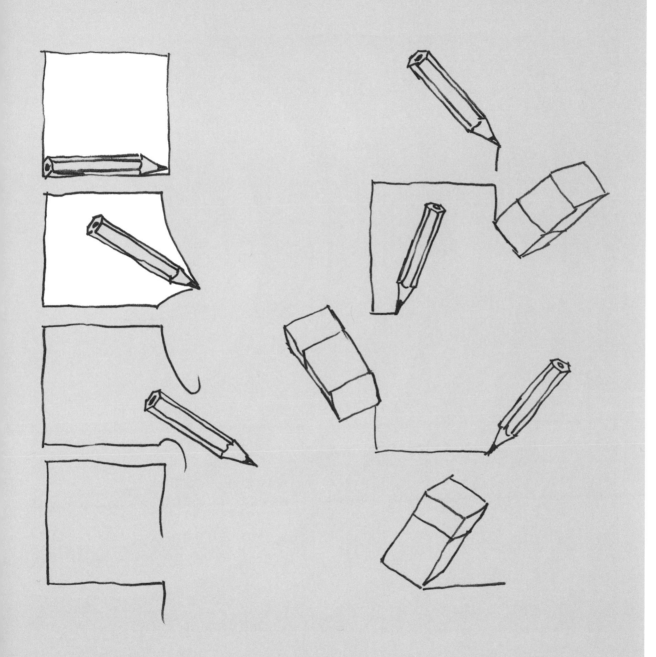

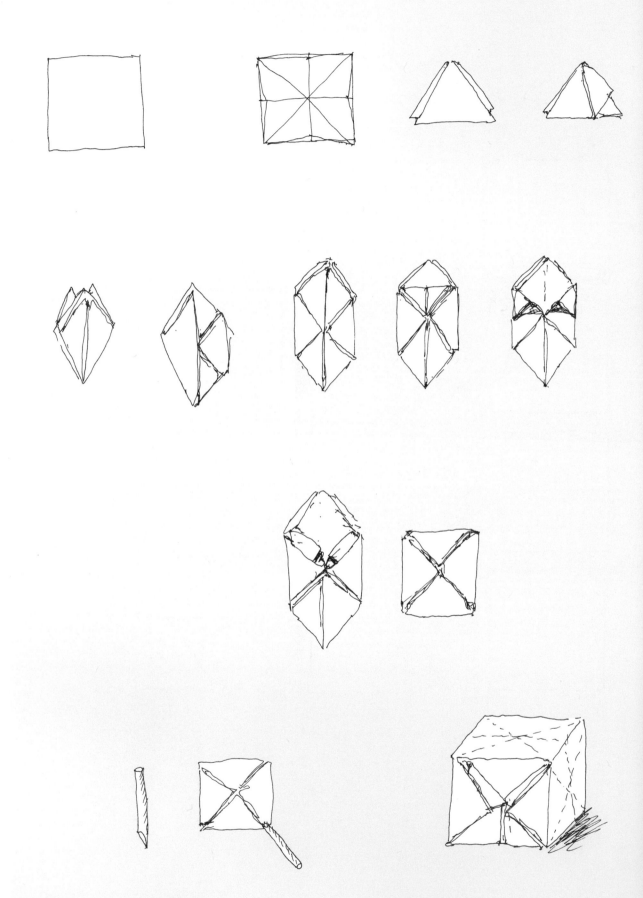

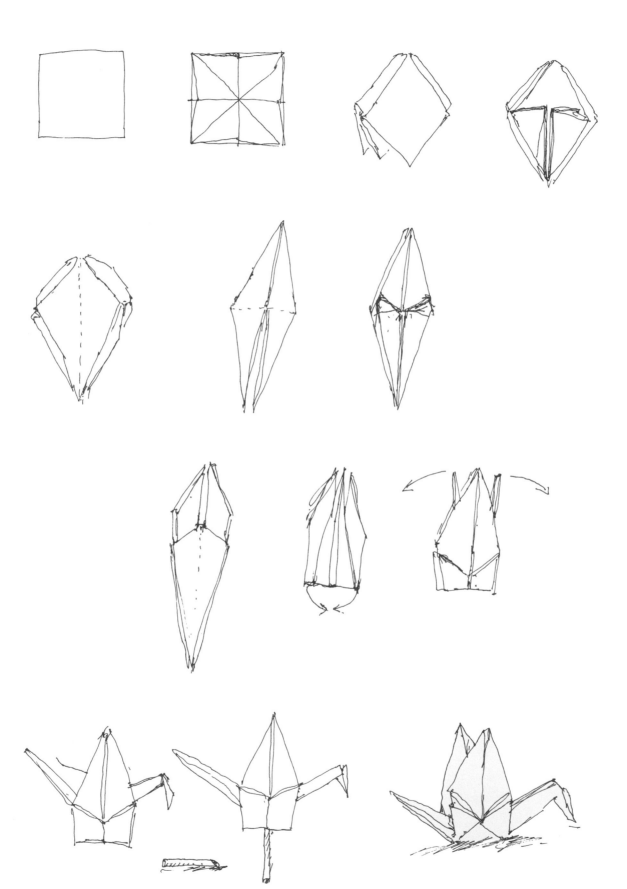

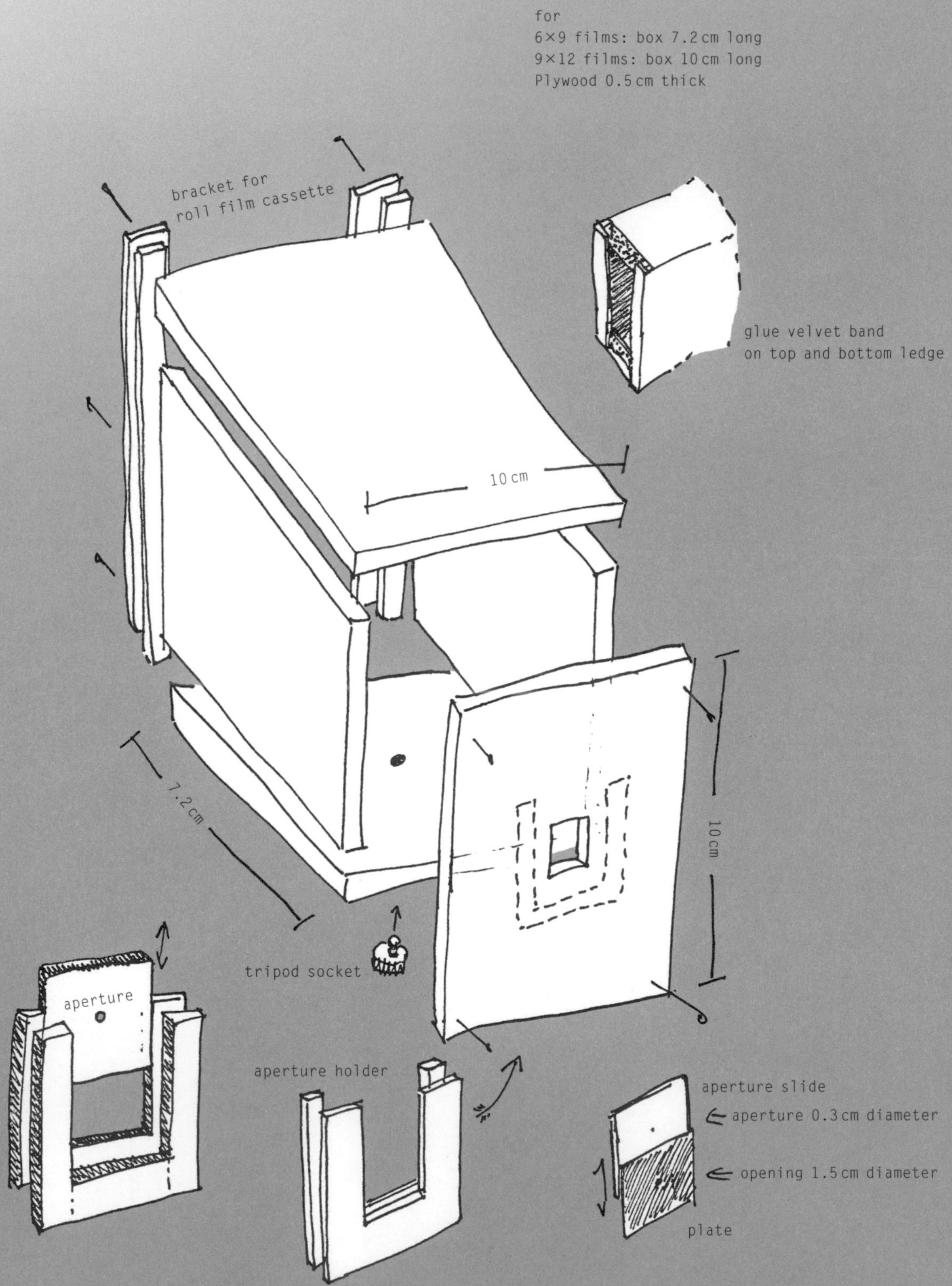

for
6×9 films: box 7.2 cm long
9×12 films: box 10 cm long
Plywood 0.5 cm thick

bracket for
roll film cassette

glue velvet band
on top and bottom ledge

10 cm

7.2 cm

10 cm

tripod socket

aperture

aperture holder

aperture slide
← aperture 0.3 cm diameter

← opening 1.5 cm diameter

plate

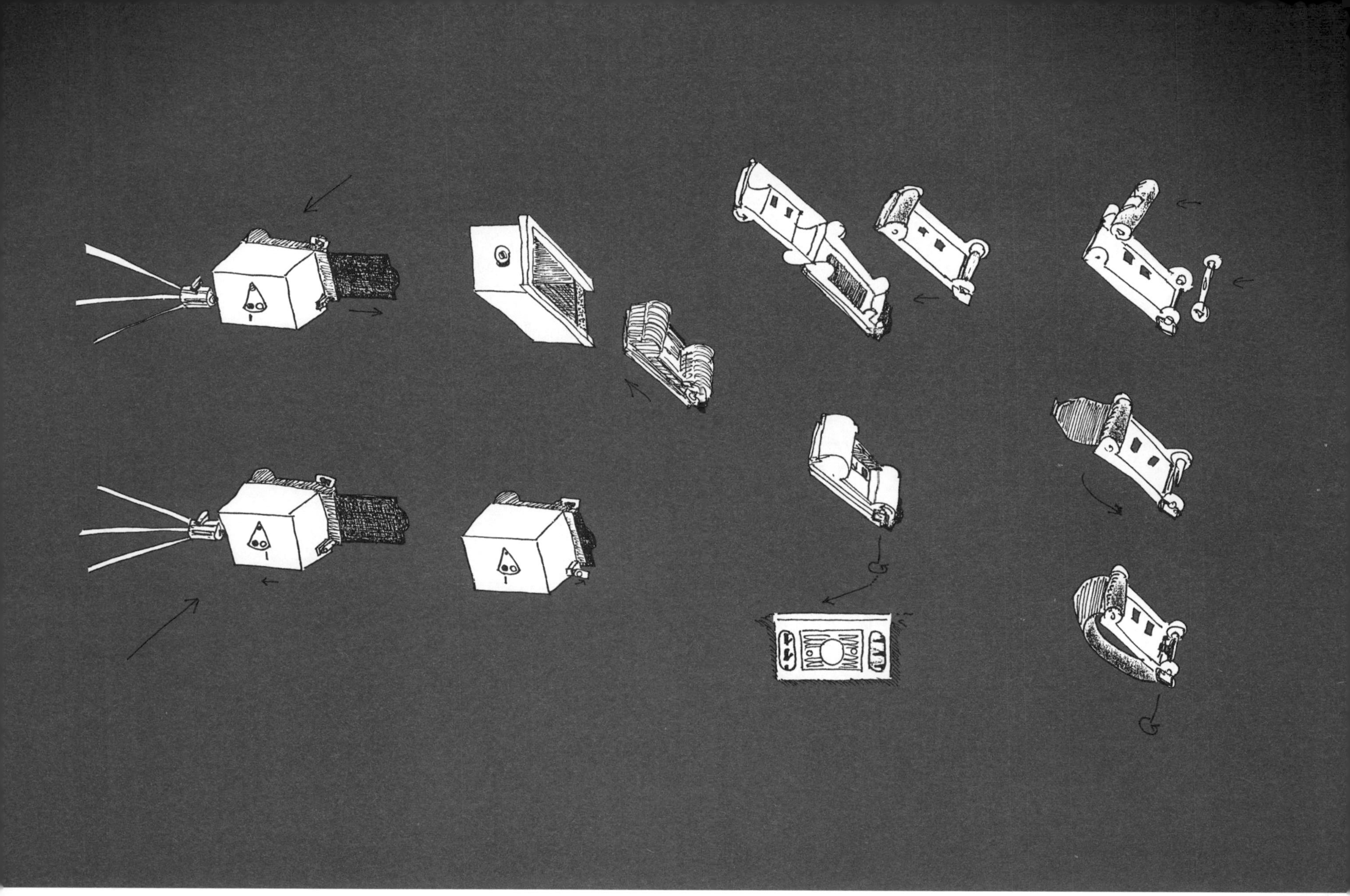

371 **SEQUENCE** How to put a roll film into a camera obscura. Uwe Friedrich

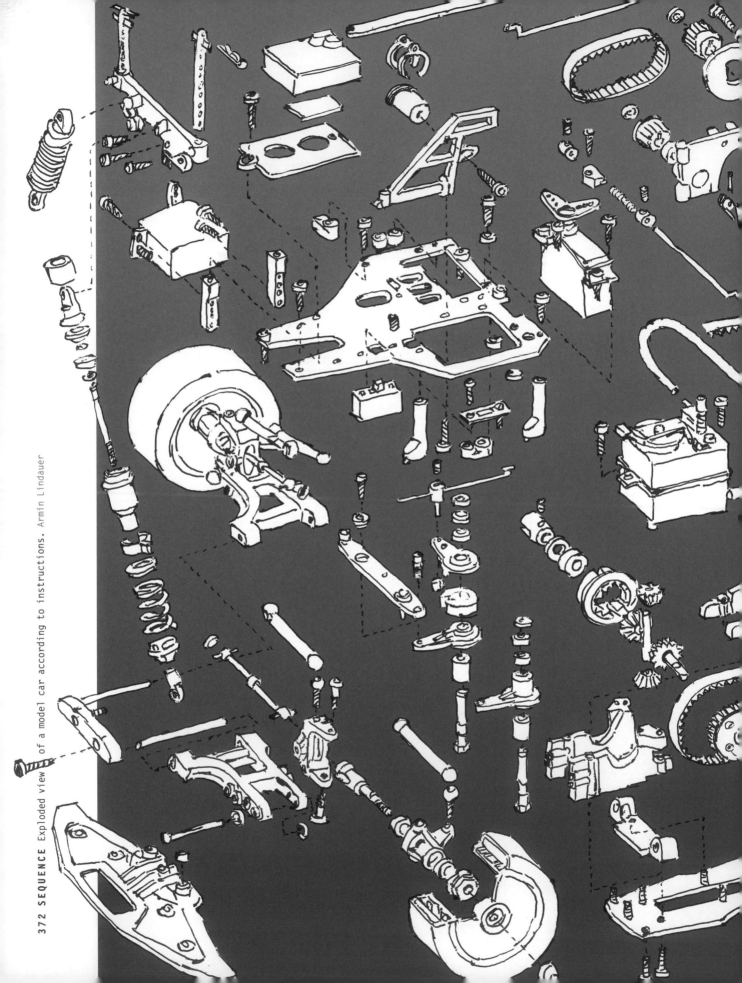

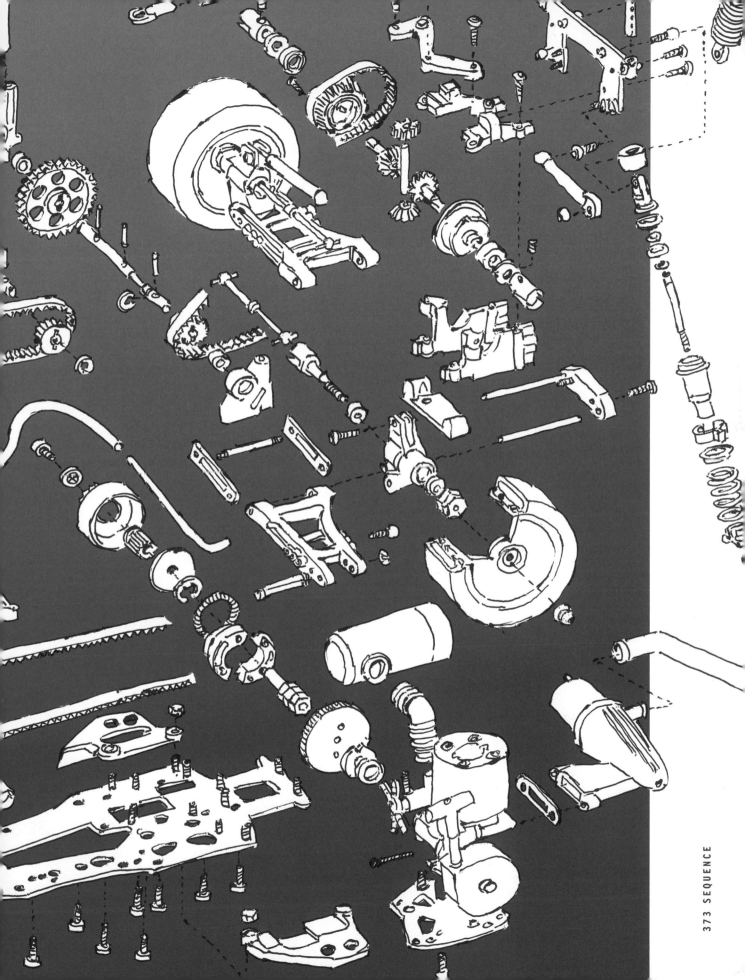

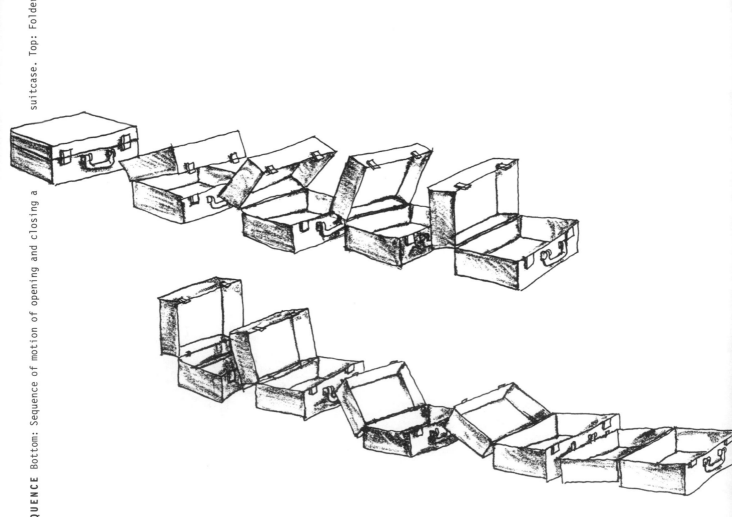

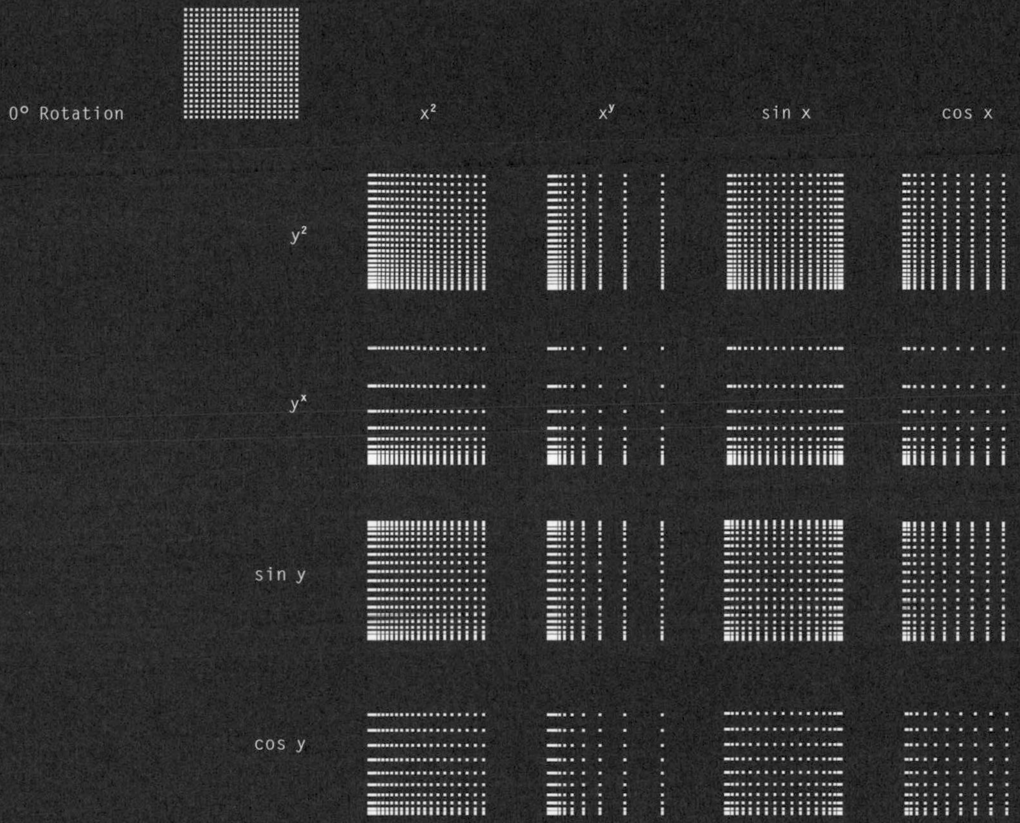

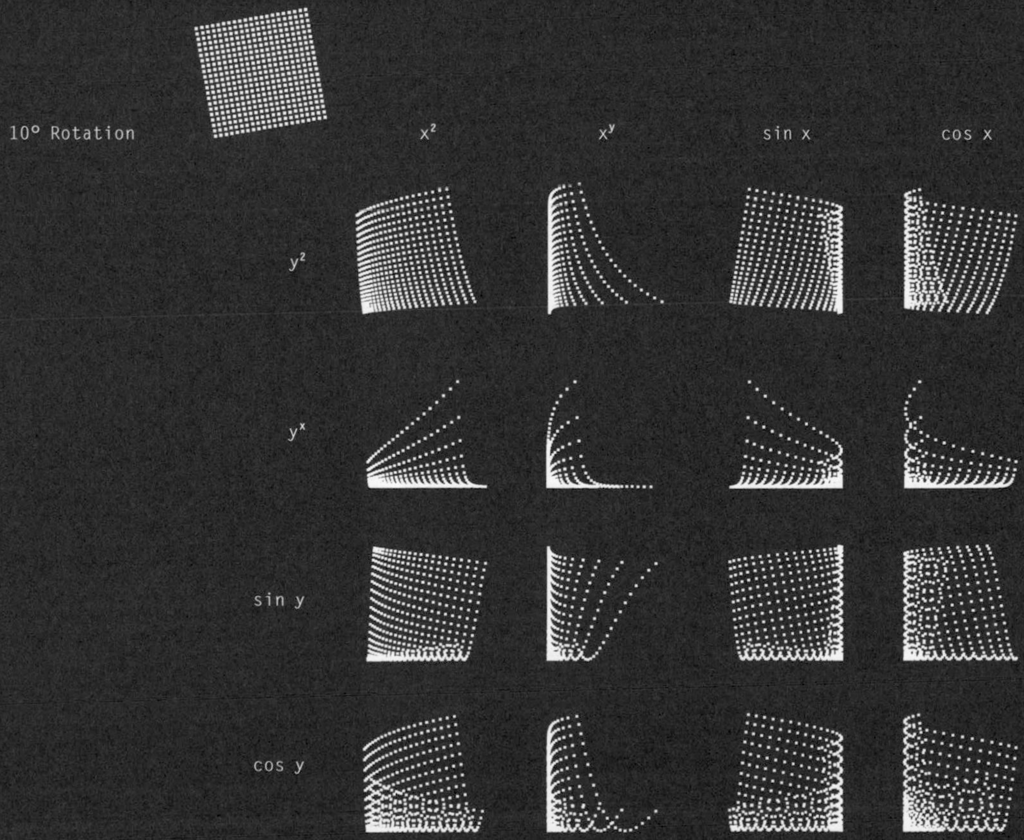

x²      x^y      sin x      cos x

y²

y^x

sin y

cos y

10° Rotation      x²      x^y      sin x      cos x

y²

y^x

sin y

cos y

375 SEQUENCE Mathematical functions are applied to a geometric form: Parabola, self-power, sinus, cosinus. Armin Lindauer, Frank Nürnberg

$$\vec{r} = \begin{pmatrix} i \\ j \end{pmatrix} \text{mit/where } i \in [1,N] \wedge j \in [1,N] \ i,j \in \mathbb{N} \qquad [1,N] \rightarrow [5,15]$$

$$\vec{r}\,' = \begin{pmatrix} \dfrac{10}{N-1} & 0 \\ 0 & \dfrac{10}{N-1} \end{pmatrix} \times \begin{pmatrix} x \\ y \end{pmatrix} + \begin{pmatrix} 5 \times \dfrac{N-3}{N-1} \\ 5 \times \dfrac{N-3}{N-1} \end{pmatrix} = \begin{pmatrix} x' \\ y' \end{pmatrix}$$

$$[5,15] \rightarrow \left[ \frac{\pi}{2}, \frac{3\pi}{2} \right] \qquad \vec{r}\,'' = \begin{pmatrix} \dfrac{\pi}{10} & 0 \\ 0 & \dfrac{\pi}{10} \end{pmatrix} \times \begin{pmatrix} x' \\ y' \end{pmatrix} = \begin{pmatrix} x'' \\ y'' \end{pmatrix}$$

$$\vec{r}\,''' = \begin{pmatrix} \cos\varphi & -\sin\varphi \\ \sin\varphi & \cos\varphi \end{pmatrix} \times \begin{pmatrix} x'' \\ y'' \end{pmatrix} = \begin{pmatrix} x''' \\ y''' \end{pmatrix} \text{mit/where } \varphi \in [0°, 90°] \qquad \vec{r}\,^* = \begin{pmatrix} \sin x''' \\ \sin y''' \end{pmatrix}$$

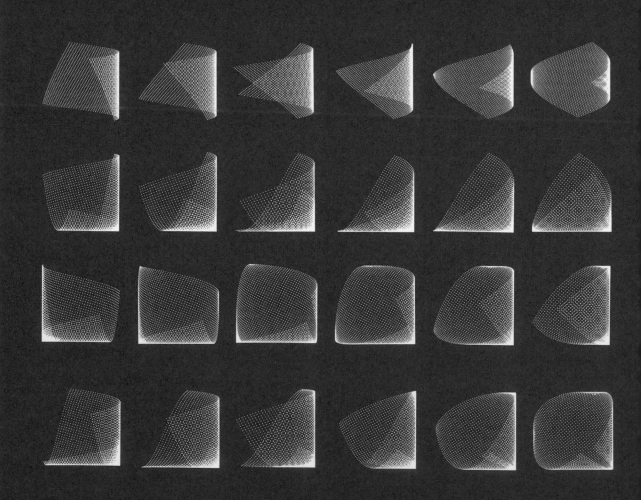

Armin Lindauer, Frank Nürnberg

**376 SEQUENCE** The algorithm creates the figures of the matrix on page 375 and the animation.

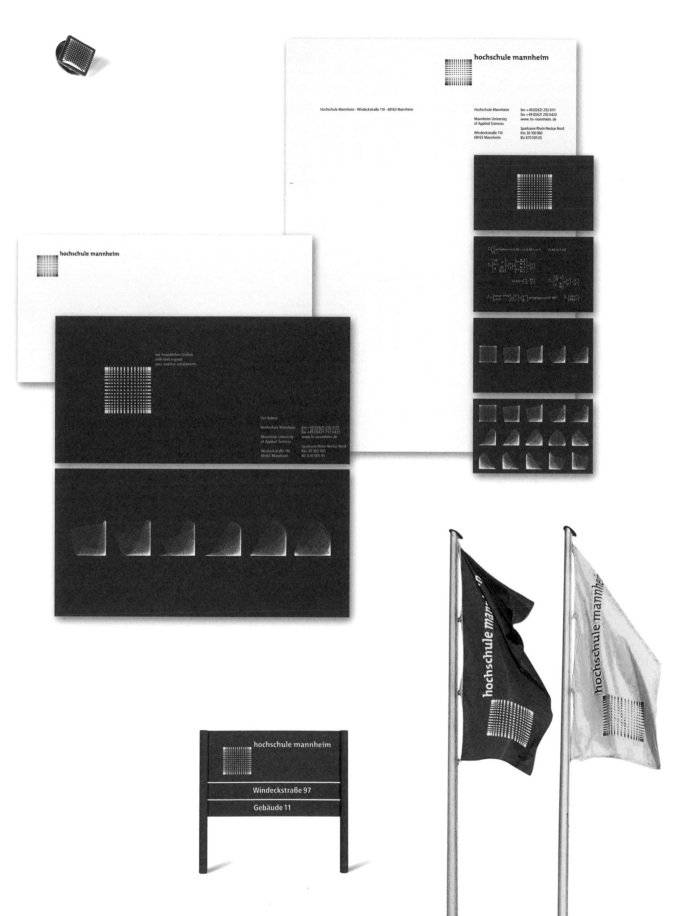

A standard chair where left and right, top and bottom are readily recognisable is systematically rotated by 30° increments around two axes. No vanishing point perspective considered.

The information content of the individual figures is clear. The two-dimensional figures contain less information.

This system can be easily transferred to other objects and can therefore help to select the required figure and information.

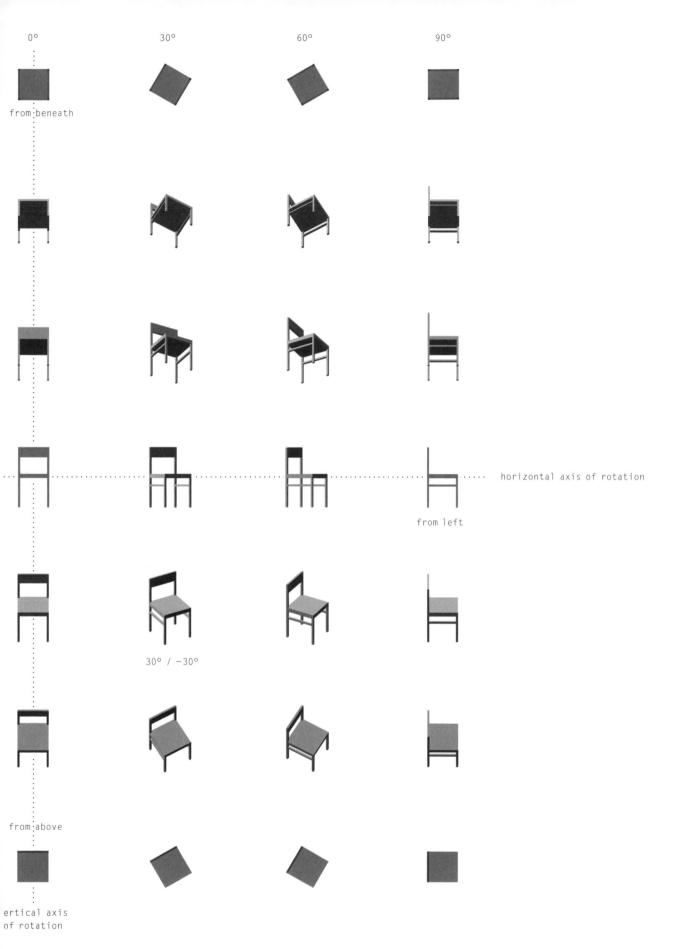

0°              30°              60°              90°

from beneath

horizontal axis of rotation

from left

30° / −30°

from above

vertical axis
of rotation

**380 SEQUENCE** Letters for the Virtual Reality Center of Mannheim University of Applied Sciences. The dimensions of space are symbolized by the letters VRC that form a coordinate system of x, y and z axis. Practical example. Concept, design: Armin Lindauer, programming: Carsten John

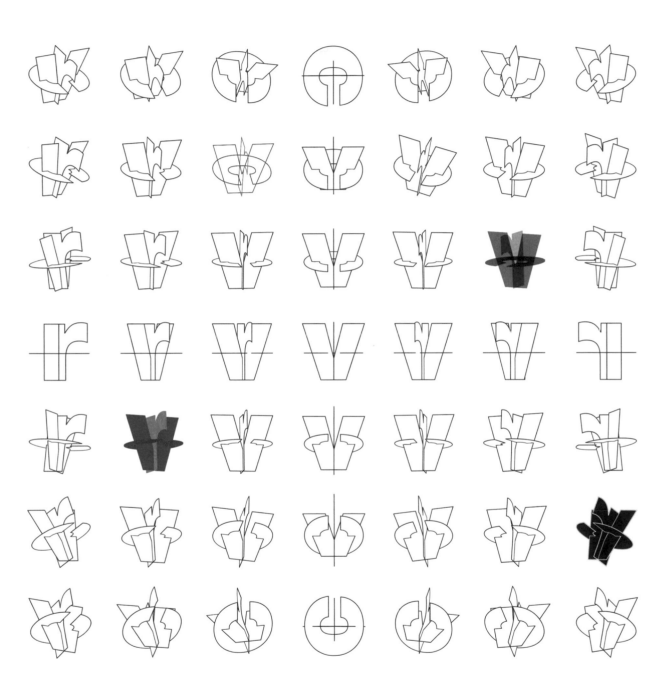

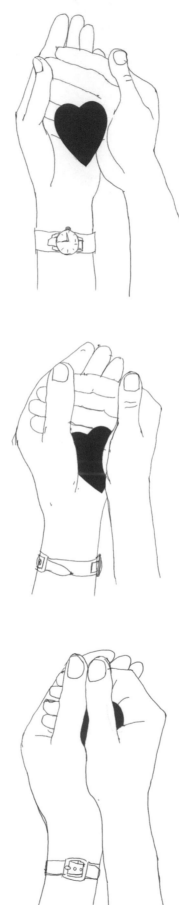

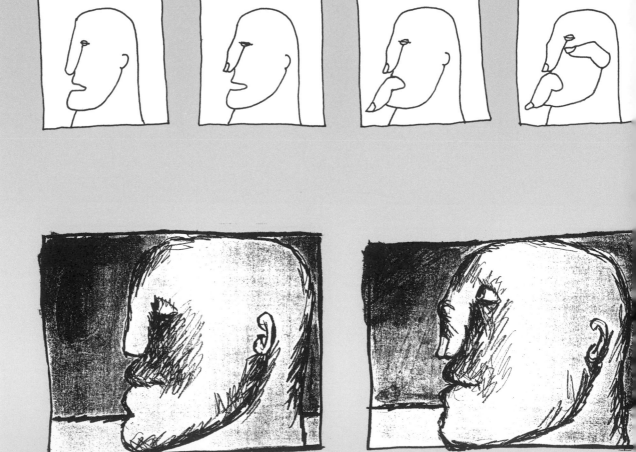

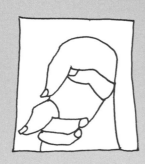

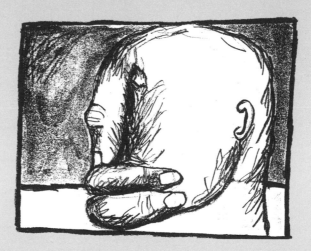

Tag. Armaturenbrett des fahrenden Lastwagens mit Blick auf die Stras-
se. Auf der Ablagefläche ein kleines Spielzeug-Lastauto. Bei der klein-
sten Strassenbiegung rutscht das Spielzeug-Lastauto hin und her.
Eine Kinderhand kommt ins Bild und nimmt das Spielzeug-Lastauto weg.

Nacht. Blick aus der Höhe von Kinderaugen in eine überfüllte, laute
Kneipe. Kamerafahrt zwischen den Tischen, an denen Männer sitzen und
Bier trinken - f Blick auf Untes Schoss

Nacht. Das Kind steht am Fenster im Spitalzimmer und starrt hinaus.

Nacht. Innenraum der Führerkabine. Das Kind schläft in der Koje. Die
Türe des Lastwagens öffnet sich. Der Vater steigt ein und legt sich
neben das Kind. f Fahrt weg

Tag. Spielzeug-Lastauto in einer Eislandschaft. Das Lastauto ist durch
und durch vereist. In der sich entfernenden Kamerabewegung erkennt man,
dass das Spielzeug-Lastauto im Gefrierfach eines Kühlschranks liegt.

Tag. Der Arzt schildert die Geschichte des Kindes in die Kamera.

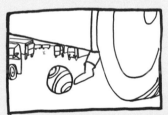

Tag. Parkplatz mit unzähligen Lastwagen. Das Kind spielt mit einem Ball.
Das spielende Kind wirkt winzig unter den Giganten, was mitunter den
Eindruck von Gefährlichkeit vermittelt, aber auch die Vertrautheit des
Kindes zu den Lastwagen zeigt.

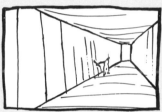

Tag. In der Dunkelheit der leeren Ladefläche des Lastwagens das spielende
Kind. Es geht den Wänden entlang und schlägt mit einem Stück Holz auf die
Blechwände. Der rhythmische Klang der Schläge übertönt seinen Dialog mit
dem Lastwagen.
Die Tür der Ladefläche öffnet sich und gleissendes Licht dringt herein.

Tag. Das Kind mit einem Spielzeug-Lastauto. Mit seinen Fingern streicht
es den Konturen des Lastautos entlang, durchforscht es.

Tag. Subjektiver Blick des Kindes aus dem fahrenden Lastwagen. Auf dem
Gehsteig schiebt eine Frau einen Kinderwagen. Cellospiele mit Cello -
husten als Pasant

Tag. Vorderfront des fahrenden Lastwagens. Der Vater rauchend am Steu-
er. Aus dem Vorhang der Schlafkoje hinzelt das noch schlaftrunkene
Gesicht des Kindes hervor. Die Kamera entfernt sich dann in Fahrtrich-
tung des Lastwagens, als das Kind im Begriffe ist neben den Vater zu
klettern.

Nacht. Das Kind klettert flink aus dem Lastwagen.

Tag. Unfallsituation mit dem zerstörten Lastwagen.

Der Vater und das Kind
prüfen die LKW's Reifen

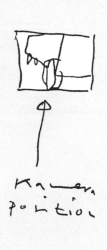

Kamera
position

Von
oben

taking cups out of cupboard

laying the table          filtering coffee          pouring coffee

breakfast

clearing the table        putting cups back into cupboard

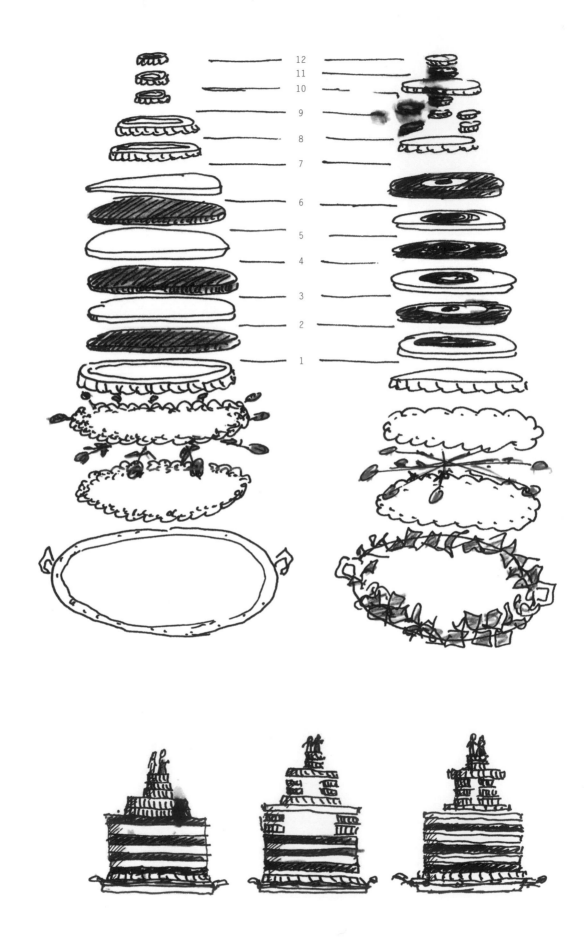

chocolate shavings

cherries

whipped cream rosettes

whipped cream coating

chocolate sponge

cream filling

chocolate sponge

cherry filling

chocolate sponge

short pastry

cherries

whipped cream rosettes

brittle chips

cream coating

sponge ring

cream filling

sponge ring

strawberry jam

sponge ring

cream ring

sponge ring

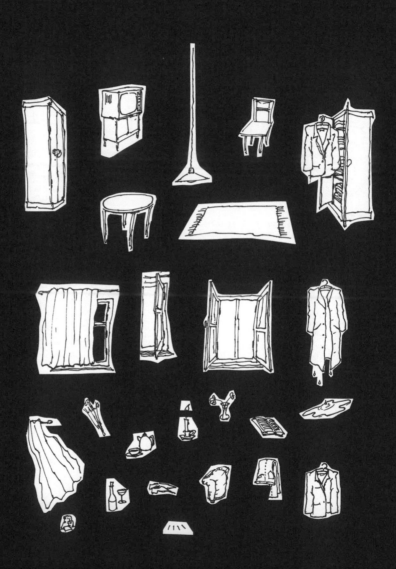

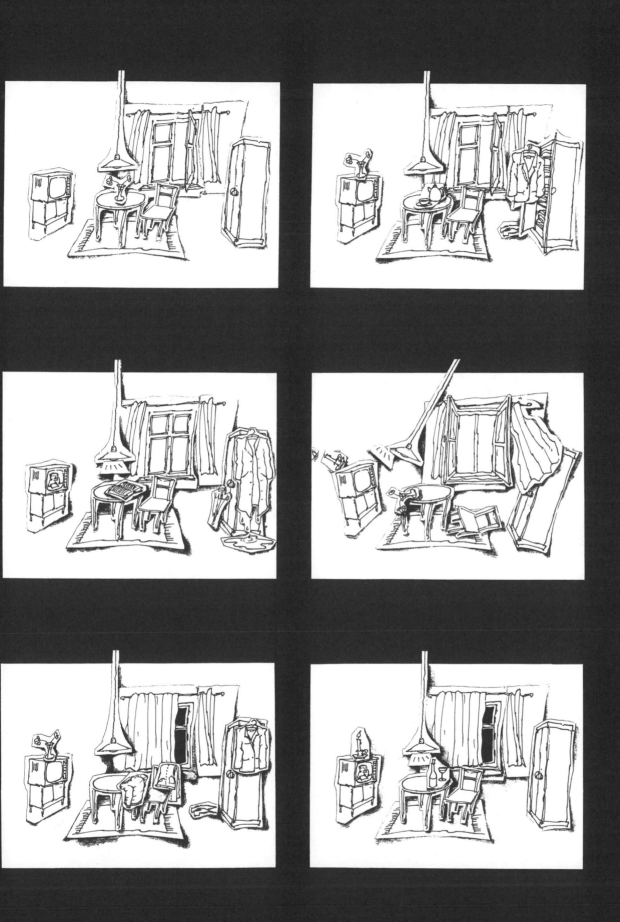

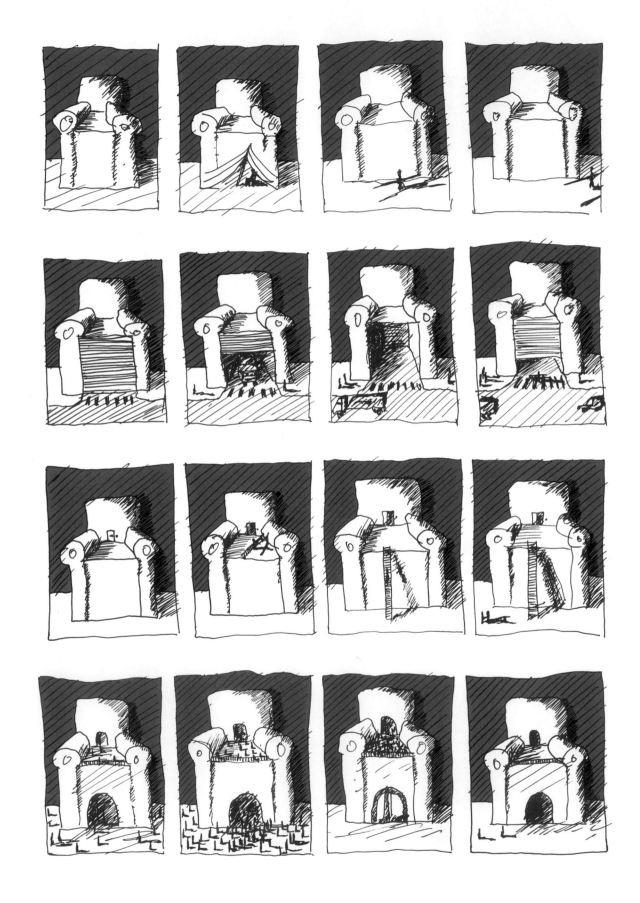

395 SEQUENCE Blue lines are the constant. Figures tell the story. Sara Midda

reinforced
balloon envelope

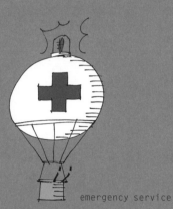

emergency service

lighting

Exploded view of a centaurus beetle (augosoma centaurus). After an illustration by Julia Carabain

401 SEQUENCE Centaurus beetle (augosoma centaurus). Photograph: John Ska

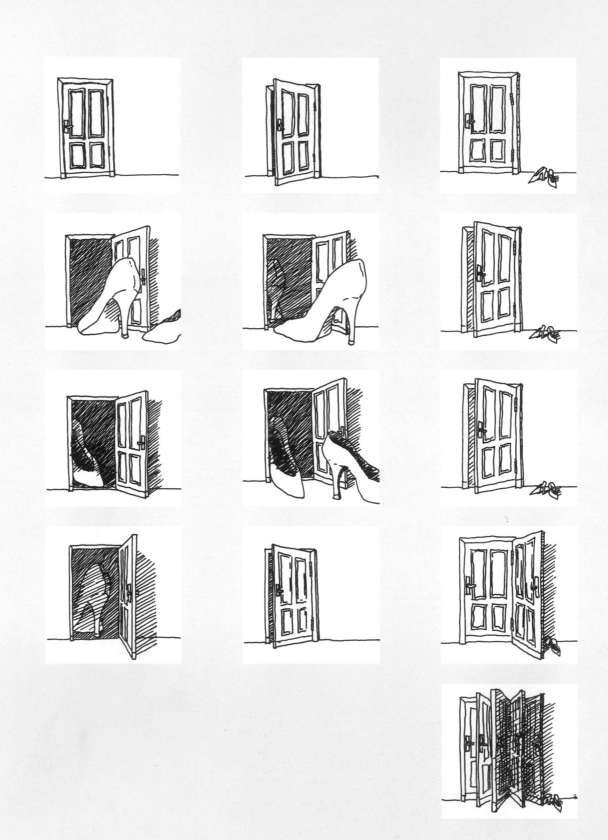

**403 SEQUENCE** Shoes and door. A surreal scene is created through 'incorrect' proportiors, polaroids. Motoko Aoki

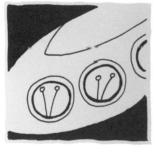

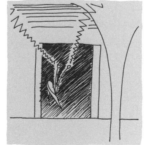

 Fulldome projection NO. 217: A man and his shadow. Julia Wiesner, Lea Weber-Schäfer, Phil Schöll

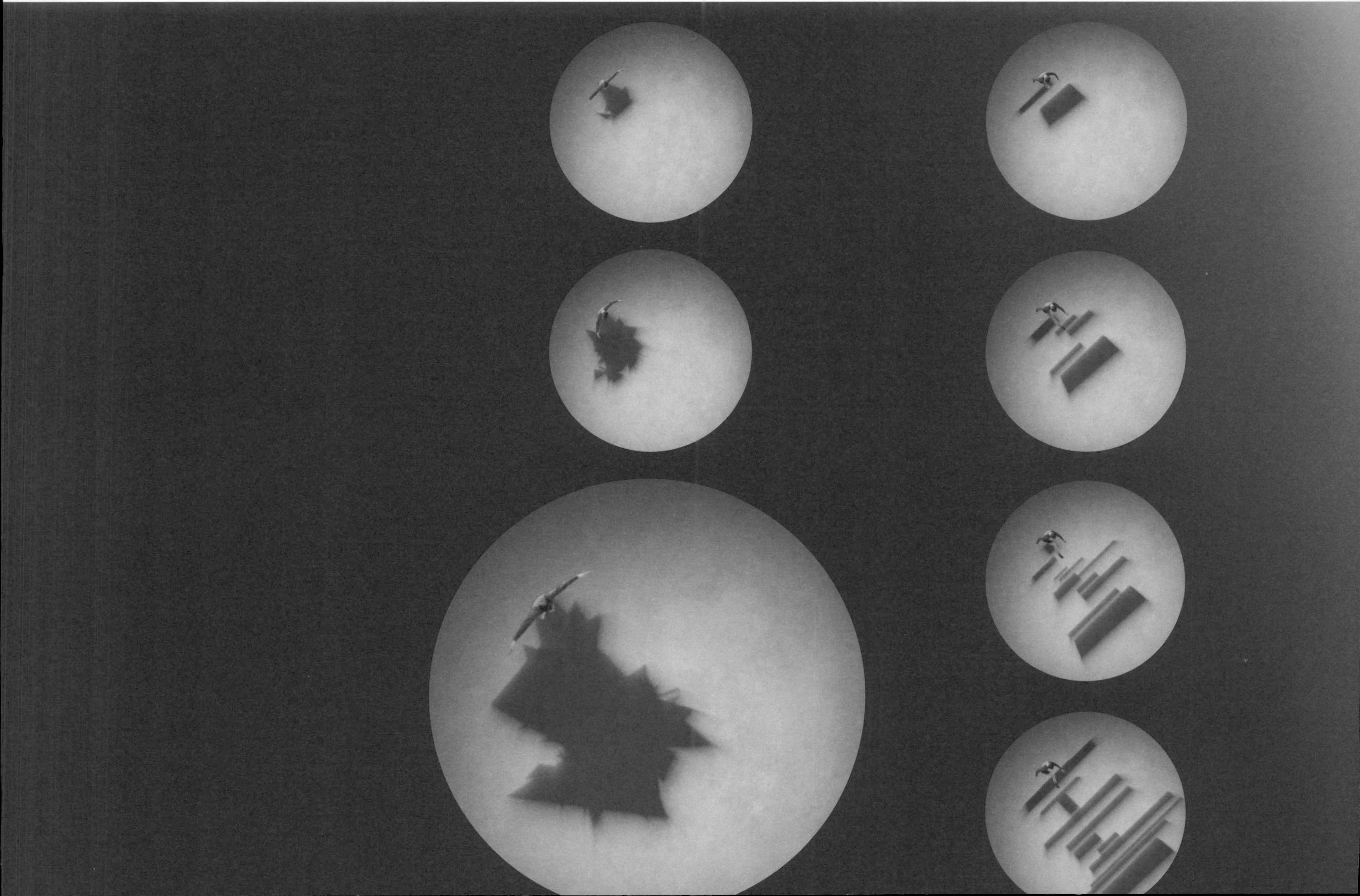

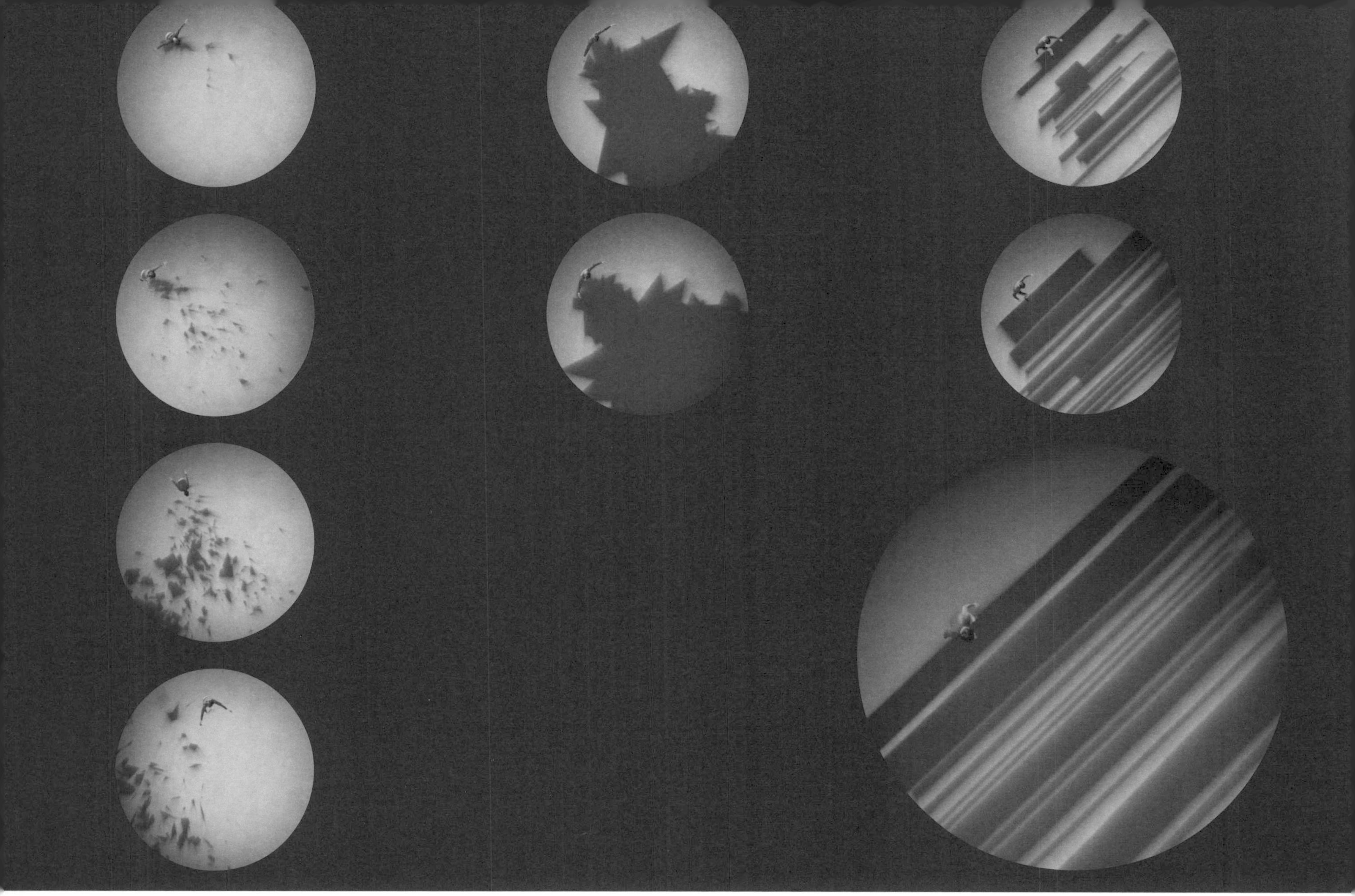

 **SEQUENCE** www.vimeo.com/23565276

Julia Wiesner, Lea Weber-Schäfer, Phil Schöll

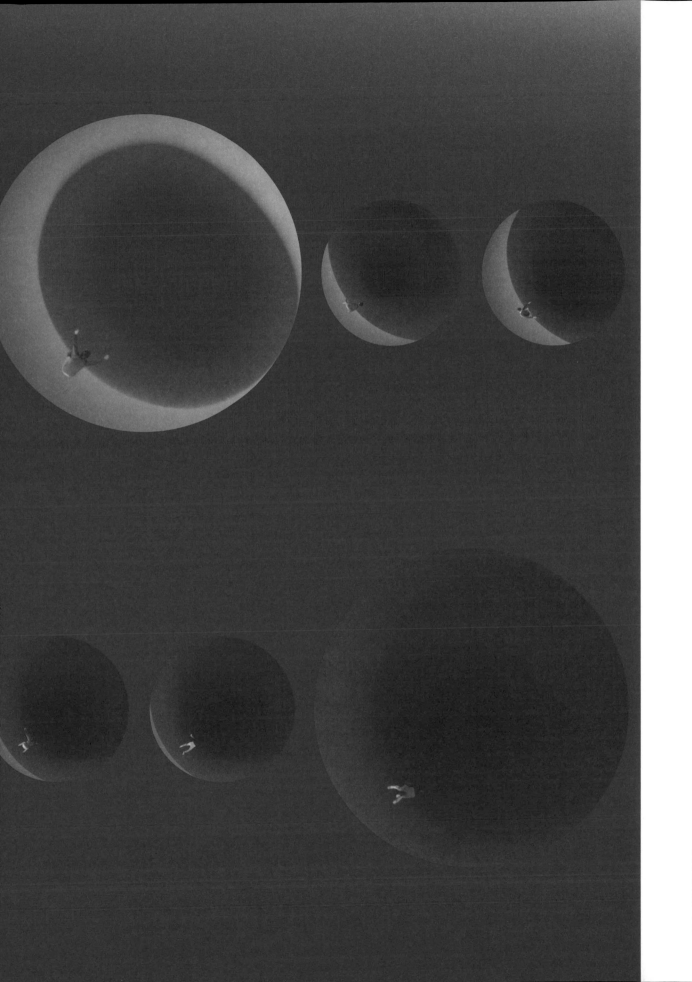

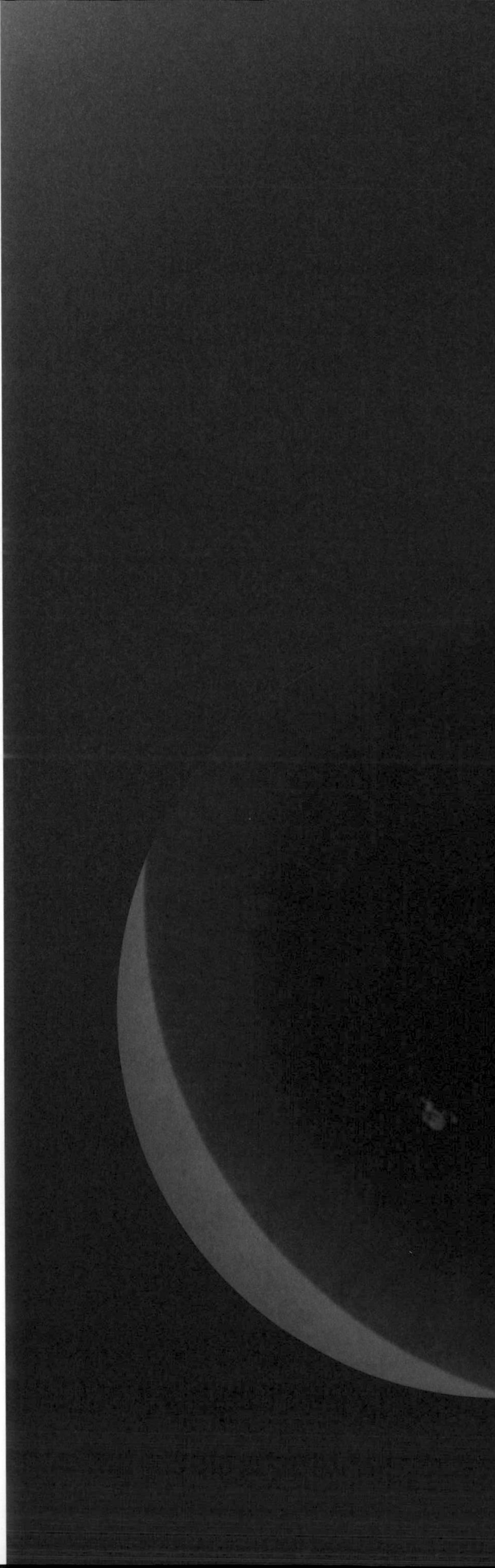

**EPILOGUE**  Our targeted research for this book began in 2004. However, the 'incubation' period of our — if not aimless, but still rather vague — searching and gathering process had begun much earlier, probably dating back to our mutual studies with Professor Helmut Lortz at the Berlin University of the Arts. At the same time, we encountered the LORTZ REIHEN[1], which are three volumes published in the mid-1970s by Eduard Roether, a small Darmstadt publishing company, without an ISBN number, and almost impossible to find in bookshops. That is why they are probably not very well known to the wider public. These books already present a number of sequences of drawings. They are only loosely connected and arranged in rows without a clearly defined structure, however the sequences still contain principles of variation and methodical procedure in many parts. The contact with this oeuvre and many other experiences during our studies, professional life and teaching activities formed the basis of this book. An initial attempt to put Lortz's analytic-systematic drawings in a certain order is portrayed in HELMUT LORTZ. DENKZETTEL[2], an excerpt from his countless drawings and sketchbooks that he had compiled over the decades, which can be described as the work of a manic graphic artist. In 2003, still with his support, I managed to complete and publish the book.

We had initially intended to collect design methods from different sources, some of which would facilitate decisions on visual quality, while others would boost our imagination and intuition. Over the years, however, we accumulated a vast, ever increasing collection that did not communicate our far from fully-fledged conceptions at the time. The vital job of classifying and categorising everything turned out to be a real challenge. Since we were able to allocate many of the works to different chapters, we were engaged in a process of permanent consideration and appraisal. We pieced the work together again and again, not only to achieve convincing results, but also to create processes that would make dramaturgical sense. The material was shaped and adapted accordingly, which is, in itself, nothing objectionable, but still needs to be pointed out, in order to prevent people from thinking that we had originally found the illustrated works in this condition. It is clear that no book can be entirely neutral or without intentions and our subjective point of view is visible throughout this publication.

It is also necessary to make some comments on the works we used from the archive of the Berlin University of the Arts. Most of the available models were monochrome copies of inferior quality. That is why they often needed to undergo comprehensive preparation and restoration, which we hope to have accomplished with the required care and sensitivity — reflecting that of the original artists. While some of the works were rearranged, others were

1 LORTZ REIHEN 1–3, Darmstadt 1972, 1973, 1974.*
2 Armin Lindauer, HELMUT LORTZ. DENKZETTEL, Mainz 2003.*

mounted on a coloured surface. We did this with the intention of clarifying
statements and improving dramaturgical processes as well as the presentation
as a whole. Many of these interventions were indispensable in defining
the core concept with increased precision. We warmly thank those artists who
supported us in our efforts and gave us their consent. Many of our own
older works had to be reworked or constructed anew in order to achieve the
desired quality.

Many drawings by different authors are simple, linear and monochrome.
We would like to stress that this has nothing to do with a specific style or
artistic gesture; the absence of half tones, shade, colour and other
differentiations rather helps to focus on the essence of the work. These
drawings[>188–189/196–201/244–245] are clear and objective and the artists often
forego their individual style, as the line has the extraordinary ability
to convey all necessary information about that which is represented, or about
the concept, with minimal means. Having said that, we are fully aware of
the fact that freedom of style and neutrality do not exist, and that this can
only be relative.

We can safely assume that a number of works presented here, particularly
significant works of art history, such as those by Courbet, Monet, Albers and
others, are familiar to most readers. This is probably true for some
advertising works, too. However, most people only know them as single works,
since they are rarely shown together and in a series. As far as we know,
there is hardly anything equal or similar to the comprehensive collections
we present in this book. This type of arrangement establishes the
desired comparability, explaining and underpinning our principles. It was
therefore essential to show them again in this context.

Despite the vast amount of pictorial material available an incompleteness
stayed identifiable. Indeed, we searched and created new works in order to
clarify the overall picture we had striven for, and to pinpoint its principles.
In the end, we had to accept the fact that some gaps would remain. Despite great
efforts by the scriptwriter DRAFTING A SYSTEM OF VISUAL METHODS, too,
remains sketchy and many issues were only briefly outlined or superficially
dealt with. Frequently, I ventured into areas that I am not very familiar with,
which is why I consulted a number of experts who checked the accuracy of my —
sometimes rather audacious — conclusions and statements. In the end, we decided
to publish the collection in its present form, despite its sketchiness, hoping
that our intentions and propositions are nevertheless clear.

**ACKNOWLEDGEMENTS** First of all, we would like to warmly thank all artists who kindly allowed us to use their works. They are named in alphabetical order in the following list. We also thank the Berlin University of the Arts, especially the archive staff Dr Dietmar Schenk and Karen Krukowski for supporting us during our research. We are extremely grateful to all scientific and artistic staff at Mannheim University of Applied Sciences, in particular to Nadine Zimmer for editing images and handling files, Marek Slipek for programming and studio photography, and Dr Nadine Schreiner-Alles for her editorial support. We also thank Mannheim and Potsdam University of Applied Sciences for allowing us to work on this project within the framework of several research semesters.

Thanks to Matthias Beyrow, Manja Hellpap and Judith Schalansky for their constructive and creative suggestions and Kerstin Forster for her detailed comments and extensive support.

We would like to thank physicist Prof Dr Frank Nürnberg for checking the lapidary remarks by the scriptwriter on statistics, light, thermodynamics and fractals, as well as for explaining combinatorics and for many other valuable hints. Our thanks also go to art historian Dr Andreas Schenk for his careful revision of the manuscript and many useful suggestions, and journalist Heike van Laak for proofreading the manuscripts many times as well as for her wise and kind advice and many linguistic tips. Last but not least, we are grateful to philologist Günter Foshag for checking grammar and spelling as well as for his many helpful comments.


Armin Lindauer and Betina Müller

**ARMIN LINDAUER**   studied Visual Communication at the Konstanz School of Arts and Crafts and the Berlin University of the Arts. He has had his own design studio in Berlin since 1984, now he also works in Mannheim. From 1984 to 1997, he taught Graphic Design, Typography and Photography at the Berlin University of the Arts. In 2000, he was appointed to a professorship for Editorial Design and Typography at Mannheim University of Applied Sciences. He has published books on design topics, such as HELMUT LORTZ. DENKZETTEL, a textbook for designers, and HELMUT LORTZ — LEICHT SINNIG, a typographically designed prize-winning book. His frequently exhibited conceptual photographs of the Berlin Wall provided the basis for his panorama photo book THE WALL — THE BEGINNING OF THE END and his leporello format book AROUND BERLIN. From 2004 to 2006, he was artistic advisor to the FIFA Organising Committee of the 2006 World Cup. Alongside his applied works, he produces drawings and paintings that are on show in many exhibitions. He has already received over 40 national and international design awards as well as the 1987 special award of 'Stadtzeichner' of Nuremberg. Armin Lindauer is a member of the Type Directors Club New York; he lives and works in Mannheim and Berlin.

**BETINA MÜLLER**   studied Visual Communication at the Berlin University of the Arts and graduated as 'master class student' of Professor Helmut Lortz. Since 1984, she has taught Basic Typography and Layout at the Berlin University of the Arts and had run her own design studio. In 1992, she was appointed to a professorship for Typographical Design at the newly established Department of Design at Potsdam University of Applied Sciences.
Betina Müller is the publisher of the Potsdam vacat verlag since 1994 and is responsible for conceptual, design-related and production management.
She has also undertaken free graphic and typographic projects and has received the 'Most Beautiful German Books' awards and was nominated for the Design Award of the Federal Republic of Germany as a representative of vacat verlag.
Betina Müller is a member of the Federal Ministry of Finance's art advisory board for commemorative postage stamps, of Forum Typografie and of the Gesellschaft zur Förderung der Druckkunst (Society for Advancement of the Printing Art in Leipzig) as well as the Verein für Schwarze Kunst (Society of Printer's Art) in Dresden. She has been responsible for the conception, organization and documentation of MACHTSPIELE — MACHT SPIELE!
15TH FORUM TYPOGRAFIE. She has numerous publications and outstanding students' work to her name. Betina Müller lives and works in Potsdam.

Aigner, Wolfgang;
Miksch, Silvia;
Schumann, Heidrun;
Tominski, Christian
**Visualization of**
**Time-Oriented Data**
London, Dordrecht,
Heidelberg, New York 2011

Albers, Josef
**Interaction of Color**
New Haven 1963

Arnheim, Rudolf
**Entropy and Art. An Essay**
**on Disorder and Order**
Berkeley, Los Angeles,
London 1971

Arnheim, Rudolf
**Art and Visual Perception.**
**The New Version**
Berlin, New York 1974

Arnheim, Rudolf
**Visual Thinking**
Berkeley 1969

Barth, Jan;
Grasy, Roman Stefan;
Leinberger, Jochen;
Lukas, Mark;
Schilling, Markus Lorenz
**Prototyping Interfaces –**
**Interaktives Skizzieren**
**mit vvvv**
Mainz 2013

Beckett, Samuel
**Das Gleiche nochmals anders.**
**Texte zur bildenden Kunst**
Frankfurt/Main 2000

Berning, Tina (Illustration)
**100 Girls on Cheap Paper**
San Francisco 2009

Bertin, Jacques
**Semiology of Graphics:**
**Diagrams, Networks, Maps**
Madison 1983

Biesele, Igildo G.
**Graphic Design International.**
**Kreatives Schaffen von**
**ausgewählten Grafikschulen**
**aus zwölf Ländern**
Zurich 1977

Binnig, Gerd
**Aus dem Nichts.**
**Über die Kreativität**
**von Natur und Mensch.**
Munich, Zurich 1989

Blake, Quentin; Cassidy, John
**Drawing for the Artistically**
**Undiscovered**
Witney 1999

Blättler, Christine (ed.)
**Kunst der Serie.**
**Die Serie in den Künsten**
Munich 2010

Boehm, Gottfried (ed.)
**Was ist ein Bild?**
Munich 1994

Bohnacker, Hartmut;
Groß, Benedikt; Laub, Julia;
Lazzeroni, Claudius (eds.)
**Generative Gestaltung.**
**Entwerfen, Programmieren,**
**Visualisieren mit Processing**
Mainz 2009

Bono, Edward de
**Lateral Thinking.**
**A Textbook of Creativity**
London 1970

Brandstätter, Ursula
**Grundfragen der Ästhetik:**
**Bild – Musik – Sprache – Körper**
Cologne, Weimar, Vienna 2008

Bredekamp, Horst
"Bildwissenschaft", in:
Pfisterer, Ulrich (ed.)
**Metzler Lexikon Kunstwissenschaft**
Stuttgart 2003

Buchmann, Mark (ed.)
**Ornament? ohne Ornament**
exhibition catalogue
Kunstgewerbemuseum Zürich
Zurich 1965

Danilowitz, Brenda
**The prints of Josef Albers.**
**A catalogue raisonné**
Manchester, New York 2010

Dilts, Robert B.; Epstein, Todd
**Tools For Dreamers: Strategies**
**of Creativity and the**
**Structure of Innovation**
Capitola CA 1991

Dürer, Albrecht
**Unterweisung der Messung mit**
**dem Zirkel und Richtscheit**
Faksimile-Neudruck der
Ausgabe Nürnberg 1525
Nördlingen 2000

Edwards, Betty
**Das neue ‹Garantiert**
**Zeichnen lernen›**
Reinbek 2000

Feyerabend, Paul K.
**Wissenschaft als Kunst**
Frankfurt/Main 1984

Feyerabend, Paul K.
**Wider den Methodenzwang**
Frankfurt/Main 1986

Fletcher, Alan
**Beware Wet Paint**
London 1996

Fletcher, Alan
**The Art of Looking Sideways**
London 2001

Gansterer, Nikolaus
**Drawing a Hypothesis.**
**Figures of Thought**
New York, Vienna 2011

Gerstner, Karl
**Designing Programmes**
Baden 2007

Goleman, Daniel;
Kaufman, Paul; Ray, Michael
**The Creative Spirit**
New York 1993

Gomez-Palacio, Bryony;
Vit, Armin
**Graphic Design, Referenced:**
**A Visual Guide to the**
**Language, Applications, and**
**History of Graphic Design**
Beverly MA 2009

Graubner, Gotthard
**Gespräch mit Josef Albers**
exhibition catalogue
Museum Quadrat Bottrop
Düsseldorf 2011

Guntern, Gottlieb
**Chaos und Kreativität.**
**Rigorous Chaos**
Zurich, Berlin, New York 1995

Guntern, Gottlieb (ed.)
**Irritation und Kreativität.**
**Hemmende und fördernde**
**Faktoren im kreativen Prozeß**
Zurich 1993

Gysin, Béatrice (ed.)
**Wozu zeichnen? Qualität und**
**Wirkung der materialisierten**
**Geste durch die Hand**
Sulgen 2010

Hofmann, Armin
**Graphic Design Manual.**
**Principles and Practice**
Teufen 1965

Holm-Hadulla, Rainer M.
**Kreativität, Konzept**
**und Lebensstil**
Göttingen 2005

Huizinga, Johan
**Homo Ludens: A Study of the**
**Play-Element in Culture**
Boston 1971

Jenny, Peter
**Zeichnen im Kopf**
Ennenda 2004

Jenny, Peter
**Anleitung zum falsch Zeichnen**
Ennenda n.y.

Jenny, Peter
**Notizen zur Zeichentechnik**
Ennenda 1999

Jenny, Peter
**Bildrezepte**
Zurich 1996

Jenny, Peter
**Bildkonzepte**
Zurich 1996

Junker, Thomas
**Die Evolution der**
**Phantasie. Wie der Mensch**
**zum Künstler wurde**
Stuttgart 2013

Junker, Thomas
**Die 101 wichtigsten**
**Fragen: Evolution**
Munich 2011

Kapitza, Petra and Nicole
**geometric**
Mainz 2008

Khazaeli, Cyrus Dominik
**Systemisches Design.**
**Intelligente Oberflächen für**
**Information und Interaktion**
Reinbek 2005

Spiller, Jürg (ed.)
**Paul Klee. Unendliche**
**Naturgeschichte**
Basel 1990

Klieber, Ulrich
**Wege zum Bild. Ein Lehrkonzept**
**für künstlerisches Gestalten**
Leipzig 2007

Koestler, Arthur
**The Act of Creation**
London 1964

Koren, Leonard;
Pasquier, Nathalie du
**Arranging Things:**
**A Rhetoric of Object Placement**
Berkeley CA 2003

Lanners, Edi
**Illusionen**
Lucerne, Frankfurt/Main 1973

Lewandowsky, Pina;
Zeischegg, Francis
**A Practical Guide to Digital
Design: Designing With
Your Computer Made Easy!**
Worthing 2003

Lewis, Richard W.
**Absolut Book. The Absolut
Vodka Advertising Story**
Boston, Tokyo 1996

Lindauer, Armin
**Helmut Lortz – Denkzettel**
Mainz 2003

Lindauer, Armin
**Helmut Lortz – leicht sinnig**
Mainz 2005

Lortz, Helmut
**Lortz Reihen, 1958–1972**
Darmstadt 1972

Lortz, Helmut
**Lortz Reihen 2, 1972–1973
Bildprotokolle**
Darmstadt 1973

Lortz, Helmut
**Lortz Reihen 3, 1973–1974**
Darmstadt 1974

Lortz, Helmut
**Helmut Lortz – Bildprotokolle**
Berlin 1975

Lortz, Helmut
**Helmut Lortz – der Lehrer**
Band 1
Berlin 1990

Lortz, Helmut
**Arheilgen – Berlin und zurück,
ein bebilderter Lebenslauf**
Darmstadt 2001

Lützau, Alan von
**Zirkeltraining**
Mainz 2011

Mandelbrot, Benoît B.
**The Fractal Geometry of Nature**
New York 1977

Márquez, Gabriel García
**Living to Tell the Tale**
London 2014

McCloud, Scott
**Reinventing Comics.
How Imagination and Technology
Are Revolutionizing an Art Form**
New York 2000

McCloud, Scott
**Understanding Comics.
The Invisible Art**
New York 1993

Metzger, Wolfgang
**Laws of Seeing**
Cambridge MA 2006

Midda, Sara
**Sara Midda's South
of France. Sketchbook**
New York 1990

Muybridge, Eadweard
**The Male and the Female
Figure in Motion. 60 Classic
Photographic Sequences**
New York 1984

Nino, Jacques
**Macht Schwarz schlank?
Über die Täuschung
unserer Wahrnehmung**
Leipzig 1999

Paál, Gábor
**Was ist schön?
Ästhetik und Erkenntnis**
Würzburg 2003

Poschauko, Thomas and Martin
**Nea Machina.
Die Kreativmaschine.
Kopf – Bauch – Hand – Computer**
Mainz 2010

Poschauko, Thomas and Martin
**Nea Machina.
Die Kreativmaschine.
Next Edition**
Mainz 2013

Pricken, Mario
**Visuelle Kreativität.
Kreativitätstechniken für
neue Bildwelten in Werbung,
3-D-Animation und Computergames**
Mainz 2003

Queneau, Raymond
**Exercises in Style**
London 1998

Richter, Jean P. (ed.)
**The Notebooks of
Leonardo da Vinci**
New York 1970
[London 1883]

Ruskin, John
**The Elements of Drawing.
In three Letters to Beginners**
Mineola 1971

Ryba, Michael
**Pig Art**
New York 1983

Sagmeister, Stefan
**Things I have learned
in my life so far**
New York 2009

Sagmeister, Stefan
**Sagmeister: Made you Look**
Mainz 2009

Scheinberger, Felix
**Illustration – 100 Wege
einen Vogel zu malen**
Mainz 2013

Scheinberger, Felix
**Mut zum Skizzenbuch**
Mainz 2009

Scheinberger, Felix
**Wasserfarbe für Gestalter**
Mainz 2011

Schwochow, Jan;
Grauel, Ralf
**Deutschland verstehen.
Ein Lese-, Lern-
und Anschaubuch**
Berlin 2012

Siegrist-Thummel, Anne-Marie
**Figürliches Zeichnen.
Methoden, Ideen, Techniken**
Sulgen 2014

Stolz, Matthias;
Häntzschel, Ole
**Die große Jahresschau.
Alles was 2010 wichtig ist**
Munich 2010

Strunk, Marion
"Kunst wie Wissenschaft.
**Wissenschaft wie Kunst"**
in: Liebig, Brigitte u. a.
(ed.)
**Mikrokosmos Wissenschaft.
Transformationen und
Perspektiven**
Zurich 2006

Teunen, Jan (ed.)
**T-Kiste: 100 Variationen zum T**
Mainz 2000

Tufte, Edward R.
**The Visual Display of
Quantitative Information**
Connecticut 2002

Tufte, Edward R.
**Beautiful Evidence**
Connecticut 2006

Tufte, Edward R.
**Visual Explanations.
Images and Quantities,
Evidence and Narrative**
Connecticut 1997

Tufte, Edward R.
**Envisioning Information**
Connecticut 1990

Tufte, Edward R.
**The Visual Display of
Quantitative Information**
Connecticut 1983

Ware, Colin
**Information Visualization
Perception for Design**
Boston 2012

Watson, James D.
**The Double Helix:
A Personal Account
of the Discovery
of the Structure of DNA**
New York 1968

Watzlawick, Paul
**The Invented Reality:
How Do We Know
What We Believe We Know?**
New York 1984

Watzlawick, Paul
**How Real Is Real?**
New York 1976

Watzlawick, Paul
**The Situation Is Hopeless,
But Not Serious. The
Pursuit of Unhappiness**
New York 1983

Wember, Martina
**Beziehungsreicher Alltag.
Perspectives on Everyday Life**
Klagenfurt, Amsterdam 2001

Wember, Martina
**Beziehungsweise Linien.
Karteibezeichnungen**
Herzogenaurach 2003

Wick, Rainer K.
**Bauhaus-Pädagogik**
Cologne 1982

Willberg, Brigitte
**Wechselspiele. Neuer Umgang
mit alten Ornamenten**
Munich 1995

Zöllner, Frank
**Leonardo da Vinci. Complete
Paintings and Drawings**
Cologne 2003

Zwimpfer, Moritz
**2d, Visual Perception**
Sulgen 1994

p. 76 based on:
Hofmann, Armin
**Methodik der Form- und
Bildgestaltung. Aufbau,
Synthese, Anwendung**
Teufen 1965

p. 105 based on:
Meunier, Alexandre
**Collection des Dessins
Topographiques exécutes par
Alexandre Meunier 1887–89**
École de Dessin, n.p.

pp. 114–115 from:
Tufte, Edward R.
**Visual Explanations.
Images and Quantities,
Evidence and Narrative**
pp. 118–119
Connecticut 1997

pp. 116–119 from:
Ryba, Michael
**Das große Schweinebuch oder:
Das Schwein in der bildenden
Kunst des Abendlandes**
Munich, Hamburg 1980

pp. 126–127
Sagmeister, Stefan
**Zumtobel
annual report 2001/02**

pp. 128–131
**Artwork courtesy
of Alfred A. Knopf**
New York

pp. 142–145
Sagmeister, Stefan
**Things I have learned
in my life so far**
Mainz, New York 2008

p. 165 from:
Barañano, Kosme de (ed.)
**Picasso – Dialogue
with ceramics**
Künzelsau 1999

Boeck, Wilhelm
**Picasso. Drawings**
Cologne 1973

Chevalier, Denys
**Picasso. Blue and pink periods**
Munich n.y.

Melcher, Ralph
**Picasso. The 50s**
Heidelberg 2007

Gauss, Ulrike
**Pablo Picasso.
His lithographic oeuvre**
Ostfildern-Ruit 2000

pp. 214–215 based on:
Thompson, D'Arcy Wentworth;
Bonner, J.T. (eds.)
**On Growth and Form**
Cambridge 1961
[1st edition 1917]

p. 216 based on:
**Zweidimensionale
Transformation eines
Tierbildes** in:
Nagel, Matthias;
Benner, Axel;
Ostermann, Rüdiger;
Henschke, Klaus
**Grafische
Datenanalyse**, p. 105
Stuttgart 1996

p. 219 from:
**Spektrum der Wissenschaft
Evolution**, p. 20
Heidelberg 1988

pp. 222–226
© **Jörg Hempel**, Aachen

pp. 254–257 from:
Lewis, Richard W.
**Absolut Book. The Absolut
Vodka Advertising Story**
pp. 44–49/61–62
Boston, Tokyo 1996

pp. 314–315/395 from:
Midda, Sara
**Sara Midda's South
of France. Sketchbook**
New York 1990

pp. 322–323 from:
Glaser, Milton
**Kunst ist Arbeit**, p. 215
Hamburg 2000

pp. 340–342 from:
Ungerer, Tomi
**Hintereinander**
Munich 1991

p. 347 based on:
Tufte, Edward
**Visual Explanations.
Images and Quantities,
Evidence and Narrative**
p. 86
Connecticut 1997
based on:
Bragdon, Claude
**A Primer of Higher Space:
The Fourth Dimension**
plate 30
Rochester NY 1913

**editors, concept, design**
Armin Lindauer and Betina Müller

**texts**
Armin Lindauer

**copy-editing, proofreading**
Kerstin Forster, Constanze Nobs

**typesetting**
Betina Müller

**assistance**
Nadine Zimmer, Marek Slipek,
Dr Nadine Schreiner-Alles

**translation**
y'plus: Marina Brandtner
*translated from the German edition
by Marina Brandtner

**proofreading English edition**
y'plus: Maria Nievoll,
Susannah Chadwick

**lithography**
Nadine Zimmer, Marek Slipek,
Armin Lindauer, Oliver Otto,
Andreas Brietzke

**printing**
H. Heenemann GmbH & Co. KG, Berlin

**binding**
Bruno Helm, Berlin

**paper**
150 g/sqm and 300 g/sqm Tauro


©2015 niggli Publishing
a brand of Braun Publishing AG
www.niggli.ch
as well as the editors and authors


ISBN 978-3-7212-0913-6
(English edition)

ISBN 978-3-7212-0912-9
(German edition)